Civil Society and Gender Relations
in Authoritarian and Hybrid Regimes

Gabriele Wilde
Annette Zimmer
Katharina Obuch
Isabelle-Christine Panreck (eds.)

Civil Society and Gender Relations in Authoritarian and Hybrid Regimes

New Theoretical Approaches and Empirical Case Studies

Barbara Budrich Publishers
Opladen • Berlin • Toronto 2018

All rights reserved. No part of this publication may be reproduced, stored in or introduced into a retrieval system, or transmitted, in any form, or by any means (electronic, mechanical, photocopying, recording or otherwise) without the prior written permission of Barbara Budrich Publishers. Any person who does any unauthorized act in relation to this publication may be liable to criminal prosecution and civil claims for damages.

You must not circulate this book in any other binding or cover and you must impose this same condition on any acquirer.

A CIP catalogue record for this book is available from
Die Deutsche Bibliothek (The German Library)

© 2018 by Barbara Budrich Publishers, Opladen, Berlin & Toronto
www.barbara-budrich.net

    ISBN 978-3-8474-0729-4
    eISBN 978-3-8474-0874-1

Das Werk einschließlich aller seiner Teile ist urheberrechtlich geschützt. Jede Verwertung außerhalb der engen Grenzen des Urheberrechtsgesetzes ist ohne Zustimmung des Verlages unzulässig und strafbar. Das gilt insbesondere für Vervielfältigungen, Übersetzungen, Mikroverfilmungen und die Einspeicherung und Verarbeitung in elektronischen Systemen.

Die Deutsche Bibliothek – CIP-Einheitsaufnahme
Ein Titeldatensatz für die Publikation ist bei der Deutschen Bibliothek erhältlich.

Verlag Barbara Budrich   Barbara Budrich Publishers
Stauffenbergstr. 7. D-51379 Leverkusen Opladen, Germany

86 Delma Drive. Toronto, ON M8W 4P6 Canada
www.barbara-budrich.net

Jacket illustration by Bettina Lehfeldt, Kleinmachnow –
    www.lehfeldtgraphic.de
Picture credits: photo: Philipp Lehfeldt
Typesetting: Anja Borkam, Jena – kontakt@lektorat-borkam.de
Printed in Europe on acid-free paper by paper & tinta, Warsaw

Table of contents

Katharina Obuch, Gabriele Wilde, Annette Zimmer
Civil Society and Gender Relations in Non-Democratic Regimes:
Democracy, Power, and Traditional Gender Roles. Introduction 7

Section 1
Theoretical foundations and methodological implications

Eva Maria Hinterhuber, Silke Schneider
Gender, Civil Society, and Non-Democratic Regimes 27

Annette Zimmer
If Not for Democracy, for What? Civil Society in Authoritarian
Settings 75

Gabriele Wilde
The Authoritarian as Discourse and Practice: a Feminist Post-structural
Approach 99

Isabelle-Christine Panreck
Analyzing the Authoritarian: Post-structural Framing-Analysis –
a Methodological Approach 119

Section 2
Case studies

Katharina Obuch
Between Militancy and Survival? The Case of the Nicaraguan Women's
Movement 137

Gabriele Wilde, Jasmin Sandhaus
The Tunisian Constitution between Democratic Claim and
Constitutional Reality 165

Joyce Mushaben
"I'm here too, Girlfriend ...": Reclaiming Public Spaces for the
Gendering of Civil Society in Turkey 185

Stephanie Bräuer
Between Provocation and Incorporation – Social Gender Activism
in the Hybrid Regime of the PRC 217

Patricia Graf
In the Shadow of Autocracy. Gender Politics in Chile 247

Authors 267

Index 269

Civil Society and Gender Relations in Non-Democratic Regimes: Democracy, Power, and Traditional Gender Roles. Introduction

Katharina Obuch, Gabriele Wilde, Annette Zimmer

1. The worldwide developments of non-democratic regimes

While the number of democratic regimes in the world reached its peak around the turn of the millennium, the last decade of the new century has been marked by a "renaissance of authoritarianism" (Bank 2009). In 2017, according to Freedom House, 61% of the global population lived in countries that are either only "partly free" or "not free" at all, marking the "12th consecutive year of decline in global freedom" (Freedom House 2018). As *Journal of Democracy* editor Marc Plattner (2017) recently stated, "Today liberal democracy is clearly on the defensive. Authoritarian regimes of various stripes are showing a new boldness, and they appear to be growing stronger as the confidence and vigor of the democracies wane" (ibid. 2017: 6). Current prominent examples include the consolidation of Vladimir Putin's rule in Russia, Recep Tayyip Erdogan's autocratic course in Turkey, the increased repression of human rights activists in China, the electoral victory of a right-wing government in Poland, and the erosion of democratic values under Viktor Orbán in Hungary. Even more, the authoritarian trend does not stop short of assumed guarantors of democracy but is apparent in the "rise of populist parties and candidates in the long-established democracies of the West" (ibid. 2017: 6). This includes, among others, the new government coalition in Austria including the far-right Freedom Party, the relative strength of Marine Le Pen's Front National in the past presidential election in France, and the success of the populist political outsider Donald Trump in the US elections.

These worldwide developments have also inspired a paradigm shift in the field of democratization studies (see Carothers 2002). Since the start of the Third Wave democratizations (Huntington 1991) with Portugal's peaceful Carnation Revolution in 1974, scholars occupied with the study of regime change have heavily focused on democratic transition (see O'Donnell et al. 1986) and, later, consolidation (Croissant and Merkel 2004: 2). Today, however, non-democratic regimes have made their way back to the center of research and academic debate (Diamond 2008; Levitsky and Way 2010; Márquez 2017).

Analyzing the ongoing global democratic recession, Diamond (2015) lists four trends that make up the renaissance of authoritarianism in the new century: The breakdown of formerly democratic regimes (e.g., Turkey, Venezuela, Philippines), the net recession of freedom in emerging-market countries (e.g., South Korea, South Africa, Mexico), the deepening of authoritarianism (e.g., China, Russia), and, last, the "decline of democratic efficacy, energy, and self-confidence in the West" (Diamond 2015: 251). At the heart of these transformations seems to be a general disaffection with liberal democracy (Plattner 2017: 8) that is also noticeable in populist discourses, electoral outcomes, and public opinion polls worldwide.

The rather unexpected proliferation of non-democratic regimes in the twenty-first century furthermore inspires a shift of attention of scholars away from the focus on institutions and elites and toward the exploration of a broader set of actors, deeper societal structures, and discourses. Especially the increasing number of "hybrid" regimes, which combine formal democratic structures with deficits regarding political and civic liberties or the rule of law (Croissant 2002), is the starting point for this book, which emerged out of our research project on "Gender Relations in Authoritarian and Hybrid Regimes," which ran from 2013–15 at the Center for European Gender Studies at Münster University (ZEUGS). The book highlights the necessity to look beyond or refine traditional approaches and offers innovative potential to bond gender, authoritarianism, and civil society in an auspicious way leading to insights into the whys and wherefores of the persistence of autocratic structures and gender inequalities worldwide. By focusing on the domains of non-institutional legitimation and power strategies, civil society comes in as a potential but so far understudied actor in the analysis of the transformation but also the persistence of non-democratic regimes.

2. Civil society as an important actor in non-democratic settings

Qustions of if, how, and to what extent civil society might exist under non-democratic, deficient, or even authoritarian governments has only recently become highly visible on the political science agenda (Teets 2016; Cavatora 2015; Heuerlin 2010; Spires 2011; Pickel 2013; Wischermann 2013). There are many reasons for this. Social, economic, and political developments obviously have a strong impact on the social sciences in general and on political science in particular. The political concept and term "civil society" was rediscovered alongside the awakening of dissident movements, which at the end of the 1970s and early 1980s stood up against the power and inhumane ideology of the so-called socialist governments in the countries behind the Iron Curtain that cut off almost half of Europe from democratic rule (Havel and Keane 1985; Keane 1998). The dissidents in Poland, Hungary, and many other Eastern European countries referred to "civil society" as a democratic and participatory alternative to non-democratic authoritarian rule. Because they did not have freedom of expression nor the possibility to legally stand up against inhumanity and authoritarian one-party governments in Eastern Europe, the term civil society became a synonym for a democratic political program and progressive utopia. As such, the concept was increasingly placed in juxtaposition to the non-democratic and illiberal political reality under socialist rule.

The discussions that took place in oppositional groups in Eastern Europe and in other regions struggling with non-democratic regimes such as Latin America and Southeast Asia strongly influenced debates on the state of the art of democratic rule and governance in the so-called Western Hemisphere. As a consequence, during the 1980s and 1990s deliberation on civil society as a topic of political theory and political philosophy moved into the center of discourses on the deepening and further development of democracy (Cohen and

Arato 1997; Taylor 1991). Civil society was used as an approach to respond to the problems of post-modern societies by key scholars arguing in a classical liberal tradition such as Ralf Dahrendorf (1991, 1999); the concept was taken up by Jürgen Habermas, who highlighted the pivotal importance of civil society as a sphere of deliberation and reasoning (Habermas 1992); civil society was also to become a cornerstone of communitarian thinking (Etzioni 1994; Walzer 1992, 2003) as well as of various facets of participatory democracy such as associational democracy (Warren 2001) or strong democracy (Barber 2004).

Although the renaissance of the term and concept of civil society was triggered by real politics in Eastern Europe, and partially in Latin America, civil society as a concept and horizon of ideas has always been closely linked to political philosophy and political theory (Kneer 2000: 235–23; Adloff 2005). Without going into detail, there are numerous interpretations and readings of the meaning of civil society and its features. For the general public and the media, civil society stands for a better life in a fairer, more democratic, and participatory society. As such the term is linked to utopian political and societal ideas. For sure, opposition and critical voices are necessary for any democratic setting in order to keep things moving and to guarantee that critique as an alternative view on the state of affairs is taken seriously. Without a utopia in terms of how government and society are supposed to advance or how the current state of government and governance should be improved, democracy does not work and modern societies reach an impasse. Civil society is also associated with "civicness," a term used to characterize societies or any human setting that is able to resolve conflicts peacefully through the acceptance of the strength of arguments. Civicness is usually supported and strengthened through the rule of law, a jurisdiction underwriting human and civil rights, and the peaceful resolution of conflict. Finally, scholars have identified the drivers of civil society action in a societal sphere that is populated by social movements, voluntary associations, initiatives, and groups, which is distinguishable from the market, the state, and the family (Kocka 2003). These groups, networks, movements, and veritable organizations constitute the infrastructure or backbone of civil society. As an ensemble, the organizations and groups form an intermediary sphere between the individual person, the society, and the respective government. Again, many features are attributed to this intermediary sphere of societal activity. Organizations might work on behalf of members and/or the general public, they might be engaged in advocacy, or they might be involved in the production of social services for the general public or for specific constituencies.

Since the mid-1970s, a growing number of scholars from various disciplines have started to take a closer look at the organizational infrastructure of civil society. Various labels are used to categorize the organizations, e.g., third sector, nonprofit, nongovernmental, and civil society organizations. Each "label" highlights a different feature. The term "third sector" signals that the respective organization belongs neither completely to the market nor to the state (Zimmer and Priller 2007: 15ff.); "nonprofit" indicates that profit gains are restricted from being distributed to members or owners of those organizations; "nongovernmental" indicates that the organization is engaged in public affairs without being a state or government entity; and a "civil society" organization signals that the respective organization works on behalf of civicness as an enactment and simultaneous underpinning of participatory or strong democracy.

Sometimes, however, terms are only "sound and smoke." This is particularly the case with the use of civil society in the general public and by the media. Lacking a refined definition, the term civil society has developed into a catchword that is referred to in many settings and circumstances. But, the popularity of the term in the media and general public significantly contrasts with its applicability and usefulness in empirical research. In other words, the very positive and democracy-friendly connotation of the term and concept of civil society might overshadow the very fact that the organizations that are populating the societal sphere characterized as civil society and situated in between the market and the state and serving as an intermediary sphere between the individual citizen and government need not necessarily be either democratic nor working on behalf of the strengthening of democratic government. It might be the case that these organizations are "under the thumb" of an authoritarian government if they are co-opted or live on public subsidies. Or, the organizations might be in accordance with authoritarianism, either in favor of charismatic leadership or in a cultural and normative sense in agreement with the ideology of the respective non-democratic regime.

Finally, many civil society organizations, in particular those that are active in service provision, might be prone not only to tolerate but also to at least indirectly support non-democratic settings. For some of these organizations, serving the community through the provision of, e.g., health care or other welfare-related activities, comes first. However, civil society organizations whose prime objective is the provision of services for the community or specific constituencies are the main arena of civic engagement of women. Indeed, some of these organizations are founded, exclusively staffed, and governed by women. Furthermore, many of these organizations perceive themselves as non-political, as mingling with politics and politicians is sometimes seen as a "dirty business." Therefore, the organizations and their women leaders tend to abstain from lobbying and advocacy. This is not to say that women's organizations are generally distancing themselves from politics. The women's movement and many initiatives and organizations around the world are a testament to the fact that since the nineteenth century women have increasingly taken the opportunity to become active and lobby on behalf of women's rights and gender justice as important components of a strong democracy. But, the success story of the women's movement should not distract our attention from the very fact that gender equality has not yet been achieved in any society around the world. Furthermore, it might also be the case that civil society organizations, in particular those with a female labor force and leadership, might not be working on behalf of a further advancement of gender justice and democracy but are, due to numerous reasons, indirectly or directly supporting authoritarianism and non-democratic rule.

With a special eye on women's organizations and initiatives, this volume aims at investigating the nexus between civil society and democracy in non-democratic settings. By doing this, the chapters follow a research design and specific approach developed by Gabriele Wilde, which serves as the theoretical framework and normative underpinning of the majority of the contributions present in this volume.

3. Gender relations and the authoritarian

Although the nexus between authoritarian politics and gender relations as an essential component and core of civil society is increasingly becoming the focus of political science analyses, it is still hardly understood theoretically or systematically. Just as gender relations were a focal point of research on democratic transformation – especially in institution-centered approaches, which focused on political participation and quotas (Norris and Inglehart 2001; Saxonberg 2000; Tripp 2001) – so too were gender relations in authoritarian regimes important for the empirical studies and country examples of authoritarianism research.

Such approaches typically conceptualize gender relations more in terms of the political order and less in terms of the social order. This is apparent, for instance, in the studies of Southeast Asia, which look at the reproduction of social elites in dynasties, scrutinize the political participation of certain women, or investigate the postcolonial legacy and significance of social diversity in gender (Robinson 1999). Other analyses have considered – against the background of the low level of political representation of women – the role of women in the construction of democratic oppositions (Fleschenberg and Hellmann-Rajanayagam 2009). Research on democratic transformation in Eastern Europe centered on how gender relations were changing on political and social levels; it examined the decreased institutional representation of women during the transition and the development of the political representation of women in democratization processes, which varied significantly across regions. In addition, gender research on Eastern Europe took up the problem of the trafficking of humans, especially women (Deutsche Gesellschaft für Osteuropakunde 2003; Hinterhuber, Fuchs, and Karbstein 2006; Hasibovic, Nickel, and Sticker 2007). Gender relations in autocracies have become the object of numerous political science analyses (for an overview, see Kreile 2009) in studies on the Middle East; scholars problematize specific and unequal forms of political participation; the degree of limited plurality (Linz 1964: 255); how political representation and parliaments function as mechanisms of authoritarian rule (Matz 1987); and the nexus between modernization, political emancipation movements, and democratization (Al-Rebholz 2014; Yesilyurt Gündüz 2002) with regard to the political and social position of women.

Beyond such studies – which focus above all on political rule and investigate how "electoral authoritarianism" (Schedler 2006) in voting procedures and parliament (Köllner 2008: 358ff.) impacts the gender order – current analyses of developments in Latin America and of the Arabic Spring have demonstrated that liberalization and formal democratization do not automatically lead to more equality or gender justice (Al-Ali 2012; Roy 2012; Antonakis 2017).

But explaining the sluggish democratization of social gender relations as the result of the stubborn persistence of patriarchal traditions and cultural religious foundations would be too easy.

Recent developments all over the world obviously show that the increasing authoritarian organizations and political power are shaking up not only societies striving for democracy. Civil society, a space for ideas of gender justice, plural gender identities, and equal life chances, is also diminishing, and its activities, responsibilities, and solidarities are limited by systemic mechanisms of discrimination, hierarchization, exclusion, and arrangements. According to this understanding, the institutions, parties, groups, and social organizations have a fundamental effect on civil society and the gender relations inscribed there. This is clearly what is happening by means of ideological, populist, discursive, and materialistic strategies, which offer traditional forms of gender identification and secure power and provide legitimation in authoritarian settings (Graf, Schneider, and Wilde 2017; Wilde and Meyer 2018).

Even in established European democracies the call has become louder for conservative family values, women's maternal role is being emphasized, and women are being precluded from political representation; the significance and function of hierarchical-patriarchal gender orders, traditional power structures, and non-governmental actors have now become more than evident: they serve the reproduction of domination structures and the stability of authoritarian regimes, as well as the democratization of gender relations (Sauer 1996: 123f.).

But research on autocracy and right-wing populism has kept quiet about this topic – the nexus between autocracies and the inscription and constituting of gender relations as social power relations falls neither into theoretical nor empirical focus in political science research, which is preoccupied with the structures and institutions of authoritarian systems, their core properties, functional logic, and maintenance mechanisms.

With the exception of post-structural and governmental approaches (Foucault 2000, 2001; Laclau and Mouffe 1991; Mouffe 2007), attention is only seldom turned to society, and even more seldom to gender, gender roles, and gender identities, a fact which has been criticized for a long time now by feminist autocracy research (Schneider and Wilde 2012). In light of political upheavals and changes aiming to turn civil society into a homogenous, enclosed entity and to inscribe gender relations as an essential and constitutive part of the questionable ideals of closed, non-pluralistic, and homophobic societies, mainstream research approaches and instruments for theoretical analyses are becoming increasingly outdated. The developing authoritarian inscriptions and mechanisms of control are far too complex to be explained by the distinction between unity parties or privileged parties and their fusions with different social organizations. And fundamental systematizations – such as Juan Jose Linz's (1964, 2000) triad of totalitarian systems, authoritarian regimes, and democracies, which is still being used in comparative empirical research, for instance, on the regimes in the Middle East (Bank 2009) – are overwhelmed and hardly perceptive given the intersection of formal democratic institutions and principles of the rule of law with authoritarian practices, as well as in view of self-contained power and domination relations. Non-institutional mechanisms for securing domination and the social foundations of authoritarian rule have not been adequately considered conceptually or methodically (Köllner 2008: 362); though feminists have criticized autocracy research exactly for this reason, it still continues to focus one-sidedly on domination mechanisms and legitimation strategies (Albrecht and Frankenberger 2010, 2011).

Feminist research on autocracy and right-wing populism fills this gap. By focusing on the domains of non-institutional legitimation and power strategies and civil society processes, it provides numerous possibilities for analyses, all of which take into account gender and gender relations systematically and conceptually. Based on an understanding of society aligned with Antonio Gramsci (1991) as the unity of political and civil society, and based on a basic understanding of power relations, feminist research emphasizes the significance and function of hierarchical gender orders and traditional-religious gender roles. In examining the retraditionalization of gender relations resulting from ideological, populist, or materialistic power and legitimation strategies, important knowledge about the reproduction of domination structures, the stability of authoritarian regimes, and the destruction of democratic relations has been acquired. By linking the establishment of political order to social conditions, retraditionalization is revealed as part of a practical life-nexus (Kreile 2016: 11); the focus becomes how phenomena of exploitation, alienation, exclusion, and violence intersect with political authorities in different domains of society. The construction of society as a closed entity inscribing gender relations as power relations becomes the central object of research and actual core of authoritarian politics.

Besides the ambivalent role of civil society organizations, a feminist perspective sees the public and private domains as powerful constructions (Wilde 2012). In this context, regulatory mechanisms are of central importance, as they posit relations between gender groups and distinguish the private from the public. It has been demonstrated that the activities of autocratic or totalitarian systems in the context of social policy, discourses about marriage and family, or the political organization of social reproduction have significant effects on the political inscription of gender relations as social power and domination relations. Signs of authoritarian policies are evident in gender identity constructions and role models in the public domain as well as – under the new negotiations of care work – in the limited self-determination and freedom of women in the private sphere.

Based on these criteria, and from a feminist standpoint, we can recognize the extent to which poverty and social inequalities are connected to the strengthening and establishing of authoritarian politics and domination relations. Also important for this project is understanding processes of socialization and the ideological upbringing of gendered subjects: how do authoritarian discourses and practices – which are in opposition to democratic ideas of equal and just gender relations – tailor gendered individuals to fit into their societies? Or, based on religious-cultural narratives and traditional family images, how is the systematic exclusion of women from the public domain and their discrimination carried out and legitimated (Schneider 2010)?

This background sketch presents new challenges for feminist research on autocracy. Notably, there must be a new examination of theoretical approaches, an elaboration of conceptual foundations, a reformulation of central categories and concepts, and the systematization of research perspectives. The aim must be to obtain concrete information about the dynamic, persistence, and weaknesses of autocracies, as well as systematic knowledge of informal and non-institutional forms of domination, which inscribe gender relations as power relations in civil societies. The anthology contributes to this project.

4. Structure of the book

In order to address the outlined issues in our anthology we combine theoretical-conceptual contributions and methodological implications (part I) with a set of case studies studying the interrelation of civil society and gender as societal power structures in different non-democratic settings and transforming regimes all over the world (part II). The compilation bonds gender, authoritarianism, and civil society in an auspicious way leading to insights into the whys and wherefores of the persistence of autocratic structures and gender inequalities worldwide. Moreover, in a second step our findings may also help to reassess gender and human rights policies designed to bring forward societal democratization.

The first part of the volume starts with the contribution by *Eva Maria Hinterhuber* and *Silke Schneider*, which provides a comprehensive overview of the multifaceted relationship between "Gender, Civil Society, and Non-Democratic Regimes." The authors scrutinized more than 200 scientific publications with the aim of detecting the ambivalent role of civil society and gender in non-democratic settings. Right at the beginning, the authors underline that civil society itself constitutes a contested terrain where "the struggle for social hegemony takes place" (p. 27). Accordingly, civil society might cleverly be used by autocratic regimes to keep women in their place, which is traditionally closely related to the private sphere and hence to the family. However, it is also true that since the very beginning of the women's movement, civil society has been "the space where the struggle for gender equality is taking place" (p. 31). Due to its ambivalence, heterogeneity, and multifunctionality, civil society should move into the focus of political science analysis that aims at shedding light on how non-democratic regimes manage to gain legitimacy and stay in power. The review of the literature by Hinterhuber and Schneider highlights that in-depth studies of gender relations in non-democratic settings as well as in societies and regimes in transition are essential for a better understanding of why and how these societies continue moving away from democracy. The chapter covers a wide spectrum of regions and countries ranging from the Middle East and Asia to Russia and Latin America; all in all, the authors draw our attention to a wide range of subtle strategies of how authoritarianism makes use of both civil society and gender relations in order to stay in power.

Annette Zimmer's contribution "If Not for Democracy, for What? Civil society in Authoritarian Settings" takes a closer look at the nexus between civil society and democracy. Civil society has been linked to considerations of the improvement of social justice and participatory democracy for decades now. Widely referred to in the media, civil society became almost synonymous with a countervailing power, if not alternative to authoritarianism. However, is it indeed the case that a lively civil society in the sense of a societal sphere populated by numerous voluntary and nonprofit organizations constitutes the bedrock of democratic government? Might it also be possible that associational life is lively and striving, although there is no democratic regime in place? The contribution addresses this topic by introducing civil society as a multidimensional concept, highlighting the variety of civil society actors, and finally by discussing from a functional perspective whether and how the concept has been used and interpreted by key scholars of political theory and philosophy. Against this background, she comes to the conclusion that civil society as a societal sphere and hence as an arena for the engagement of voluntary organizations and nonprofits need not necessarily go along with democracy.

In the chapter "The Authoritarian as Discourse and Practice: A Feminist Post-Structural Approach," *Gabriele Wilde* addresses a desideratum in autocracy research, which still holds tight to a state- and institution-centered perspective and thus masks the non-institutional mechanisms of securing domination and social power relations as the foundation of authoritarian rule. Starting with the question concerning the nexus between autocracies or hybrid political systems and the inscription of gender relations as social power relations, this contribution presents a feminist theoretical approach grounded in political science. Organized civil society, the public and private domains, and specific knowledge discourses make up the four central areas in which various mechanisms of inclusion and exclusion, as well as social equality and inequality processes, are put into place by regimes. With this focus, the chapter shows how the inscription of social gender relations – in particular their significance for the power and domination of autocracies – can be systematically examined.

In the chapter "Analyzing the Authoritarian: Post-structural Framing-Analysis – a Methodological Approach," *Isabelle-Christine Panreck* introduces post-structural framing-analysis as an instrument for feminist authoritarianism research. This chapter aims to show how the post-structural framing approach can be used for the analysis of authoritarian discourse and gender relations as relations of power and domination. Through the example of the Serbian invocation of women as "Mother of the Nation," *Panreck's* contribution demonstrates how framing can be applied to examine the concatenation of different discourse levels as strategies to establish gender power relations in authoritarian regimes.

Katharina Obuch introduces the second part of the volume with her chapter titled "Between Militancy and Survival? The Case of the Nicaraguan Women's Movement." She presents findings from her interviews with women's activists and civil society experts in Nicaragua, a country historically known for its strong and belligerent women's movement. Examining the movement's historical evolution, its major wings, and the particular challenges faced by Nicaraguan women's organizations in the context of today's hybrid regime structures, she highlights the movement's ambiguous potential: it is a pioneer of societal democratization yet often promotes traditional gender roles. More precisely, her findings demonstrate that civil society can play an important role in the overcoming of power relations (e.g., as an agent of change, school of democracy, or democratic watchdog) as well as in their reinforcement – in the form of conservative and unprogressive (antifeminist) movements, dubious entanglements with government structures, or simply as depoliticized service providers.

In "The Tunisian Constitution between Democratic Claim and Constitutional Reality" G*abriele Wilde* and *Jasmin Sandhaus* consider the implications and effects of Tunisia's constitutional process for democratic gender relations. Focusing on the development process of the constitution and constitutional texts, they reflect on the integration of women's associations and the significance of gender equality and question the prevalence of struggles for gender equality and to what extent the views of actors and interest groups were portrayed and unequal gender relations discussed and negotiated. This chapter concludes that the Tunisian Constitution can be understood as a hegemonic construction using traditional ideas to establish gender relations as domination relations and confirms the subordinate role of women.

The contribution by *Joyce Marie Mushaben* provides a multifaceted picture of the women's movement in Turkey. The article draws our attention to the fact that Turkish society is extremely heterogeneous, which is reflected by numerous factions and diverse groups of the women's movement, as well as by a multitude of very different NGOs and civil society organizations working on behalf of women's issues. Despite many hurdles and significant difficulties related to class, ethnicity, and regional provenience of women activists and key protagonists, the author clearly identifies space and opportunities for the development of a shared and coherent identity of the Turkish women's movement. The title of Mushaben's contribution, "'I'm here too, Girlfriend …': Reclaiming Public Spaces for the Gendering of Civil Society in Turkey," signals a positive development toward a further empowerment of women in Turkey with the goal of standing up for their rights. However, in between the lines there are also indicators of how fragile and vulnerable the Turkish women's movement still is. It is an open question whether the heterogeneous women's movement that is furthermore divided along class and ethnic cleavages will be able to speak up and to build a more or less uniform bulwark against repression, nationalism, and arbitrary use of power.

Stephanie Bräuer's chapter, "Between Provocation and Incorporation – Social Gender Activism in the Hybrid Regime of the PRC," focuses on the Beijing anti-domestic violence (ADV) movement as a case study of social gender activism in China. Analyzing the evolution and tactical alignment of ADV activists in the capital, she highlights how traditional, professional organizations with well-established links to the political system have laid the ground for the recent awakening of a provocative and confrontational activism seeking to raise public awareness. Still, she concludes that in the given context of autocratic structures and recently increasing hard crackdowns on social gender activists, a non-confrontational, unprovocative tactical approach seems to be better suited to influence policy decision-making in China.

Finally, *Patricia Graf* shows in her chapter, "The Shadow of Autocracy. Gender Politics in Chile," how the authoritarian gender regime in Chile was only partially reformed in the country's transition process, as traditional gender roles are extremely persistent up until today. While access to positions of power and resources have changed, the conservative discourses and gender images of the old military dictatorship were carried over to the new democratic regime. Analyzing the particular role of women's movements during the transition, she points out how feminist demands were successfully weakened by establishing a state feminism and enforcing the division between radical groups and "institutionalists."

References

Bargetz, Brigitte et al. (2017): Geschlechterverhältnisse als Machtverhältnisse. In: Femina Politica 26, 1, pp. 11-24.
Adloff, Frank (2005): Zivilgesellschaft. Theorie und politische Praxis. Frankfurt am Main: Campus Studium.
Al-Ali, Nadje (2012): Gendering the Arab Spring. In: Middle East Journal of Culture and Communication 5, 1, pp. 26-31.
Albrecht, Holger/Frankenberger, Rolf (Eds.) (2010): Autoritarismus Reloaded. Neuere Ansätze und Erkenntnisse der Autokratieforschung. Baden-Baden: Nomos.
Albrecht, Holger/Frankenberger, Rolf (2011): Die „dunkle Seite" der Macht: Stabilität und Wandel autoritärer Systeme. In: Albrecht, Holger/Frankenberger, Rolf/Frech, Siegfried (Eds.): Autoritäre Regime: Herrschaftsmechanismen, Legitimationsstrategien, Persistenz und Wandel. Schwalbach: Wochenschau Verlag, pp. 17-45.
Al-Rebholz, Anil (2014): Das Ringen um die Zivilgesellschaft in der Türkei: intellektuelle Diskurse, oppositionelle Gruppen und Soziale Bewegungen seit 1980. Bielefeld: Transcript.

Antonakis, Anna (2017): In Transformation? – Renegotiating Gender and State Feminism in Tunisia between 2011 and 2014: Power, Positionalities and the Public Sphere. Berlin: Freie Universität.

Bank, Andre (2009): Die Renaissance des Autoritarismus. Erkenntnisse und Grenzen neuerer Beiträge der Comparative Politics und Nahostforschung. In: Hamburg Review of Social Sciences 4, 1, pp. 10-41.

Barber, Benjamin (2004): Strong Democracy: Participatory Democracy for a New Age. Berkeley: Univ. of California Press.

Carothers, Thomas (2002): The End of the Transition Paradigm. In: Journal of Democracy 13, 1, pp. 5-21.

Cohen, John L./Arato, Andrew (1997): Civil Society and Political Theory. Cambridge/Mass.: MIT-Press.

Croissant, Aurel (2002): Einleitung: Demokratische Grauzonen – Konturen eines Forschungszweigs. In: Bendel, Petra (Eds): Zwischen Demokratie Und Diktatur. Zur Konzeption und Empirie Demokratischer Grauzonen. Opladen: Leske und Budrich, pp. 9-47.

Croissant, Aurel/Merkel, Wolfgang (2004): Introduction: Democratization in the Early Twenty-First Century. In: Democratization 11, 5, pp. 1-9.

Dahrendorf, Ralf (1991): Die gefährdete Civil Society. In: Michalski, Krzysztof (Ed.): Europa und die Civil Society. Castelgandolfo-Gespräche 1989. Stuttgart: Klett-Cotta, pp. 247-263.

Dahrendorf, Ralf (1999): Impulse für die Bürgergesellschaft. Die Kraft des Dritten Sektors. In: Reflexion und Initiative. Hamburg, pp. 10-15.

Deutsche Gesellschaft für Osteuropakunde (2003): Osteuropa. In: Zeitschrift für Gegenwartsfragen des Ostens 53, 5, pp. 633-733.

Diamond, Larry (2008): The Democratic Rollback. The Resurgence of the Predatory State. In: Foreign Affairs 87, 36, pp. 36-48.

Diamond, Larry (2015): Facing up to the Democratic Recession. In: Journal of Democracy 26, 1, pp. 141-155.

Cavatorta, Francesco (2015): Civil Society Activism under Authoritarian Rule. A Comparative Perspective. London: Routledge.

Etzioni, Amitai (1994): Spirit of Community, New York: Simon & Schuster.

Fleschenberg, Andrea/Hellmann-Rajnayagam, Dagmar (2008): Female Political Power in Asia: Dynasties, Religion, Sacrifices. Some Introductory Remarks. In: Fleschenberg, Andrea/Hellmann-Rajnayagam, Dagmar (Eds.): Goddesses, Heroes, Sacrifices: Female Political Power in Asia. Berlin, pp. 13-27.

Foucault, Michel (2000): Die Gouvernementalität. In: Bröckling, Ulrich/Krasmann, Susanne/Lemke, Thomas (Eds.): Gouvernementalität der Gegenwart. Studien zur Ökonomisierung des Sozialen. Frankfurt am Main: Suhrkamp, pp. 41-67.

Foucault, Michel (2001): In Verteidigung der Gesellschaft. Frankfurt am Main: Suhrkamp.

Freedom House (2018): Freedom in the World 2018. Democracy in Crisis. https://freedomhouse.org/report/freedom-world/freedom-world-2018 (10.01.2018).

Introduction 23

Graf, Patricia/Schneider, Silke/Wilde, Gabriele (2017): Geschlechterverhältnisse und die Macht des Autoritären. In: Femina Politica 26, 1, pp. 70-88.

Gramsci, Antonio (1991): Gefängnishefte, Bd. 1-10. Berlin/Hamburg: Argument-Verlag.

Habermas, Jürgen (1992): Faktizität und Geltung. Frankfurt am Main: Campus.

Hasibovic, Sanin/Nickel, Manja/Sticker, Maja (2007): Gender und Transition im Raum Südosteuropa. In: Arbeitspapiere und Materialien der Forschungsstelle Osteuropa der Universität Bremen 85 (Regimewechsel und Gesellschaftswandel in Osteuropa), pp. 133-136.

Havel, Vaclav/Keane, John (Eds.) (1985): The Power of the Powerless: Citizens Against the State in Central Eastern Europe. London: Taylor and Francis.

Heuerlin, Christopher (2010): Governing Civil Society: The Political Logic of NGO – State Relations Under Dictatorship. In: Voluntas 21, 2, pp. 220-239.

Hinterhuber, Eva Maria/Fuchs, Gesine/Karbstein, Inga (Eds.) (2006): Geschlechterpolitik nach der EU-Osterweiterung. In: Femina Politica 15, 1, pp. 9-98.

Huntington, Samuel P. (1991): Democracy's Third Wave. In: Journal of Democracy 2, 2, pp. 12-34.

Keane, John (1998) Civil Society: Old Images, New Visions. Stanford: Stanford Univ. Press.

Kneer, Georg (1997): Zivilgesellschaft. In: Kneer, Georg et al. (Eds.): Soziologische Gesellschaftsbegriffe II. Stuttgart: UTB, pp. 229-251.

Kocka, Jürgen (2003): Zivilgesellschaft in historischer Perspektive. In: Forschungsjournal Neue Soziale Bewegungen 16, 2, pp. 29-37.

Köllner, Patrick (2008): Autoritäre Regime – Ein Überblick über die jüngere Literatur. In: Zeitschrift für Vergleichende Politikwissenschaft 2, 2, pp. 351-366.

Kreile, Renate (2009): Transformation und Gender im Nahen Osten. In: Beck, Martin/Harders, Cilja/Jünemann, Annette/Stetter, Stephan (Eds.): Der Nahe Osten im Umbruch: Zwischen Transformation und Autoritarismus. Wiesbaden: Springer VS, pp. 253-276.

Kreile, Regina (2016): Die verdrängte Demokratie. Essays zur politischen Theorie. Baden-Baden: Nomos.

Laclau, Ernesto/Mouffe, Chantal (1991): Hegemonie und radikale Demokratie. Wien: Passagen Verlag.

Levitsky, Steven/Way, Lucan A. (2010): Competitive Authoritarianism. Hybrid Regimes after the Cold War. Cambridge et al.: Cambridge University Press.

Linz, Juan Jose (1964): An Authoritarian Regime: The Case of Spain. In: Arland, Erik/Littunen, Yrjo (Eds.): Cleavages, Ideologies and Party Systems. Helsinki, pp. 291-341.

Linz, Juan J. (2000): Totalitarian and Authoritarian Regimes. Boulder, Colorado: Lynne Rienner Publishers.

Márquez, Javier (2017): Non-democratic Politics. Authoritarianism, Dictatorship, and Democratization. London: Palgrave, Macmillan Education.

Matz, Ulrich (1987): Zur Dialektik von totalitärer Ideologie und pluralistischer Gesellschaft. In: Funke, Manfred/Jacobsen, Hans-Adolf/Knütter, Hans-Helmut/Schwarz, Hans-Peter (Eds.):

Demokratie und Diktatur. Geist und Gestalt politischer Herrschaft in Europa. Bonn: Bundeszentrale für politische Bildung, pp. 554-566.

Mouffe, Chantal (2007): Über das Politische. Wider die kosmopolitische Illusion. Frankfurt am Main: Suhrkamp.

Norris, Pippa/Inglehart, Ronald (2001): Women and Democracy. Cultural Obstacles to Representation. In: Journal of Democracy 12, 3, pp. 126-140.

O'Donnell, Guillermo A./Schmitter, Philippe C./Whitehead, Laurence (Eds.) (1986): Transitions from Authoritarian Rule. Baltimore: Johns Hopkins University Press.

Pickel, Susanne (2013): Demokratie, Anokratie, Autokratie und die Verwirklichung der Rechte von Frauen – Wechselwirkung zwischen Gender Empowerment, Wertestrukturen und Regimepersistenz. In: Kailitz, Steffen/Köllner, Patrick (Eds.): Autokratien im Vergleich. Sonderheft 47 der PVS. Baden-Baden: Nomos-Verlag, pp. 438-476.

Plattner, Marc (2017): Liberal Democracy's fading Allure. In: Journal of Democracy 28, 4, pp. 5-14.

Robinson, Kathryn (1999): Women. Difference versus Diversity. In: Emmerson, Donald K. (Ed.): Indonesia beyond Suharto. Polity, Economy, Society, Transition. New York: ME Sharp Inc., pp. 237-261.

Roy, Olivier (2012): The Transformation of the Arab World. In: Journal of Democracy 23, 3, pp. 5-18.

Sauer, Birgit (1996): Transition zur Demokratie? Die Kategorie „Geschlecht" als Prüfstein für die Zuverlässigkeit von sozialwissenschaftlichen Transformationstheorien. In: Kreisky, Eva (Ed.): Vom patriarchalen Staatssozialismus zur patriarchalen Demokratie. Wien: Verlag für Gesellschaftskritik, pp. 131-168.

Saxonberg, Steven (2000): Women in East European Parliaments. In: Journal of Democracy 11, 2, pp. 145-158.

Schedler, Andreas (Ed.) (2006): Electoral Authoritarianism. The Dynamics of Unfree Competition. Boulder: Lynne Rienner Publishers.

Schneider, Silke (2010): Verbotener Umgang – Ausländer und Deutsche im Nationalsozialismus. Diskurse um Sexualität, Moral, Wissen und Strafe. Baden-Baden: Nomos.

Schneider, Silke/Wilde, Gabriele (2012): Autokratie, Demokratie und Geschlecht: Geschlechterverhältnisse in autoritären Regimen. In: Femina Politica. Zeitschrift für feministische Politik 2, 1, pp. 9-16.

Spires, Anthony (2011): Contigent Symbosis and Civil Society in an Authoritarian State: Understanding the Survival of China's Grassroots NGOs. In: American Journal of Sociology 117, 1, pp. 1-45.

Taylor, Charles (1991): Die Beschwörung der Civil Society. In: Michalski, Krzysztof (Ed.): Europa und die Civil Society. Castelgandolfo-Gespräche 1989. Stuttgart: Klett-Cotta, pp. 52-81.

Teets, Jessica C. (2016): Civil Society under Authoritarianism: The China Model. Cambridge: Cambridge Univ. Press.

Tripp, Aili Mari (2001): Women and Democracy. The New Political Activism in Africa. In: Journal of Democracy 12, 3, pp. 141-155.

Walzer, Michael (1992): Zivile Gesellschaft und amerikanische Demokratie. Berlin: Rotbuch Verlag.

Walzer, Michael (2003): A Better Vision: The Idea of Civil Society. In: Hodgkinson, Virginia A./Foley, Michael W. (Eds.): The civil society Reaser. Hanover/London: Univ. Press of England, pp. 306-321.

Warren, Mar E. (2001): Democracy and Associations. Princeton: Princeton Univ. Press.

Wilde, Gabriele (2012): Totale Grenzen des Politischen: Die Zerstörung der Öffentlichkeit bei Hannah Arendt. In: Femina politica. 21, 1, pp.17-29.

Wilde, Gabriele/Meyer, Birgit (2018): Angriff auf die Demokratie. In: Femina Politica 27, 1.

Wischermann. Jörg (2013): Zivilgesellschaften als Stütze autoritärer Regime. Das Fallbeispiel Vietnam. In: Kailitz, Steffen/Köllner, Patrick (Eds.): Autokratien im Vergleich, Sonderheft 47 der PVS. Baden-Baden: Nomos-Verlag, pp. 324-353.

Yesilyurt Gündüz, Zuhal (2002): Die Demokratisierung ist weiblich. Die türkische Frauenbewegung und ihr Beitrag zur Demokratisierung der Türkei. Osnabrück: Der Andere Verlag.

Zimmer, Annette/Priller, Eckhard (2007): Gemeinnützige Organisationen im gesellschaftlichen Wandel. Wiesbaden: VS Verlag.

Gender, Civil Society, and Non-Democratic Regimes

Eva Maria Hinterhuber and Silke Schneider

1. Introduction

In contemporary political science, research on authoritarianism emphasizes the role of the state and of institutions for the maintenance of dominance, but largely neglects the significance of non-institutional influences. As a consequence, the role of civil society – although described as a sphere in which the struggle for social hegemony takes place – is most often not taken into adequate consideration. At the same time, despite the fact that studies have shown the crucial contribution of gender in the making of the nation-state, gender relations are rarely included in reasoning about autocracies. In this chapter, we bring together current research on gender, civil society, and non-democratic regimes in order to establish a new perspective on the function and persistence of authoritarianism. Our theoretical starting point is Gabriele Wilde's innovative theoretical approach to authoritarianism (Wilde in this volume; see also Schneider and Wilde 2012). Placing civil society at the core of a new understanding of the political, Wilde reflects on the organization of gender relations in civil society in four main ways: she focuses on civil society organizations (in the tradition of Tocqueville); the plural public (with reference to Arendt); familial privacy (in accordance with Pateman); and citizenship as discursive practice (as developed by Mouffe). On this basis Wilde develops a specific research framework for the analysis of hegemonic gender relations in autocracies.

Against this theoretical background the aim of this chapter is to lay the foundation for future empirical research that shall help to fill the initially mentioned research gap in authoritarianism studies. This first calls for a solid account of what has been done so far; the basis of our contribution is therefore a systematic review of existing literature on gender, civil society, and non-democratic regimes of more than 200 scientific publications mostly published in the last two decades. In our chapter we take up Wilde's notion of the political, which focuses on civil society, and review research that systematically applies a gender perspective to the concept of civil society. Grounded in a Gramscian concept of civil society, we examine how other studies on gender relations in authoritarian and hybrid regimes have focused on how gender inequality serves to legitimize and stabilize authoritarianism in society.

In the following section, we elaborate on the organization of gender relations in civil society in non-democratic regimes. First, the possibilities for gendered subjects to organize themselves under authoritarianism are examined with particular regard to the development and specificity of women's movements. Second, the complex relationship between gender, civil society, and the public sphere under the aggravating circumstances of authoritarianism is discussed. Third, the effect of (an emerging) civil society on the notion of privacy in authoritarian regimes is considered from a gender perspective. Last but not least, it is discussed in what sense discursive practices on gender relations contribute to the maintenance of power in autocracies. In conclusion, we discuss the results of our systematic literature analysis and examine the importance of the inclusion of gender relations in analyses of civil society for understanding the maintenance of power in non-democratic regimes. Moreover, we develop hypotheses and end with further research desiderata for the future exploration of the subject area.

2. Focusing on civil society: toward a new understanding of the political

An understanding of the political that focuses on civil society perceives societal power relations not primarily as an effect of action but as a result of the struggle for social supremacy within civil society itself. Civil society is therefore not placed beyond power relations but is the site where the battle for hegemony is located. This becomes especially clear when a gender perspective is applied. The combination of civil society and gender have been researched in manifold ways in feminist theory, mainly with regard to the dichotomy between public and private spheres. Furthermore, a Gramscian understanding of civil society plays an important role for gender-sensitive research. The influence of gendered, dominant states on civil society, as well as on its internal organization, are also subjects of the respective literature.

3. Civil society, the public, and the private

A central starting point of feminist research on the topic "civil society" is the examination of the public and private spheres, which have been prominent in the history of feminist theory since their inception (see Pateman 1989: 118). Feminist theorists have thoroughly examined the gendered dichotomy between public and private running through the history of Western theories. Susan Moller Okin's (1998: 116–141; see also Hagemann 2008: 29; Howell 2005: 12–13; Klein 2001: 190) work examines their strong impact on the perception of civil society. Okin points out that the juxtaposition of "public" and "private" includes the distinction between state and society as well as that between domestic and non-domestic life. In the first distinction, civil society is assigned to the private sphere, whereas it is attributed to the public in the second. Against the background of the gendered character of the dichotomy, the second perspective shows civil society as a "male" area from which women are absent or even excluded (see also Phillips 2002: 72) – women are still traditionally located in the private, domestic sphere, and essentialist arguments are called forth to justify their responsibility for reproductive work.

In Carole Pateman's (1988) "sexual contract," she convincingly argues that the gender-specific division of labor is an essential prerequisite for a "social contract." In this context, the boundary between "public" and "private" becomes a social construct (Hagemann 2008: 28), which is variable and subject to change.[1] At the same time, the autonomous subject of civil society, the citizen, is always conceptualized as male (see also Wilde 2009: 43). Only when the sexual contract is no longer a precondition for a social contract can civil society be constructed as a place of freedom and self-determination (see Wilde 2009: 46). As a political structure, the sexual contract still characterizes contemporary political systems (see Wilde 2009: 42). A mere revaluation of domains traditionally ascribed to women thus remains in the dichotomy that underlies the sexual contract. In contrast, a "concept that assigns to civic policy [exclusively] the task to formulate basics for the common political identity of subjects" offers a possible alternative, especially from a gender perspective (Wilde 2009: 44, with reference to Mouffe 1992; translation by authors).[2]

---

[1] Empirical proof offers the changes of the relationship between public and private in postsocialist transition states. Their effects on gender relations were analyzed by Pateman (1989) in a second piece of work, which refers to the emergence of civil society parallel to the shift to a "free" market economy.

[2] The feminist critique of the widespread "conceptual separation of civil society in a democracy-relevant, political-public and a seemingly less significant to democracy, social-private branch" (Ruppert 1998: 501; translation by authors) also derives from the discussion of "public" and "private." Young comes to a similar conclusion, which leads to her distinction between a "literary-cultural and a political-public sphere" of civil society on a conceptual level (cf. Young 1999; cited in Hagemann 2008: 32). Given the social division of labor between men and women, both distinctions are deeply gendered. The higher weight of a political to a social or "literary-cultural branch" (Hagemann 2008: 32) of civil society again reflects hierarchical gender relations. Accordingly, the conceptual assumption of such "separate civil societies" (Ruppert, 1998: 500; translation by authors) is dismissed by feminist scholars, yet to varying degrees: one side evaluates social engagement only as part of civil society when in addition to social services advocacy functions are also fulfilled (cf. Appel, Gubitzer, and Sauer 2003: 14–15). Other voices go further: social organizations create the foundations for political participation, hold a politicization potential, and may even initiate processes of social change – potentially also in terms of gender relations (Sifft and Abels 1999: 27; for an empirical study on the topic see Hinterhuber 2012).

4. Gender and civil society: recourse to Gramsci

In addition to the analysis of the gendered character of the distinction between public and private and its consequences not least for the definition of civil society, another strand of feminist theory refers to Antonio Gramsci's model of civil society (cf. Appel et al. 2003; Cohen 1999; Fraser 1996; Hagemann 2008; Phillips 2002; Sauer 2004; Sänger 2007; Wilde 2009; Wilde 2013). Although Gramsci's concept focused originally on class struggle, it can also be applied to the "battle of the sexes." It stands to reason whether it can be adapted to other social categories that structure society and constitute social power relations. Thus, Gramsci's terminology has been taken up by feminists and activists alike and applied to hierarchical gender relations in order to overcome them.

As mentioned, Gramsci understands civil society as a terrain "on which social domination and power relations are contested" (Sänger 2007: 19; translation by authors). Thus, he deserves credit for defining "the dimension of conflict over the cultural power of interpretation in modern civil societies" (Adloff 2005: 43; translation by authors), which cannot be underestimated, especially from a gender perspective. Fraser's theoretical design of "subaltern counterpublics" (1997: 81) can be interpreted in a Gramscian tradition. According to her model, subaltern counterpublics are "parallel discursive arenas where members of subordinated social groups invent and circulate counterdiscourses, which in turn permit them to formulate oppositional interpretations of their identities, interests, and needs" (Fraser 1997: 81). Furthermore, Young's (2000) model of the public sphere resembles Gramsci's understanding of civil society: "a locus/space for conflicts and struggles about inclusion and exclusion of marginalized social groups in democracy, as well as for contestation and negotiation of political discourses, policies and visions for the future of the polity" (Mokre and Siim 2013: 26).

Since legal achievements of recent decades have not been able to overcome the hierarchical character of gender relations, the goal of gender equality cannot be realized exclusively at the state level. Thus, from a gender perspective, civil society is the space where the struggle for gender equality is taking place (cf. Phillips 2002: 79). "Gender-sensitive, anti-patriarchal hegemony, e.g., new labor relations, equal social, and economic rights for men and women, must be fought for and enforced in civil society" (Sauer 2003: 132; translation by authors). Moreover, Gramsci's concept of power clearly reveals the ambivalence of civil society: "It is at the same time a moment of domination and of resistance" (Schade 2002: 15; translation by authors). Against this background, civil society cannot be perceived in opposition to a gendered and dominant state as "a sphere of free communitization," but must be viewed as "an area where time and again a women-friendly order must be created anew" (Appel et al. 2003: 11–12; translation by authors).

Civil society is not only inclusive but also exclusive. From a gender perspective, the most obvious examples of the exclusive character of civil society are in organizations such as the Freemasons, Rotarians, Lions Club, etc., whose career networks are still almost exclusively relevant for men (cf. the concept of the "male bond," Kreisky 1994). Furthermore, the gendered nature of civil society manifests itself in many ways: Gender differences exist in relation to female/male dominance in certain civil society areas (e.g., in the social sphere), and, consequently, exert an influence on society; the nature and extent of civic engagement as well as the positions of women and men in civil society organizations follow gendered patterns. In sum, hierarchical gender relations are also dominant and (re-)produced in civil society.

At the same time, civil society represents a space where gender concerns and perspectives can be articulated. Women's struggle for equality often begins in civil society, if only because they do not possess full citizenship rights (cf. Reverter-Bañón 2006: 8). Whether the access threshold to civil society is actually lower in comparison to institutionalized politics, as it is often claimed, and whether unconventional participation is particularly attractive for women are controversial matters. In any case, the dominant and traditional division of labor between the sexes creates different conditions for civic engagement (see above; see Gubitzer 2003: 173).

Nevertheless, there is consensus that women shape the face of civil society, especially when it comes to social issues of local interest (cf. Phillips 2002:

73).³ Due to the fact that women have long been excluded from institutionalized politics and to this day are not represented to the same extent as men (see Inter-Parliamentary Union 2013),⁴ civic engagement of women has a long historical tradition. Several reasons for their high level of participation are considered: the innovative potential of civil society is underlined as facilitating gender-political activities by many scholars, in opposition to the impervious state and market (cf. Phillips 2002: 78). And the pluralism of civil society – a quality clearly less pronounced in the state and the market – corresponds to the pluralistic character of feminism (see Phillips 2002). Besides, civil society engagement offers women a variety of training facilities, the opportunity to network, and possible job prospects (see Gubitzer 2000: 16). Moreover, if understood as a space where social groups can pool their interests and introduce them to the public sphere (cf. Habermas 1992: 443–444), civil society provides a number of starting points in terms of gender policy.

Whether civil society is a "female ghetto of underpaid jobs and little power" (Liborakina 1998: 57) or has emancipatory potential depends on the following decisive criterion: the question of political participation (Gubitzer 2000, 2003; Appel et al. 2003), i.e., whether civic engagement grants women political subject status, thus enabling them to shape society and actively participate in politics (Appel et al. 2003: 7).

5. Gender, civil society, and non-democratic regimes

As discussed, research on civil society and gender generally deals with the opportunities and constraints in the public and private spheres; civil society as a place for negotiation of political discourses and their concrete implementation in a polity; and the gendered nature of civil society itself. These issues coincide

---

3   As mentioned above, this fact should also be taken into consideration when conceptualizing civil society – not least in order to not reproduce social relations of power on a theoretical level.
4   Holland-Cunz argues that the disproportional representation of women in institutionalized politics worldwide is as relevant as the right to vote (cf. Holland-Cunz 1999: 213).

with the four subject areas developed by Wilde (in this volume) to analyze the constitutive relationship between autocratic systems and societal gender relations, i.e., civil society organizations, the plural public, familial privacy, and citizenship as discursive practice.[5]

In the following section we examine the current literature on women's civic activism, in particular women's liberation movements in autocracies, in periods of transition from authoritarianism to democracy or the converse, which is followed by a review of publications on political rights, representation, and women's participation in non-democratic regimes. Consequently, literature on the issue of privacy from a gender perspective in authoritarian regimes is assessed. In a fourth step, gender, citizenship, and discursive practices in non-democratic regimes are presented systematically.

6. Women's political activism in times of change: from authoritarianism to democracy and vice versa

Studies about women's liberation movements and women's civic engagement in female dominated or feminist civil society organizations are at the intersection of research on gender, civil society, and political systems. And there are a range of country-specific studies not only on full democracies (e.g., Denmark: Andersen 2004; Japan: Shigematsu 2012; Czech Republic: Forst 2006),[6] but also on so-called flawed democracies.[7] Furthermore, there are publications on

---

5 Wilde presents these topics in a different sequence.
6 For the following systematization, cf. Democracy Index, The Economist's Intelligence Unit (2011).
7 Poland: see for example Fuchs (2003, 2013); Bulgaria: Luleva (2006); Croatia: Kunovich and Deitelbaum (2004); Croatia and Serbia: Grsak et al. (2007); South Africa: Hirschmann (1998); Hassim and Gous (1998); Botswana: Cailleba and Kumar (2010); India: Berglund (2011), Datta (2007), Gibson (2012), Kilby (2011), MCDuie Ra (2007), Unterhalter and Dutt (2001); Philippines: Reese (2010); Taiwan: Chang (2009) and Lo and Fan (2010); South Korea: Ruhlen (2007); Mexico: Brickner (2006, 2010, 2013), Marquardt (2005), and Reininger et al. (2013).

Gender, Civil Society, and Non-Democratic Regimes 35

civil society and gender in various hybrid regimes[8] and – in terms of our interest – in authoritarian regimes.[9] Many of the authors are especially interested in the gendered nature of transition periods, both from autocracy to democracy and vice versa.[10]

The spectrum of research is exemplified by changes in Eastern European countries; the emphasis here is placed on the Russian Federation, as there are studies on women's gender policy activism during the transition to formal democracy in the Soviet Union, its authoritarian predecessor, and on Russia's reclassification as an authoritarian political system.

There are numerous studies on women's movements under Soviet rule, e.g., Köbberling (1993) covers both state and dissident gender policy activism (see also Attwood 1990). Pateman had already characterized the gendered transition from state socialism to a market economy in 1989. She described the emergence of civil society as the transition from a "paternalistic" to a "fraternalistic" patriarchy and thus explained why the changes of the political system went hand in hand with a radical change in gender relations in post-socialist countries. And Watson (1995, 1993) shows how, alongside the state, the "second society," which filled the vacuum caused by the oppression of civil society, contributed to the maintenance and reinforcement of traditional gender roles (see also Hinterhuber 2012: 56).

Immediately after the collapse of the Soviet Union, several authors wrote about the history of national women's movements, including numerous women's organizations that were founded in the course of the transformation

---

8   Singapore: Lyons (2005); Cambodia: Mona (2013); Ukraine: Hankivsky (2012), Phillips (2008); Albania: Binaj (2006); Turkey: Akdeniz-Taxer (2011).
9   Egypt: Krause (2008); Algeria: Cheriet (1996); China: Howell (2003, 2004); Jordan and Syria: Rabo (1996); Yemen: Destremau (2011); Pakistan: Weiss (2011); Russia: Caiazza (2002), Godel (2002), Hemment (2007a, 2007b), Hinterhuber (1999, 2011, 2012), Kay (2000), Ritter (2001), Salmenniemi (2005, 2008), and Schmitt (1997); United Arab Emirates: Krause (2012).
10 The following authors provide an overview of Central and Eastern European states: Einhorn and Sever (2003), Mueller and Funk (1993), Pető and Szapor (2004), and Sloat (2005). The publications of Al-Ali (2005), Beck et al. (2009), Klein-Hessling (1998, 1999), Ghodsee (2007), and Sharify-Funk (2008) deal with Muslim women's organizations. For the European Union see also Agustín (2008), Halsaa (2012), and Lister (2006).

processes (e.g., Schmitt 1997). Against the background of a neo-traditional gender climate and sharp cuts in gender-specific political, social, and civil rights, it was particularly interesting to see how women seized the new opportunities for participation and organized themselves in civil society organizations (see, e.g., Racioppi and O'Sullivan 1997; Kay 2000; Hemment 2007a), thus proving that women were involved in the transformation process. In the face of the Chechen wars in the 1990s, other studies focused on the civic engagement of women for peace (cf. Hinterhuber 1999; Eremitcheva and Zdravomyslova 2001; Caiazza 2002; Hapke 2009). In the first years of the new century, at a time when the democratization process in Russia was at least formally completed, feminist researchers were interested in how activists of the "new" women's movement in Russia defined democracy and emancipation (cf. Godel 2002).

The results of the research on women's organizations in Russia in terms of their topics, objectives, and degree of organization and of political participation will be presented here in a nutshell. In comparison to czarist Russia, women were able to gain broader rights in the aftermath of the October Revolution of 1917, e.g., concerning suffrage, marital, reproductive, and, above all, labor rights. The dominance of communism gave center stage to the integration of women into the labor force – and not equal opportunities (which was perceived as a "side contradiction"). Without downplaying their achievements (such as literacy and improvements in health care), socialist state feminism went along with the divestiture of the bottom-up women's liberation movements (proletarian and liberal) founded at the turn of the millennium (Köbberling 1993: 44). In 1930, it was declared that women's liberation had been achieved in a tactical move to further exploit the female workforce: the double (or triple) burden of women as unpaid care workers and laborers under extreme conditions such as food shortage was ignored and unchallenged (cf. Attwood 1990: 118). Soviet gender policy then changed in conjunction with economic and demographic necessities, i.e., either women's traditional roles and duties or their equal participation in the workforce were emphasized. Women's activism was strictly regulated and organized by the state, and feminist dissidents were repressed or forced to emigrate. The above stated instrumentality of gender policy became especially visible before and after the collapse of the Soviet

Union at the beginning of the 1990s, when the greater part of women's civil, political, and economic rights was taken away.

But the emerging civil society opened doors to civic participation and gender policy activism: the "new" Russian women's movement came into being (cf. Hinterhuber 2012a). From its inception, it covered a broad range of subjects from the working world, welfare, education, and health to culture and politics (among them environmental and human rights organizations). Females dominated in particular organizations in the field of social work. The broad array of subjects corresponded to the interests of women's organizations. In response to the narrow or broad sense of "women's movement," women focused on practical or strategic gender needs (cf. Molyneux 1985). Notably, women's organizations also promoted further democratization, building a civil society, and a strong rule of law.

Organizations with large numbers of members were and are still rare in Russia's civil society. The negative connotation of "feminism" also accounts for the weak position of the women's movement in the Russian population. In this context, the widespread funding from Western countries had an additional negative effect (see Funk 2007; cf. Horn 2008; Fabian 2010). Nevertheless, Russia's women's organizations were able to achieve some gender-political success (cf. Hinterhuber 2012a), thus proving that it was possible to publicly articulate issues such as gender discrimination and sexualized violence against women.

On a meso-level, the national and international networking of women's organizations can be highlighted. The success at the macro-level, however, was moderate: it was possible to influence legislation on gender equality, but implementation of the relevant provisions is still lacking. Setbacks under the increasingly authoritarian "Putin system" (Mommsen and Nußberger 2008), such as the recent tightening of the laws on homosexuality, could not be prevented. And the massive presence of women in civil society has not led to increased female representation in institutionalized politics. Women's organizations, apace with other non-governmental organizations, are more and more affected by state repression. The future development has yet to be seen.

In a large-scale international comparative study, Waylen (2007) investigated under what circumstances transformation processes of state socialist or authoritarian systems can go along with gender policy improvements. Among others, she analyzed the role of women's civil society organizations and their different roles in non-democratic regimes, during their collapse, in transitional contexts, and after the transition (Waylen 2007: 45). A correlation between the existence and the strength of women's organizations still under authoritarian conditions and their gender-political achievements in the context of transformation could not be proven by the study. Waylen concluded that the gender-political success of women's organizations largely depends on the state and other institutional actors, as well as on a favorable international context (Waylen 2007: 204). Cohen and Arato, however, argued that the success of women's organizations depends on certain strategies, namely, whether they apply a "dual logic." A feminist dual logic includes both "a communicative, discursive politics of identity and influence that targets civil and political society," and "an organized, strategically rational politics of inclusion and reform that is aimed at political and economic institutions" (Cohen and Arato 1992: 550).

7. Political rights, representation, and participation of women in non-democratic regimes

On an empirical level, women's formal and substantive access to the public sphere in authoritarian systems is of interest. In this context, we focus, in a first step, on women's political rights and their development under the different shapes of authoritarian rule. In a second step, women's political representation in non-democratic regimes takes center stage. We focus on how it affects the character of a gender regime and on the maintenance, undermining, or destabilization of authoritarian rule.

7.1 Women's political rights

Women's suffrage is a traditional field of gender research, not only in democracies but also in authoritarian settings. Recent studies focus on its specific constellation in Arab states (Manea 2011) and women and women's rights activism in Islamic countries (Al-Ali 2003, 2013; Budianta 2002, 2012; Fleschenberg and Derichs 2011; Jamal and Langohr 2009; Holike 2011). And studies on women's political rights in China (Edwards 2008; Howell 2003) draw attention to the latest research questions and theoretical approaches. For instance, how loud are women's voices in the political arena of autocracies and hybrid regimes, where there is no egalitarian political culture, if they are allowed to articulate themselves as political subjects at all?

Al-Ali analyzes women's movements in the Middle East and points out their close affiliation with nationalist movements and their common political struggle against the repression of civil society and authoritarian structures (Al-Ali 2003, 2013). Women political activists in the Middle East, according to Al-Ali, fight for increased social justice, gender equality, and "their rights and political space within a broader civil society" (Al-Ali 2003: 228). They foster an egalitarian political culture that depends on the social and political spaces constituting civil society, which are restricted by authoritarian regimes. Al-Ali's main idea is that women's movements in the Middle East mostly fight in order to improve their situation, namely, to be able to act politically. This conclusion is in agreement with Jamal and Langohrs assertion that, according to the fourth wave World Values Survey, gender attitudes in the Arab world are the most inegalitarian in the world (2009: 3; Fish 2002). While focusing on Jordan, Morocco, Kuwait, and Yemen, Jamal and Langohr stated that authoritarian regimes could improve the status of women by changing their degree of equality in the constitutions, women's personal status laws, laws against gender-based violence, or women's participation in politics and society. Interestingly, the authors underline the commitment of many unelected leaders to greater gender equality in legislation; they found that "unelected leaders are often more committed to more egalitarian legislation than members of lower houses elected in somewhat free elections" (Jamal and Langohr 2009: 17).

They concluded that regimes – not social movements – play central roles in advancing the condition of women in Arab countries (Jamal and Langohr 2009: 31). Their conclusion underlines the specific relation between democratization and women's liberation in the Arab world. It seems that autocracies grant fewer political and social rights to women than democracies (Pickel 2013), but this general truth may be worth questioning.

Ellen R. Judd (2002) focuses on the organizational changes concerning women's interests in China and points out that their political activism is divided between a strong, officially designed party mass organization, the All-China Women's Federation (ACWF), and the more limited, newer women's organizations that began emerging in the 1980s and 1990s. These organizations have, according to Judd, an "implicit political agency" and are "symbolically important" (2002: 191), even if they do not act primarily for political change.

Moreover, the increasing diversity among women in Chinese society, especially during the years of economic reforms, according to Judd, has led to the pluralization and diversification of social interests, increased social differentiation and stratification, the breakdown of urban-rural barriers, and new forms of associational life (2002: 193). Whereas rural migrant women are confronted with poor employment conditions, sexual harassment, and urban prejudices, urban females who were formerly employed by state and collective enterprises before the reforms were established were confronted with age and gender discrimination in the free labor market. Finally, female sex workers in the growing Chinese sex industry were confronted with male violence, sexually transmitted diseases, and economic exploitation (see Judd 2002: 194). Some of these issues made it onto the agenda of the ACWF, which Judd described as "the best placed of all women's organizations to influence policy-making" (2002: 207) for its location in the party structure. As a result, legislative changes that benefit women were introduced. During the reform period the political space for non-governmental actors widened.

The rights of rural Chinese women, their participation in community development, and the effects of changing rural work patterns on the gender division of labor have been analyzed since the late 1990s (Judd 1999, 2002, 2007). Juanhong concludes that the "current educational, scientific, and technical levels of our rural women are not sufficient for the requirements of rural modernization; they lag behind that of men" (1999: 56). This reflects the patriarchal nature of current rural social structures and prejudices against women. Women's political opportunities may increase within authoritarian regimes if selectively incorporated into state projects, for instance, via women's party organizations.

The different elements of citizenship – civil, political, and social rights – did not develop linearly; rather, their evolution was a variable and contingent process. In an overview on Latin American development in the twentieth century, Dore (2000) correctly finds that these processes must be analyzed in a historical and cultural-specific manner if the democratic developments are to be understood.

7.2 Women's representation and participation

Many recent studies on women's political representation look at African countries (Bauer and Britton 2006). Moreover, authoritarian regimes are the topic of more general analytical approaches (Bauer and Tremblay 2011). Does a high number of women representatives in national parliaments improve the situation of women in these countries? Does a high number of women representatives in parliament indicate increased women's participation? Does it point to shifting social hierarchies between the sexes (Burnet 2008)?

Studies on women's representation in Asia want to clarify the complexity of gender, politics, and democracy in a very diverse region (Fleschenberg and Derichs 2011). How did failed democratization and authoritarian regression in Asia influence gender relations? The role of heterogeneous identity politics is important to understand the specific discussion of women's rights and religious standards (Holike 2011). How could women seek representation and participation, taking into account their diversity, age, ethnicity, and socioeconomic status (Fleschenberg and Derichs 2011: 2)? Case studies on Malaysia (Budianta 2012) and Cambodia (Chap 2011) show how specific hurdles to women's political representation are supported by a network of patriarchal, sexist, and authoritarian structures, which impact the motivation and the chances of women's participation and representation.

The service of well-known women acting as political leaders in Asia, such as Megawati Sukarnoputri or Aung San Suu Kyi, is judged differently. Some authors see them as being the "main feminist issue," whereas others do not consider these chairwomen an "indication of feminist advances" in the region (Budianta 2002: 143). But, as Fleschenberg and Derichs state:

> "[T]he importance of visible and audible women politicians and women activists cannot be underestimated, because they open up the political space for other women and even grant them socially acceptable access to politics and state institutions in highly gender-segregated and/or violent ridden political contexts." (Fleschenberg and Derichs 2011: 11)

Studies on women's representation in Africa paint a different picture. There are far fewer leading women from domestic elites, but a high percentage of women representatives. With the election of thirty-nine women to the Chamber of Deputies in post-genocide Rwanda in 2003, the East African country "displaced Sweden as the country with the world's highest percentage of women in its lower or single house of parliament" (Longman 2006: 133). High percentages of women's representation in general lead to increasing gender equality over time, which is observable in Scandinavian countries and other Western democracies. Secularization, extended welfare states, educational attainment, and labor force participation, on the one hand, and women's pressure groups and gender quotas in political parties, on the other, are seen as promoting such development (Dahlerup 2004; cited in Bauer and Britton 2006: 1). But case studies on Rwanda show that the meaning of the increasing participation of women in politics and the increasing representation of women in national parliaments for authoritarian, single-party states is unclear (Longman 2006; Burnet 2008). Burnet explores the dramatic increase in women's participation in public life and representation in governance and the increasing authoritarianism of the Rwandan state under the guise of "democratization." She concludes that while women's participation has increased for the time being, their ability to influence policy making has decreased. However, increased female representation in government in the long-term could transform over time political subjectivity and pave the way for their meaningful participation in a genuine democracy (Burnet 2008: 361). When the leading party Rwandan Patriotic Front (RPF) linked gender to nationalism, women began influencing the character and content of political debates, and this linkage contributed to the transformation of the collective cultural imagination of wives and daughters into a wider range of social and political agency (Burnet 2008: 386).

The questions that have emerged in recent case studies on women's representation in autocracies have been discussed within feminist political theory for a long time. Here, the presence of women in national parliaments is the first step toward female representation, and is followed by women's political agencies and the systematic integration of gender equality into the political process. At the same time, feminist scholars criticized essentialist categories of (gender) identity in concepts of representation and refer to the diversity of needs and interests among women (Squires 2007).

8. Privacy and authoritarianism

Degrees of privacy in authoritarian regimes are indicators of the freedom to engage in resistance. At the same time, power relations and hierarchies within families and between genders can stabilize and legitimize autocratic rule (cf. Wilde's contribution in this volume). This chapter will thus concentrate on familial and gender relations and the degrees of privacy in authoritarian regimes. When considering gender relations, the focus will be on family policy, households, domestic violence, divorce, and abortion rights in autocracies. The knowledge at the core of feminist criticism, for Molyneux, is the "private or reproductive sphere, lying at the interface between state and civil society ... the social terrain upon which gender divisions and inequalities are constituted" (Molyneux 2000: 34). This also means that one has to look behind the naturalization of gender relations and work within the private sphere, which continues to be a central aim of women's movements until today. Authoritarian regimes often referred to the traditional family order (and thus gender) as metaphors for their government. At the core of authoritarian legitimation strategy is the construction of an ideal society by means of the ideal family. Women's reproductive rights contradict such strategies. For example, one of General Pinochet's last acts of legislation was a constitutional change aiming to enshrine the principle of protecting life in order to stop the liberalization of abortion law (Molyneux 2000: 62).

Studies on the operation of gender relations within the state, such as those on family policy, show developments within various authoritarian regimes and how different role models contribute to the stabilization or destabilization of those regimes. Recent case studies on Latin American countries and their transformations give an overview of the constellation of public and private spheres, changing gender relations, and feminist policies (Haas 2010; Macdonald and Mills 2010). Family and body politics in Arab countries show that in spite of granted suffrage rights, women are often discriminated against by the state in their private life (Manea 2011). Studies on the politics of gender relations in family and society show how women's organizations can interact with women representatives to change legislation in order to improve women's power within these relations (Britton 2006; Disney 2006; Schäfer 2012). Central issues are households and property rights within marriages and families, divorce, domestic violence, and abortion rights.

Recent research on the impact of family law reforms on gender relations is especially focused on African, Arab, and Latin American countries. Disney focuses on the Mozambique Family Law of 2004. The Mozambique Parliament had one of the highest percentages of women representatives in the 2000s but one of the lowest gender development indexes (Disney 2006: 31). On the one hand, the family law challenged traditional family structures by overturning patriarchal privilege and shared property within the family, reforming divorce, and acknowledging non-civil marriages (Disney 2006: 44ff.). On the other, it acknowledged the cultural diversity of Mozambique, which Disney discusses using the example of polygamy: the family law does not judge polygamy but tries to protect the rights of women and children of polygamous marriages (Disney 2006: 48). During the transition from a one-party state to a liberal-democratic state, the family law has established women's legal equality and expanded their power in family and society. Women representatives' interaction with women's organizations in civil society has been crucial to initiate and push through the reform (Disney 2006: 53).

Other studies identify sexual violence (and the racialization of sexual violence) as the crucial point of putting women's rights on the political agenda and negotiating gender equality as well as equality in general terms (Budianta 2012: 162; Dhawan 2013).

9. Socioeconomic development and gender equality

The persistence of authoritarian regimes relies on cultural and political attitudes and economic conditions. This part will focus on the relation between socioeconomic development and gender equality in authoritarian regimes and how the role of women changes as societies develop economically. Inglehart and Norris (2003) argue that better education, work outside the home, smaller families, and the right to vote are all features of industrialized countries. Put simply, economic changes result in attitude shifts. This evidence is contradicted by recent studies on Arab countries (Jamal and Langohr 2009).

Economic benefits, (higher) education, knowledge, and the improvement of skills and confidence all serve to empower women, which can result in their political demands for more power within the family and society as well as political rights and political representation (Ong 1991; Chap 2011; Kreile 2012; Pickel 2013).

Dictatorships are sometimes associated with the transition to neoliberalism, which Molyneux (2000: 63) calls a "new political economy" of dictatorship. She finds that the burden of restructuring the economy fell disproportionately on poor women, which led to radical criticism by feminist economists like Diane Elson (1991).

In consideration of the dynamic effects of gender inequality in socioeconomic terms, the research focused on women's activism in economic crises. Even when connected to traditional family models emphasizing "motherhood, nutrition of the family and charity" (West and Blumberg 1991: 15; cited in Budianta 2012: 152), women's activism in economic crises questions the male breadwinner model, which Budianta identified as taking place during Indonesia's post-1998 democratization, the "reformasi years" (Budianta 2012: 152-

158). Here, Budianta sees motherhood as a "discursive strategy [which] was not only adopted in the face of state paternalism and militarism, but also makes activism more acceptable to a wider spectrum of women" (Budianta 2012: 158).

Finally, the case of state socialism illustrates the persisting traditional gender order despite more socioeconomic equality between the sexes. State socialism proposed to remove the basis of the traditional gender order by giving women new rights and the means to achieve economic autonomy through employment, as Molyneux (2000a) points out in her case study on the Cuban women's party organization Federación de Mujeres Cubanas (FMC). Cuban socialism, according to Molyneux, changed social relations, mobilized women into considerable activity in public life, and thus "created a distinctive kind of women's movement, albeit one that was a creature of the state" (Molyneux 2000a: 313). But the social division of labor with its unequal gender order never changed, causing feminists to criticize the gender policies of Cuban socialism for maintaining patriarchal privileges, sexual inequality, and machismo and for lacking the aim of real social transformation (Molyneux 2000a: 314).

10. Civil society and the family

The family is also subject to the structures of dominance and subordination within the prevailing gender relations (see, e.g., Ostner 1997; Ginsbourg 2005; Hagemann 2008: 33ff.); moreover, queer theory identifies the family as a site of heteronormativity. Sänger rejects the mere integration of the family and the private in general, stressing the "relational dimension of the relationship between private and public" (2007: 19; translation by authors). In other words, the two spheres do not have to be protected from each other, but rather have to be regularly questioned regarding social domination and power relations. In the end, it is "the question of the separation of the spheres of the private and the public itself [that becomes] the subject of democratic decisions" (Klein 2001, 194–195; translation by authors; cf. Cohen and Arato 1992; cf.

Habermas 1992). Therefore, including the family into a definition of civil society is not without controversy, not even in feminist theory.

From a gender perspective, the arguments presented above challenge the conventional definition of "civil society." To overcome such gender blindness, it is suggested that the private, and the family in particular, be included in the definition of "civil society" (cf. Phillips 2002: 74–75). Numerous authors, among them Habermas (1992), have consequently included the family into their concept of civil society. Cohen and Arato (1992: 631) even perceive the family as a "key institution in civil society," where autonomous individuals are able to develop "civic virtue and responsibility" (see also Cohen 1993). Yet, Cohen (1993) sought to reformulate the liberal core of the private without its gender-hierarchical connotations in order to do justice to the existing differences between the two spheres.

Reflecting on these different perspectives of the family, privacy, and the opportunities and challenges of civil society in terms of familial, gendered, and heteronormative structures and relations clarifies the importance of family and gender policy in authoritarian regimes: on the one hand, family is a central issue used to legitimate "natural" hierarchies and on the other it is a potential place to develop confrontation, e.g., if women have the opportunity to participate in politics and society, they have the opportunity to develop spaces of political opposition and resistance.

11. Gender, citizenship, and discursive practices in non-democratic regimes

This section connects questions about the public sphere and discourses and thus focuses on political culture in authoritarian regimes. We will ask if and how relations of power and social inequality are dealt with by those regimes in public and society, and which discursive constructions of gendered subjects can be analyzed in constitutional texts, laws, political programs, and the media. Which underlying conflicts can be identified?

An examination of the discursive practices of authoritarian regimes requires further discussion of the concept of the public. Underlying Wilde's approach, which is being applied here, is the concept of the "plural public" by Hannah Arendt. The concept of the plural public sphere as a basis for political and free discussions was developed by Arendt based on her analysis of totalitarian regimes (Arendt 1986; cf. Wilde in this volume). For Arendt, the destruction of public space and pluralism between people is a central feature of total domination; therefore, the following question arises when exploring authoritarian regimes: To what degree is the public space restricted and what niches exist? It is therefore important to clarify not only the concept of the public but also the concept of discourse. Discourses – assuming a genealogical, Foucault-oriented basis – are not necessarily associated with a democratic or plural public. Instead, they describe the development and generation of knowledge and a concept of society in view of a good political order or gender relations. This occurs in different social and state realms, such as in various scientific disciplines via the development of certain knowledge systems, which in turn can have an impact on (civil) societal notions of order and government practices. Against which background do individual, familial, and societal concepts of society develop?

12. Individual predispositions and political culture: gender roles and gender relations under authoritarian rules

For the analysis of gender relations, the processes in societies under authoritarian governance are important features. Definitions of authoritarianism following Linz (2000) emphasize dominating diffuse mentalities and the lack of extensive and intensive political mobilization. The analysis of social processes, social sites of power, and social power relations makes it necessary to take a closer look at the relations of individuals, society, and state and their gender impacts. Thus, it is necessary to pay attention to recent research on authoritarianism in the field of political psychology (Stenner 2005, 2009; Feldman

2003). Some aspects of this political-psychological approach continue thoughts of the classic study of Adorno et. al. "The Authoritarian Personality. Studies on Prejudice" in political culture research (Rippl, Seipel, and Kindervater 2000; Rensmann, Hagemann, and Funke 2011). For instance, what does the intolerance of social diversity mean for women's rights, women's amount of freedom, and the formation of gender images and role models? Do inegalitarian attitudes affect gender outcomes, and if so, how? Prejudice and intolerance, especially against homosexuals, are related to authoritarian tendencies within the theoretical framework of authoritarianism and the authoritarian personality. Regarding authoritarian tendencies in democracies, traditional gender role models are a central feature, for instance, in right-wing party programs. However, conservatism does not automatically mean authoritarianism. According to Stenner, authoritarianism is the "predisposition to intolerance of difference that somehow brings together certain traits: obedience to authority, moral absolutism, intolerance and punitiveness toward dissidents and deviants, racial and ethnic prejudice" (Stenner 2009: 142).

For Stenner, authoritarianism is a timeless individual predisposition influencing individual attitudes and social behavior. It is fueled by a longing for "common authority (oneness) and shared values (sameness)" (Stenner 2009: 143). There are other personal predispositions like "openness to experience ... verbal ability ... intelligence and knowledge" (Stenner 2009: 145), which are all influenced by education and social surroundings (these may also reduce authoritarian predispositions). But she underlines that in the end authoritarianism is a "normative 'worldview' about the social value of obedience and conformity" (Stenner 2009: 143) and is therefore much more than a personal distaste. Even more, some expressions of authoritarianism, such as racial intolerance, have to be analyzed according to definite social and historical conditions: "[A]lthough I have argued that authoritarianism is a universal phenomenon that always produces the same characteristic attitudes ... those same inclinations are bound to be expressed somewhat differently by majority and minority respondents" (Stenner 2009: 150). Whereas Stenner underlines authoritarianism as a universal and timeless individual predisposition, Rippl et al. claim that the appearance of authoritarianism depends on family socialization, class, and cultural background (Rippl, Kindervater, and Seipel 2000: 24ff.; for the context of class, see Hopf 2000; for cultural background, see Lederer 2000 and Meloen 2000; for an international comparative perspective, see Rensmann, Hagemann, and Funke 2011: 199ff.).

In an attempt to distinguish between conservatism and authoritarianism, Stenner sees one of the main differences as related to the perception of social change. Authoritarianism is not aversion to social change; on the contrary, it may even claim to bring about social change. Stenner's ideas are quite convincing, as they confirm the results of other branches of political science research. Although a look at the broad research on fascist movements may be sufficient, Behrends (2012) provides a current and compact overview. Political scientists should thus not be at all surprised by Stenner's results that "authoritarians are perfectly willing to embrace massive social change in pursuit of greater oneness and sameness" (Stenner 2009: 155). So, one problem with the research on authoritarianism seems to be a kind of mutual blindness – within the discipline of political science as well as interdisciplinary perspectives.

Other core elements of authoritarianism are social threats and fears. Threat activates authoritarianism (Feldman 2003); it can also reveal authoritarian tendencies within democracies. The perceived threat of homosexual marriage and gay adoption has been used to measure authoritarian effects in the USA and to analyze which political forces benefit from increasing public fears (Weiler and Hetherington 2013).

Regarding the research history of dictatorships, autocracies, and authoritarian regimes, the central categorization and thus the core distinction is between dictatorships and democracies. Political science autocracy research has traditionally focused on how dictatorships prevail and the kinds of structures that may support dictatorship. In distinguishing and comparing patterns of rule, political science has developed at least two perspectives that can be summarized as "Leviathan" versus "Behemoth" (Behrends 2012: 10). Both perspectives emerged with a strong desire to explain the twentieth century totalitarian dictatorships in Europe: Hitler's National Socialist Germany and Stalin's Soviet Union. Both perspectives apply the concepts of "Leviathan" and "Behemoth" to comprehend the state. Both perspectives still shed light on analytic categories of autocracy research. According to the first classical political theory, national socialism is explained by Behrends using the "Leviathan" model of Ernst Fraenkel, who in *Der Doppelstaat* distinguished between the "*Normenstaat*" and the "*Maßnahmenstaat*" – the latter being characteristic of national socialist dictatorship. The second classical political theory is Franz Neumann's "Behemoth." Neumann argues that there is no state but an unruly collection of different kinds of authorities such as leaders, parties, and the army. For Neumann, national socialism is a new kind of rule that destroys the state and ignores frontiers between state and society. Neumann's perspective influenced Arendt's studies on totalitarianism (Behrends 2012: 12), whose view of destroyed privacy and destroyed social structures in totalitarianism has recently been reviewed by Wilde (2012) in an examination of the destruction of political spaces as spaces of individual freedom and political agency.

When examining gender relations and the processes of how gendered hierarchies are established and legitimated in civil society within authoritarian regimes, referring to a Gramscian concept of civil society is productive, as was shown earlier in this text. This allows us to question the development of subaltern counterpublics (Fraser 1997) and to analytically frame the question of struggle and conflict within civil society as discourses.

13. Civil society and/or the state – promoting or impeding gender equality?

Another branch of feminist theory examines the gendered and dominant state and its relation to civil society: "Civil society has no meaning unless it is conceived of in relation to the state" (Reverter-Bañón 2006: 9). Initially, feminist theorists as well as the protagonists of the new women's liberation movement(s) perceived the state mainly as a power authority responsible for the maintenance of the hierarchical gender relations (cf. Phillips 2002: 84). According to the advocates of this "interdependentist position," the state appears to be the "maximum representative of the patriarchal system" (Reverter-Bañón 2006: 20), while civil society holds a positive connotation. From a gender perspective, though, the state is not only an instrument of domination and power, but also an authority of redistribution, and can therefore be used to promote gender equality (cf. Phillips 2002: 82). From an "interventionist position" (Reverter-Bañón 2006: 20), the state should promote gender equality and also take regulatory measures in relation to civil society. Therefore, the state not only has legislative means at its disposal, but can also exert influence via redistributive measures (Reverter-Bañón 2006: 21), e.g., in the context of civil society it could refuse to subsidize anti-women organizations, as proposed by Okin (2002: 183; cf. Reverter-Bañón 2006: 21). For gender democracy, it is not about "less" state, but about "which state" (cf. Sauer 2004). Sauer's dictum can also be applied to civil society: from a gender perspective, it is not automatically about "more" civil society but about "what civil society."

From a feminist perspective, civil society also has to measure to what extent gender as a structural category (as well as other social structural categories such as ethnicity or class) influences citizen participation. Even civil society is gendered. Compared to the state, civil society does not always perform better in terms of gender democracy, especially because anti-discriminatory legal provisions often only partially extend to civil society structures (see Phillips 2002: 81).

14. State formation

To understand gender-state relations, one must study the social dimensions of state power. The state's legislation as well as social and economic policies play important roles in the public order, private affairs, family life, and individual relationships. Law, social welfare, and economic and social policy influence social norms, which may also be regulated (see following chapters). Studies on state formation as a gendered process show how social processes and gender relations effect transitions to authoritarian regimes and then to democracies. For instance, the examination of state formation in Latin America, both comparatively and historically, identifies moments of transition in which gender relations were significant factors or changed significantly (Dore and Molyneux 2000). Women's movements, for instance, have contributed to ending military rule (Molyneux 2000: 63). These processes of democratization and the different ways gender-state relations may alter state formation itself are of interest not only in the Latin American region but also in Arab countries (Manea 2011: 18ff.).

Gender research is inspired by Foucault's work on the social and decentered dimensions of power. The ideal society of authoritarian states involves uniformity – an idea which trickles down to the ideal family. Studies on populist and socialist governments show how the climate of political mobilization affects political activism and the rights of women. According to Molyneux, populist governments in Latin America not only appealed to women as political subjects but also continued to support traditional family values, i.e., female dependency, service, and subordination (Molyneux 2000: 56), thus maintaining the gender order. Moreover, some regimes "used familial and patriarchal symbolism as metaphors of state rule" (Molyneux 2000: 57). Military rule is exemplary in this regard, as Molyneux convincingly describes. Military rule is a gendered rule of domination, which produces gendered forms of resistance. Feminists are born enemies of military rule, because they threaten the state order by criticizing naturalized gender roles and family values. Feminists are considered subversive and are targeted by the state, which leads to torture in the form of sexual abuse and erotized violence against prisoners. In the view of the military, the family should produce obedient citizens. Authority should be restored through retraditionalized, privatized families (Molyneux 2000: 62). The contradiction was the state's claim to form and control such ostensible private spaces.

Studies on democratization and gender relations indicate the complexity of the relationship between state and society and their interactions. Valiente (2003) focuses on the state's influence on the feminist movement and its organizational features, goals, and strategies in Spain. Following Joan Scott's call to examine the mutual construction of gender and politics, Dore (2000) frames the (gendered) state formation in Latin America in a gendered historical perspective. She points out that there was no linear development in de-colonization and liberalization (Dore 2000: 26). According to her historical overview of the nineteenth century state formation, "[I]t was the rise of organizations of and for women – feminist organizations – around the turn of the twentieth century that pushed states to move more consistently in the direction of dismantling patriarchal privileges" (Dore 2000: 26).

15. Conclusion and outlook

In accordance with Wilde, we positioned civil society at the analytical core of our research on authoritarian regimes. Hence our literature review looked at civil society and its relation to gender and authoritarian regimes. We identified central analytical approaches and policy fields to help to crystallize further research aims; our review also contributes to comprehensive research on the maintenance of dominance and the establishment of hierarchies in authoritarian regimes and their societies.

After examining recent research on civil society, gender, and authoritarian regimes, we found four main fields of interest for further research: Does gender equality play an important role in authoritarian strategies of establishing and maintaining power? How do differences and hierarchies within civil society influence its function in authoritarian regimes? How is female opposition against authoritarian regimes organized and subsequently treated? Finally, how do authoritarian and hybrid regimes differ with regard to gender hierarchies and gender equality?

The first research question – Does gender equality play an important role in authoritarian strategies of establishing and maintaining power and how does this happen? – can be elaborated to include the following questions: How does the political representation of women change gender hierarchies in authoritarian regimes? What roles do women, women's movements, women's organizations, and women politicians have in transition processes from dictatorship to democracy and vice versa? Which variables cause gender policy improvements under authoritarian regimes and within transformation processes? To which degree does the success of women's organizations depend on the support of the (authoritarian) state and how do authoritarian states improve the status of women? And, in this context, which long-term consequences are the result of the gender policies of state socialism?

Gender, Civil Society, and Non-Democratic Regimes 55

The second question – How do differences and hierarchies within civil society influence its role and function in authoritarian regimes? – can be elaborated to include the following questions: Is there a certain quality of or a certain place for the struggle against gender injustice and for gender equality under authoritarian rule? Which insights can we gain on the effects of hierarchies within civil society, on its strategies and their success?

An elaboration of the third research question – How is female opposition against authoritarian regimes organized and subsequently treated? – would include all questions concerning the situation of females and feminist opposition under authoritarian rule. Where is there space to develop opposition in general and feminist opposition in particular? Furthermore, we have to take a closer look at the diversity of women in authoritarian regimes and how such diversity influences the participation and representation of women. How common are, for instance, social justice and gender justice as political aims? Which factors that work for an egalitarian political culture can be identified within civil society?

Questions concerning the comparison of gender relations and civil society in authoritarian and hybrid regimes could include analyses of gender discrimination, the legal position of women, sexual exploitation, and sexualized violence. For further comparison, the identification of collective images of women, wives, and daughters in authoritarian regimes, and discursive practices of forming gender-related knowledge and hierarchies and how they differ over time seems fruitful. These questions would take into consideration not only democracies and authoritarian regimes but also different autocracies and their developments over time.

Following these four analytical approaches not only contributes to empirical knowledge about gender relations, discursive practices, civil society, and family and women's rights in authoritarian regimes, but also to the further development of the political theory of authoritarianism. These analytical approaches could – so we assume – be part of a prolific interdependency between empirical studies and theoretical considerations.

Civil society plays an ambivalent role in the stabilization and alteration of authoritarian and hybrid regimes. In this field of research, regardless of approach, we will have to deal with an underlying question concerning democracy theory: Is gender justice an indispensable democratic feature?

Bibliography

Abels, Gabriele (2008): Geschlechterpolitik. In: Heinelt, Hubert/Knodt, Michèle (Eds.): Politikfelder im EU-Mehrebenensystem. Baden-Baden: Nomos, pp. 293-310.

Abels, Gabriele/Mushaben, Joyce Marie (Eds.) (2012): Gendering the European Union. New Approaches to Old Democratic Deficits, Houndmills. Basingstoke: Palgrave Macmillan.

Adorno, Theodor W./Frenkel-Brunswick, Else/Levinson, Daniel J./Sanford, R. Nevitt (1950): The Authoritarian Personality. New York: Harper and Brothers.

Adloff, Frank (2005): Zivilgesellschaft. Theorie und politische Praxis, Frankfurt am Main/New York: Campus-Verlag.

Agustín, Louise Rolandsen (2008): Civil society participation in EU gender policy-making: framing strategies and institutional constraints. In: Parliamentary Affairs 61, 3, pp. 505-517.

Akdeniz-Taxer, Annika (2011): Öffentlichkeit, Partizipation, Empowerment. Wiesbaden: Springer VS.

Al-Ali, Nadje (2003): Gender and Civil Society in the Middle East. In: International Feminist Journal of Politics 5, 2, pp. 216-232.

Al-Ali, Nadje, (2005): Gender and civil society in the Middle East. In: Howell, Jude/Mulligan, Diane (Eds.): Gender and civil society: transcending boundaries. New York: Routledge, pp. 101-116.

Al-Ali, Nadje (2013): Iraq: Gendering Authoritarianism. http://www.opendemocracy.net/5050/nadje-al-ali/iraq-gendering-authoritarianism (02.08.2013)

Al-Labadi, Fadwa (2007): Zur Rolle von Zivilgesellschaft und Frauenorganisationen im Friedensprozess. In: Klein, Ansgar/Roth, Silke (Eds.): NGOs im Spannungsfeld von Krisenprävention und Sicherheitspolitik. Wiesbaden: VS-Verlag, pp. 275-283.

Alpermann, Björn (2013): Soziale Schichtung und Klassenbewußtsein im Chinas autoritärer Modernisierung. In: Zeithistorische Forschungen 10, 2, pp. 283-296.

Andersen, John (2004): The politics of inclusion and empowerment: gender, class and citizenship. Basingstoke: Palgrave Macmillan.

Appel, Margit/Gubitzer, Luise/Sauer, Birgit (Eds.) (2003): Zivilgesellschaft – ein Konzept für Frauen?. Frankfurt am Main: Lang.

Appel, Margit/Gubitzer, Luise/Sauer, Birgit (2003): Zivilgesellschaft – ein Konzept für Frauen? Eine Einführung. In: Margit Appel/Luise Gubitzer/Birgit Sauer (Eds.), Zivilgesellschaft - ein Konzept für Frauen? Frankfurt am Main: Lang, pp. 7-15.

Arendt, Hannah (1986): Elemente und Ursprünge totaler Herrschaft. München: Piper Verlag.

Arriobas Lozano, Alberto/Álvarez Veinguer, Aurora/García-Gonzalez, Nayra (2013): Intersectionality and the Discourses of Women's Social Movement Organizations across Europe. In: Siim, Birte/Mokre, Monika (Eds.): Negotiating Gender and Diversity in an Emergent European Public Sphere. Basingstoke/New York: Palgrave Macmillan, pp. 43-59.

Art, David (2012): What Do We Know About Authoritarianism After Ten Years? In: Comparative Politics 44, 3, pp. 351–373.

Attwood, Lynne (1990): The New Soviet Man and Women. Sex-Role Socialization in the USSR. London.

Backes, Uwe (2013): Vier Grundtypen der Autokratie und ihre Legitimierungsstrategien. In: Kailitz, Steffen/Köllner, Patrick (Eds.): Autokratien im Vergleich. PVS Sonderheft 47. Baden-Baden: Nomos Verlag, pp. 157-175.

Banaszak, Lee Ann/Beckwith, Karen/Rucht, Dieter (2003): When Power Relocates: Interactive Change in Women's Movements and States. In: Banaszak, Lee Ann/Beckwith, Karen/Rucht, Dieter (Eds.) (2003): Women's Movements Facing the Reconfigured State. Cambridge: Cambridge University Press, pp. 1-29.

Bank, André (2009): Die Renaissance des Autoritarismus. Erkenntnisse und Grenzen neuerer Beiträge der Comparative Politics und Nahostforschung. In: Hamburg Review of Social Sciences 4, 1, pp. 10-41.

Bauer, Gretchen/Britton, Hannah E. (Eds.) (2006): Women in African Parliaments. Boulder, Colorado: Lynne Rienner Publishers.

Bauer, Gretchen/Tremblay, Manon (Eds.) (2011): Women in Executive Power. A Global Overview. London, New York: Routledge.

Bayulgen, Oksan (2008): Muhammad Yunus, Grameen Bank and the Nobel Peace Prize: What Political Science Can Contribute to and Learn From the Study of Microcredit. In: International Studies Review 10, 3, pp. 525-547.

Beck, Martin/Harders, Cilja/Jünemann, Annette/Stetter, Stephan (Eds.) (2009): Der Nahe Osten im Umbruch. Zwischen Transformation und Autoritarismus. Wiesbaden: VS-Verlag.

Becker, Ruth/Kortendiek, Beate (Eds.) (2010): Handbuch Frauen- und Geschlechterforschung. Wiesbaden: VS-Verlag.

Behrends, Jan C. (2012): Diktatur: Moderne Gewaltherrschaft zwischen Leviathan und Behemoth, Version: 1.0. In: Docupedia-Zeitgeschichte, 6. 6.2012. http://docupedia.de/zg/ (24.06.2013)

Bellamy, Richard (1988): Introduction. In: Bobbio, Norberto: Which Socialism? Oxford: University of Minnesota Press, pp. 1-30.

Benhabib, Sheyla (1996): Democracy and Difference. Princeton: Princeton Univ. Press.

Benz, Arthur/Dose, Nicolai (2010): Governance – Modebegriff oder nützliches sozialwissenschaftliches Konzept?. In: Benz, Arthur/Dose, Nicolai (Eds.): Governance - Regieren in komplexen Regelsystemen: Eine Einführung. Wiesbaden: VS-Verlag, pp. 13-36.

Berglund, Henrik (2011): Hindu Nationalism and Gender in the Indian Civil Society A Challenge To The Indian Women's Movement. In: International Feminist Journal of Politics 13, 1, pp. 83-99.

Beyme, Klaus von (1994): Systemwechsel in Osteuropa. Frankfurt a.M: Suhrkamp.
Binaj, Delina (2006): Die politische Partizipation von Frauen in Albanien. In: Südosteuropa Mitteilungen 5/6, pp. 68-76.
BMFSFJ (Ed.) (2010): Hauptbericht des Freiwilligensurveys. München.
Bobbio, Norberto (1988): Which Socialism? Marxism, Socialism, and Democracy. Oxford: University of Minnesota Press.
Bode, Ingo/Evers, Adalbert/Klein, Ansgar (Eds.) (2009): Bürgergesellschaft als Projekt: Eine Bestandsaufnahme zu Entwicklung und Förderung zivilgesellschaftlicher Potenziale in Deutschland. Wiesbaden: Springer VS.
Brandt, Mark J./Henry, P.J. (2012): Gender Inequality and Gender Differences in Authoritarianism. In: Personality and Social Psychology Bulletin 38, 10, pp. 1301-1315.
Brickner, Rachel K. (2006): Mexican union women and the social construction of women's Labor rights. In: Latin American Perspectives 33, 6, pp. 55–74.
Brickner, Rachel K. (2010): Feminist Activism, Union Democracy and Gender Equity Rights in Mexico. In: Journal of Latin American Studies 42, pp. 749–777.
Brickner, Rachel (2013): Gender conscientization, social movement unionism, and labor revitalization: a perspective from Mexico. In: Labor History 54, 1, pp. 21–41.
Britton, Hannah E. (2006): South Africa: Mainstreaming Gender in a New Democracy. In: Bauer, Gretchen/Britton, Hannah E. (Eds.): Women in African Parliaments. Boulder, Colorado: Lynne Rienner Publishers, pp. 59-84.
Brömme, Norbert/Strasser, Hermann (2001): Gespaltene Bürgergesellschaft? Die ungleichen Folgen des Strukturwandels von Engagement und Partizipation. In: Aus Politik und Zeitgeschichte B25-26, pp. 6-14.
Browers, Michaelle (2012): Staat und Zivilgesellschaft im arabischen politischen Denken: Liberale, sozialistische und islamistische Interventionen. In: Zapf, Holger/Klevesath, Lino (Eds.): Staatsverständnisse in der islamischen Welt. Baden-Baden: Nomos, pp. 117-140.
Budianta, Melani (2002): Gender, Culture and Security: Old Legacies, New Visions. In: Asian Exchange 2001/2002.
Budianta, Melani (2012): The Blessed Tragedy: The Making of Women's Activism During the Reformasi Years. In: Heryanto, Ariel/Mandal, Sumit K. (Eds.): Challenging Authoritarianism in Southeast Asia. Comparing Indonesia and Malaysia. New York: Routledge, pp. 145-177.
Burnell, Peter/Schlumberger, Oliver (2010): Promoting Democracy – Promoting Autocracy? In: Contemporary Politics 16, 1, pp. 1–15.
Burnet, Jennie E (2008): Gender Balance und the Meanings of Women in Governance in Post-Genocide Rwanda. In: African Affairs 107, pp. 361-386.
Butterwegge, Christoph/Lösch, Bettina/Ptak, Ralf (2008): Neoliberalismus. Analysen und Alternativen. Wiesbaden: Springer VS.
Buttigieg, Joseph A. (1994): Gramscis Zivilgesellschaft und die civil-society-Debatte. In: Das Argument 206, pp. 529-554.

Caiazza, Amy (2002): Mothers and soldiers: gender, citizenship**Fehler! Textmarke nicht definiert.**, and civil society in contemporary Russia. New York: Routledge.

Cailleba, Patrice/Kumar, Rekha A. (2010): When customary laws face civil society organisations: Gender issues in Botswana. In: African Journal of Political Science and International Relations 4, 9, pp. 330-339.

Chang, Doris T. (2009): Women's movements in twentieth-century Taiwan. Urbana: University of Illinois Press.

Chap, Sopanha (2011): Women's Involvement in Polical Implementation: Experiences from Gender Mainstreaming Policy on Community Fisheries Management in Cambodia. In: Fleschenberg, Andrea/Derichs, Claudia (Eds.): Women and Politics in Asia. A Springboard for Democracy? Zürich u.a.: Lit-Verlag, pp. 149-165.

Cheriet, Boutheina (1996): Gender, civil society and citizenship in Algeria In: Middle East Report 198/26, pp. 22-26.

Cohen, Jean L./Arato, Andrew (Eds.) (1992): Civil society and political theory. Cambridge: MIT Press.

Cohen, Jean (1993): Zur Neubeschreibung der Privatsphäre. In: Menke, Christoph/Seel, Martin (Eds.): Zur Verteidigung der Vernunft gegen ihre Liebhaber und Verächter. Frankfurt am Main: Suhkamp, pp. 300-332.

Cohen, Jean (1999): Trust, Voluntary Association and Workable Democracy: The Contemporary Discourse of Civil Society. In: Warren, Mark E. (Ed.): Democracy and Trust. Cambridge: Cambridge Univ. Pr., pp. 208-248.

Croissant, Aurel/Lauth, Hans-Joachim/Merkel, Wolfgang (2000): Zivilgesellschaft und Transformation: Ein internationaler Vergleich. In: Merkel, Wolfgang (Ed.): Systemwechsel. Opladen: Leske+Budrich, pp. 9-50.

Crouch, Colin (2011): Das befremdliche Überleben des Neoliberalismus. Frankfurt am Main: Suhrkamp.

Crouch, Collin (2008): Postdemokratie. Frankfurt am Main: Suhrkamp.

Datta, Kusum (2007): Women's studies and women's movement in India since the 1970s: an overview. Kolkata: The Asiatic Society.

Derichs, Claudia (Ed.) (2010): Diversity and Female Political Participation: Views on and from the Arab World. Heinrich Böll Stiftung. Publication Series on Democracy 21. Berlin.

Derichs, Claudia (2010): Introduction. Diversity and Political Partizipation in the Arab World. In: Derichs, Claudia (Ed.): Diversity and Female Political Participation: Views on and from the Arab World. Heinrich Böll Stiftung. Publication Series on Democracy 21, Berlin, pp. 9-26.

Destremau, Blandine (2011): Women and civil society capacity building in Yemen: a research perspective on development. Sanaa.

Dhawan, Nikita (2013): Postkoloniale Gouvernementalität und "die Politik der Vergewaltigung": Gewalt, Verletzlichkeit und der Staat. In: Femina Politica 22, 2, pp. 85-104.

Disney, Jennifer Leigh (2006): Mozambique: Empowering Women Through Familiy Law. In: Bauer, Gretchen/Britton, Hannah E. (Eds.): Women in African Parliaments. Boulder, Colorado: Lynne Rienner Publishers, pp. 31-57.

Dore, Elizabeth (2000): One Step Forward, Two Steps Back. Gender and the State in the Long Nineteeth Century. In: Dore, Elizabeth/Molyneux, Martine (Eds.): Hidden Histories of Gender and the State in Latin America. Durham and London: Duke University Press, pp. 3-32.

Dore, Elizabeth/Molyneux, Martine (Eds.) (2000): Hidden Histories of Gender and the State in Latin America. Durham and London: Duke University Press.

Dutoya, Virginie (2012): Féminisation des parlements, quotas et transformation de la représentation au Pakistan et en Inde. In: Critique Internationale 55, pp. 137-158.

Dutoya, Virginie (2013): From Women's Quota to 'Women's Politics': The Impact of Gender Quotas on Political Representations and Practices in the Pakistani National Parliament. In: Femina Politica 22, 2, pp. 17-34.

Edwards, Louise P. (2008): Gender, Politics, and Democracy: Women's Souffrage in China. Standford: Stanford University Press.

Einhorn, Barbara/Sever, Charlotte (2003): Gender and Civil Society in Central and Eastern Europe. In: International Feminist Journal of Politics 5, 2, pp. 163-190.

El-Ghawary, Karim (2011): Arabischer Frühling. In: die tageszeitung (28.01.2011).

Elson, Diane (1991): Male Bias in the Development Process. Manchester: Manchester University Press.

Erdmann, Gero/Bank, André/Hoffmann, Bert/Richter, Thomas (2013): International Cooperation of Authoritarian Regimes: Toward a Conceptual Framework. Hamburg: GIGA Working Papers 229/2013.

Eremitcheva, Galina/Zdravomyslova, Elena (2001): Die Bewegung der Soldatenmütter – eine zivilgesellschaftliche Initiative. Der Fall St. Petersburg. In: Ritter, Martina (Ed.): Zivilgesellschaft und Gender-Politik in Russland. Frankfurt am Main/New York: Campus, pp. 224-248.

Fabian, Katalin (2010): Mores and gains: The EU's influence on domestic violence policies among its new post-communist member states. In: Women's Studies International Forum 33, 1, pp. 54-67.

Feldman, Stanley (2003): Enforcing Social Conformity: A Theory of Authoritarianism. In: Political Psychology 2003 24, 1, pp. 41- 74.

Fish, Steven (2002): Islam and Authoritarianism. In: World Politics 55, 1, pp. 4-37.

Fleschenberg, Andrea (2011): South and Southeast Asia. In: Bauer, Gretchen/Tremblay, Manon (Eds.): Women in Executive Power. A Global Overview. London, New York: Routledge, pp. 23-44.

Fleschenberg, Andrea/Derichs, Claudia (Eds.) (2011): Women and Politics in Asia. A Springboard for Democracy? Münster et.al/Singapore: LIT-Verlag/ISEAS.

Fleschenberg, Andrea/Derichs, Claudia: (2011): Women and Politics in Asia: A Springboard for Democracy? A Tentative Introduction & Reflection. In: Fleschenberg, Andrea/Derichs,

Claudia (Eds.): Women and Politics in Asia. A Springboard for Democracy? Zürich u.a.: Lit-Verlag, pp. 1-17.

Forest, Maxime (2006): Emerging gender interest groups in the new member states: The case of the Czech Republic. In: Perspectives on European Politics and Society 7, 2, pp. 170-184.

Fraenkel, Ernst (2012) [1941]: Der Doppelstaat. Hamburg: Europäische Verlagsanstalt.

Frankenberger, Rolf (2013): Mikrophysik und Makrostruktur. Überlegungen zu einer Analytik der Macht in Autokratien. In: Kailitz, Steffen/Köllner, Patrick (Eds.): Autokratien im Vergleich. PVS Sonderheft 47. Baden-Baden: Nomos Verlag, pp. 60-85.

Fraser, Nancy (1996): Öffentlichkeit neu denken. Ein Beitrag zur Kritik real existierender Demokratie. In: Elvira Scheich (Ed.): Vermittelte Weiblichkeit. Feministische Wissenschafts- und Gesellschaftstheorie. Hamburg: Hamburg Ed., pp. 151-182.

Fraser, Nancy (1997): „Rethinking the Public Sphere: A Contribution to the Critique of Actually Existing Democracy". In: Fraser, Nancy: Justice Interruptus: Critical Reflections on the „Postsocialist"Condition. New York/London: Routledge, pp.69-98.

Fraser, Nancy (2001): Die halbierte Gerechtigkeit. Frankfurt am Main: Suhrkamp.

Fuchs, Gesine (1999): Strategien polnischer Frauenorganisationen, In: Berliner Osteuropa Info 12/1999, pp. 10-14.

Fuchs, Gesine (2002): Polnische Frauenorganisationen in der Demokratisierung. Strategien und Erfolgsfaktoren. Diss. Hannover.

Fuchs, Gesine (2003): Die Zivilgesellschaft mitgestalten. Frauenorganisationen im polnischen Demokratisierungsprozess. Frankfurt am Main.

Fuchs, Gesine (2013): Using strategic litigation for women's rights: Political restrictions in Poland and achievements of the women's movement. In: European Journal of Women's Studies 20, 1, pp. 21-43.

Fuchs, Gesine/Hinterhuber, Eva Maria (2003): Demokratie von unten? Unverfasste politische Partizipation von Frauen in Polen und Russland. In: Osteuropa 53, 5, pp. 704-719.

Fuchs, Gesine/Hinterhuber, Eva Maria (2006): EU-Geschlechterpolitik nach der Osterweiterung. In: Femina Politica 15, 1, pp. 9-19.

Fuhrmann, Nora (2005): Geschlechtpolitik im Prozess der Europäischen Integration. Wiesbaden: Springer VS.

Funk, Nanette (2007): Women's NGOs in Central and Eastern Europe and the Former Soviet Union: the Imperialist Criticism. In: Femina Politica 16, 1, pp. 68-83.

Gabovitsch, Mischa (2013): Putin kaputt?! Russlands neue Protestkultur. Frankfurt am Main: Surhkamp.

Gal, Susan/Kligman, Gail (2000): The Politics of Gender after Socialism. Princeton/New Jersey: Princeton Univ. Press.

Gerhard, Ute (1996): „Atempause: Die aktuelle Bedeutung der Frauenbewegung für die zivile Gesellschaft". In: Aus Politik und Zeitgeschichte B 21-22/96, pp. 3-14.

Ghodsee, Kristen (2007): Religious freedoms versus gender equality: Faith-based organizations, Muslim minorities, and Islamic headscarves in the new Europe. In: Social Politics 14, 4, pp. 526-561.
Gibson, Christopher (2012): Making Redistributive Direct Democracy Matter: Development and Women's Participation in the Gram Sabhas of Kerala, India. In: American Sociological Review 77, 3, pp. 409-434.
Ginsbourg, Paul (2005): The Politics of Everyday Life. London: Yale University Press.
Godel, Brigitta (2002): Auf dem Weg zur Zivilgesellschaft: Frauenbewegung und Wertewandel in Rußland. Frankfurt am Main: Campus.
Goebel, Christian (2011): Authoritarian Consolidation. In: European Political Science, 10, pp. 176-190.
Gosewinkel, Dieter (2003): Zivilgesellschaft – Eine Erschließung des Themas von seinen Grenzen her. Berlin: WZB.
Grsak, Marijana/Reimann, Ulrike/Franke, Kathrin (2007): Frauen und Frauenorganisationen im Widerstand in Kroatien, Bosnien und Serbien. Lich: Edition AV.
Gubitzer, Luise (2000): Ausbeutung oder Gestaltungsteilnahme?, In: kfb 1/2000, pp. 13-16.
Gubitzer, Luise (2003): Zur Ökonomie der Zivilgesellschaft In: Margit Appel/Luise Gubitzer/Birgit Sauer (Eds.): Zivilgesellschaft - ein Konzept für Frauen?. Frankfurt am Main et al.: Peter Lang, pp. 137-177.
Haas, Liesl (2010): Feminists Policymaking in Chile. Pennsylvania State University Press.
Habermas, Jürgen (1992): Faktizität und Geltung. Frankfurt am Main: Suhrkamp.
Habermas, Jürgen (2011): Ein Pakt für oder gegen Europa? In: Süddeutsche Zeitung (07.04.2011).
Hagemann, Karen (2008): Civil Society Gendered: Rethinking Theories and Practices. In: Hagemann, Karen/Michel, Sonya/Budde, Gunilla (Eds.): Civil society and gender justice: historical and comparative perspectives. New York: Berghahn Books, pp. 17-42.
Hagemann, Karen/Michel, Sonya/Budde, Gunilla (2008): Civil society and gender justice: historical and comparative perspectives. New York: Berghahn Books.
Hakena, Helen (2006): NGOs and post-conflict recovery: the Leitana Nehan Women's Development Agency Bougainville. Canberra: Asian Pacific Press Anu.
Halsaa, Beatrice et al. (Eds.) (2012): Remaking Citizenship in Multicultural Europe: Women's Movements, Gender and Diversity. New York: Palgrave Macmillan.
Hankivsky, Olena (2012): Gender, politics, and society in Ukraine. Toronto: University of Toronto Press.
Hapke, Andrea (2009): The Responsibility of 'Mothers'. Gendered Discourses of Women's Peace Organisations in the North-Caucasus/Russia. In: Christine Eifler/Ruth Seifert (Eds.): Gender Dynamics and Post-Conflict Reconstruction. Frankfurt a. M.: Peter Lang.
Hassim, Shireen/Gouws, Amanda (1998): Redefining the public space. In: Politikon, 25, 2, pp. 53-76.
Haussmann, Melissa/Sawer, Maria/Vickers, Jill (Eds.) (2010): Federalism, Feminism and Multilevel Governance. Farnham: Ashgate.

Heins, Volker (2002): Das Andere der Zivilgesellschaft. Bielefeld: transcript.
Hemment, Julie (2007a): Empowering women in Russia: activism, aid, and NGOs. Bloomington: Indiana Univ. Press.
Hemment, Julie (2007b): Public anthropology and the paradoxes of participation: Participatory action research and critical ethnography in provincial Russia. In: Human Organization 66, 3, pp. 301-314.
Heryanto, Ariel/Mandal, Sumit K. (Eds.) (2012): Challenging Authoritarianism in Southeast Asia. Comparing Indonesia and Malaysia. New York: Routledge.
Heydemann, Steven/Leenders, Reinoud (2011): Authoritarian Learning and Authoritarian Resilience: Regime Responses to the "Arab Awakening". In: Globalization 8, 5, pp. 647–653.
Hinterhuber, Eva (1999): Die Soldatenmütter Sankt Petersburg. Zwischen Neotraditionalismus und neuer Widerständigkeit. Münster: Lit-Verlag.
Hinterhuber, Eva Maria (2002): Women in Civil Society: History. Philosophy. Policy. Konferenz vom 6. bis 8. Juni in St. Petersburg/Russland. In: Femina Politica 11, 2, pp. 143-144.
Hinterhuber, Eva Maria (2011): Engendering Democracy in Russia? Women's Voluntary Engagement in Social Civil Society Organizations. In: Saarinen, Aino/Kulmala, Meri/ Jäppinen, Maija (Eds.): Gazing at Welfare, Gender and Agency in Post-socialist Countries. Cambridge: Cambridge Scholars Publishing, pp. 200-231.
Hinterhuber, Eva Maria (2012a): Zwischen Überlebenssicherung und Partizipation: zivilgesellschaftliches Engagement von Frauen im Bereich Sozialwesen in Russland. Baden-Baden: Nomos.
Hinterhuber, Eva Maria (2012b): ‚Pussy Riot': feministischer Widerstand gegen das System Putin. In: Femina Politica 21, 2, pp. 141-147.
Hinterhuber, Eva Maria/Fuchs, Gesine (2016): „New gender-political impulses from Eastern Europe: The case of ‚Pussy Riot'". In: Schwabenland, Christina/Lange, Chris/Nakagawa, Sachiko (Eds.): The role of civil society in the emancipationFehler! Textmarke nicht definiert. of women: challenging or supporting the status quo? Bristol/Chicago: Policy Press, pp. 89-112.
Hinterhuber, Eva Maria/Wilde, Gabriele (2007): Cherchez la Citoyenne! Eine Einführung in die Diskussion um „Bürger- und Zivilgesellschaft" aus geschlechterpolitischer Perspektive. In: Femina Politica 16, 2, pp. 9-18.
Hirschmann, David (1998): Civil society in South Africa: Learning from gender themes. In: World Development 26, 2, pp. 227-238.
Holike, Christine (2011): The State of Islam – Negotiating Democracy, Muslim Women's Rights and Morality in Indonesia and Malaysia. In: Fleschenberg, Andrea/Derichs, Claudia (Eds.): Women and Politics in Asia. A Springboard for Democracy? Zürich u.a.: Lit-Verlag, pp. 90–122.
Holike, Christine/Scheiterbauer, Tanja (2012): Feministische Perspektiven auf Islam, Staat und Geschlecht. In: Zapf, Holger/Klevesath, Lino (Eds.): Staatsverständnisse in der islamischen Welt. Baden-Baden: Nomos, pp. 253-274.

Holland-Cunz, Barbara (1999): Sieben Thesen zu einer feministischen Theorie der Demokratie. In: Sifft, Stefanie/Abels, Gabriele (Eds.): Demokratie als Projekt: feministische Kritik an der Universalisierung einer Herrschaftsform. Frankfurt a.M./New York: Campus, pp. 213-230.

Holland-Cunz, Barbara (2003): Die alte neue Frauenfrage. Frankfurt am Main: Suhrkamp.

Hopf, Wulf (2000): Soziale Schichtung und Autoritarismus. Oder: Sind Arbeiter besonders autoritär? In: Rippl, Susanne/Seipel, Christian/Kindervater, Angela (Eds.): Autoritarismus. Kontroversen und Ansätze der aktuellen Autoritarismusforschung. Opladen: Leske+Budrich, pp. 93-118.

Horn, Denise M. (2008): Setting the Agenda. US and Nordic Gender Policies in the Estonian Transition to Democracy. In: International Feminist Journal of Politics 10, 1, pp. 59-77.

Howell, Jude (Ed.) (2004): Governance in China. Lanham: Rowman & Littlefield Publishers.

Howell, Jude (2003): Women's organizations and civil society in China making a difference. In: International Feminist Journal of Politics 5, 2, pp. 191-215.

Howell, Jude (2005): Gender and Civil Society. In: Glasius, Marlies/Kaldor, Mary/Anheier, Helmut (Eds.): Global Civil Society Yearbook 2005/2006. London: Sage, pp. 38-63.

Howell, Jude (2007): Gender and civil society: Time for cross-border dialogue. In: Social Politics 14, 4, pp. 415-436.

Howell, Jude/Mulligan, Diane (2005): Gender and civil society: transcending boundaries. London: Routledge.

Inglehart, Ronald/Norris, Pippa (2003): Rising Tide. Gender Equality and Cultural Change Around the World. Cambridge: Cambridge University Press.

Inter-Parliamentary Union (2013): Women in National Parliaments. http://www.ipu.org/wmn-e/world.htm (30.08.2013).

Ishkanian, Armine/Lewis, Jane (2007): Gender, Civil Society, and Participation: Introduction to the Special Issue of Social Politics. In: Social Politics: International Studies in Gender, State and Society 14, 4, pp. 407-414.

Jacka, Tamara (2006): Rural Women in Urban China: Gender, Migration, and Social Change. New York: East Gate.

Jamal, Amaney/Langohr, Vickie (2009): Moving Beyond Democracy: What Causes Variations in the Level of Gender Equality across Arab States? (Paper was prepared for the Middle East Politics Working Group Workshop, Cornell University, March 27-28, 2009). http://www.princeton.edu/~ajamal/Jamal_Langohr.pdf (2.8.2013)

Juanhong, Fei (1999): The Rural Reform of Our Country and the Gender Division of Labor. In: Judd, Ellen R. (Ed.): Rural Women in Reform Era China. Chinese Sociology and Anthropology, Winter 1998/99, 31, 2, pp. 42-56.

Judd, Ellen R. (Ed.) (1999): Rural Women in Reform Era China. Chinese Sociology and Anthropology, Winter 1998/99, 31, 2.

Judd, Ellen R. (2002): The Chinese Women's Movement between State and Market. Stanford: Stanford University Press.

Gender, Civil Society, and Non-Democratic Regimes

Judd, Ellen R. (2007): No Change for Thirty Years: The Renewed Question of Women's Land Rights in Rural China. In: Development and Change. 38, 4, pp. 689–710.

Kailitz, Steffen/Köllner, Patrick (Eds.) (2013): Autokratien im Vergleich. PVS Sonderheft 47. Baden-Baden: Nomos Verlag.

Kailitz, Steffen/Köllner, Patrick (2013): Zur Autokratieforschung der Gegenwart: Klassifikatorische Vorschläge, theoretische Ansätze und analytische Dimensionen. In: Kailitz, Steffen/Köllner, Patrick (Eds.): Autokratien im Vergleich. PVS Sonderheft 47. Baden-Baden: Nomos Verlag, pp. 9-34.

Kay, Rebecca (2000): Russian women and their organizations: gender, discrimination and grassroots women's organizations, 1991-96. Basingstoke: Palgrave Macmillan.

Keller, Franziska (2012): (Why) Do Revolutions Spread?, Paper prepared for Presentation at the 2012 Annual Meeting of the American Political Science Association, New Orleans, 30 August - 2 September.

Kerchner, Brigitte/Schneider, Silke (Eds.) (2010): Governing Gender. Feministische Studien zum Wandel des Regierens, Schwerpunktheft der Femina Politica. 2/2010. Berlin.

Kilby, Patrick (2011): NGOs in India: the challenges of women's empowerment and accountability. London: Routledge.

Klein, Ansgar (2001): Der Diskurs der Zivilgesellschaft. Opladen: Leske+Budrich.

Klein, Uta (2006): Geschlechterverhältnisse, Geschlechterpolitik und Gleichstellungspolitik in der Europäischen Union. Wiesbaden: Springer VS.

Klein-Hessling, Ruth (1998): Muslimische Frauenorganisationen und Internationale Frauenpolitik. Working Paper 296. Bielefeld.

Klein-Hessling, Ruth (1999): Zivilgesellschaft, Frauenorganisationen und Netzwerke. Working Paper 320. Bielefeld.

Köbberling, Anna (1993): Zwischen Liquidation und Wiedergeburt. Frauenbewegung in Russland von 1917 bis heute. Frankfurt a.M./New York: Campus.

Kohler-Koch, Beate/Quittkat, Christine (2011): Die Entzauberung partizipativer Demokratie. Zur Rolle der Zivilgesellschaft bei der Demokratisierung von EU-Governance. Frankfurt am Main/New York: Campus.

Köllner, Patrick (2008): Autoritäre Regime – Ein Überblick über die jüngere Literatur. In: Zeitschrift für Vergleichende Politikwissenschaft 2, pp. 351-366.

Kooiman, Jan (2003): Governing as Governance. London: Sage.

Kraatz, Susanne/Nève, Dorothée de/Steinsdorff, Silvia von (2003): Osteuropaforschung ohne Frauen? In: Osteuropa 5, pp. 635-646.

Krause, Wanda (2008): Women in civil society: the state, Islamism, and networks in the UAE. New York: Palgrave Macmillan.

Krause, Wanda (2012): Civil society and women activists in the Middle East: Islamic and secular organizations in Egypt. London: Palgrave Macmillan.

Kreile, Renate (2009): Transformation und Gender im Nahen Osten. In: Beck, Martin/Harders, Cilja/Jünemann, Annette/Stetter, Stephan (Eds.): Der Nahe Osten im Umbruch. Zwischen Transformation und Autoritarismus. Wiesbaden: Springer VS, pp. 253-276.

Kreile, Renate (2012): Neoliberalismus, Staat und Gender in der Türkei. In: Femina Politica 21, 1, pp. 73-85.

Kreisky, Eva (1994): Das ewig Männerbündische? Zur Standardform von Staat und Politik. In: Leggewie, Claus (Ed.): Wozu Politikwissenschaft? Über das Neue in der Politik. Darmstadt: Wissenschaftliche Buchgesellschaft, pp. 191-208.

Kunovich, R. M./Deitelbaum, C. (2004): Ethnic conflict, group polarization, and gender attitudes in Croatia. In: Journal of Marriage and Family 66, 5, pp. 1089-1107.

Lachenmann, Gudrun (1996): Weltfrauenkonferenz und Forum der Nichtregierungsorganisationen in Peking: internationale Frauenbewegungen als Vorreiterinnen einer globalen Zivilgesellschaft? Working Paper. Bielefeld.

Lamla, Jörn (2005): Kontexte der Politisierung des Konsums. Die Zivilgesellschaft in der gegenwärtigen Krisenkonstellation von Politik, Ökonomie und Kultur. In: Adloff, Frank/Birsl, Ursula/Schwertmann, Philipp (Eds.): Wirtschaft und Zivilgesellschaft. Wiesbaden: Springer VS, pp. 127-156.

Langohr, Vickie (2004): Too Much Civil Society, Too Little Politics: Egypt and Liberalizing Arab Regimes. In: Comparative Politics 16, 2, pp. 181-204.

Lederer, Gerda (2000): Autoritarismus und Fremdenfeindlichkeit im deutsch-deutschen Vergleich: Ein Land mit zwei Sozialisationskulturen. In: Rippl, Susanne/Seipel, Christian/Kindervater, Angela (Eds.): Autoritarismus. Kontroversen und Ansätze der aktuellen Autoritarismusforschung. Opladen: Leske+Budrich, pp. 199-214

Lemke, Christiane (1996): „Frauen und Politik in den Transformationsprozessen Osteuropas" In: Penrose, Virginia/Ruppert, Uta et al. (Eds.): Frauenbewegung und Frauenpolitik in Osteuropa. Frankfurt a. M./New York: Campus, pp. 15-33.

Lenz, Ilse (2008): Frauenbewegungen: Zu den Anliegen und Verlaufsformen von Frauenbewegungen als sozialen Bewegungen. In: Becker, Ruth/Kortendiek, Beate (Eds.): Handbuch Frauen- und Geschlechterforschung. Theorie, Methoden, Empirie. Wiesbaden: Springer VS, pp. 859 – 869.

Levitsky, Steven/Way, Lucan (2010): Competitive Authoritarianism: Hybrid Regimes After the Cold War. Cambridge: Cambridge University Press.

Liborakina, Marina (1998): The Unappreciated Mothers of Civil Society. In: Transitions 5, 1, pp. 52-57.

Lilja, Mona (2013): Resisting gendered norms: civil society, the juridical and political space in Cambodia. Aldershot: Asgate.

Linz, Juan J. (2000): Totalitarian and Authoritarian Regimes. Boulder, Colorado: Lynne Rienner Publishers.

Lister, Marjorie (2006): New pathways in international development: gender and civil society in EU policy. Aldershot: Ashgate.

Lo, Ming-Cheng M./Fan, Yun (2010): Hybrid Cultural Codes in Nonwestern Civil Society: Images of Women in Taiwan and Hong Kong. In: Sociological Theory 28, 2, pp. 167-192.

Locke, John (1977) [1690]: Zwei Abhandlungen über die Regierung, Frankfurt am Main: Suhrkamp.

Longman, Timothy (2006): Rwanda: Achieving Equality or Serving an Authoritarian State?. In: Bauer, Gretchen/Britton, Hannah E. (Eds.): Women in African Parliaments. Boulder, Colorado: Lynne Rienner Publishers, pp. 133-150.

Luleva, Ana (2006): Transformation and gender arrangements in postsocialist Bulgaria. In: Ethnologia Bulgarica 3, pp. 12-22.

Lyons, Lenore (2005): Transient Workers Count Too? The Intersection of Citizenship and Gender in Singapore's Civil Society, Sojourn 20, 2, pp. 208-248.

Macdonald, Laura/Mills, Lisa (2010): Gender, Democracy and Federalism in Mexico: Implications for Reproductive Rights and Social Policy. In: Haussmann, Melissa/Sawer, Maria/Vickers, Jill (Eds.): Federalism, Feminism and Multilevel Governance. Farnham: Ashgate, pp. 187-198.

Manea, Elham (2011): The Arab State und Women's Rights. The Trap of Authoritarian Governance. London, New York: Routledge.

Marquardt, M. F. (2005): From shame to confidence - Gender, religious conversion, and civic engagement of Mexicans in the US South. In: Latin American Perspectives 32, 1, pp. 27-56.

Marx Ferree, Myra/Martin, Patricia Yancey (Eds.) (1995): Feminist organizations: harvest of the new women's movement. Philadelphia: Temple Univ. Press.

McDuie-Ra, Duncan (2007): The Constraints on Civil Society beyond the State: Gender-based Insecurity in Meghalaya, India. In: Voluntas 4/2007, pp. 359-384.

Meloen, Jos D. (2000): Die Ursprünge des Staatsautoritarismus. Eine empirische Untersuchung der Auswirkungen von Kultur, Einstellungen und Politik im weltweiten Vergleich. In: Rippl, Susanne/Seipel, Christian/Kindervater, Angela (Eds.): Autoritarismus. Kontroversen und Ansätze der aktuellen Autoritarismusforschung. Opladen: Leske+Budrich, pp. 215-236.

Merkel, Wolfgang (2010): Are Dictatorships Returning? Revisiting the "Democratic Rollback" Hypothesis. In: Contemporary Politics 16, 1, pp. 17–31.

Merkel, Wolfgang/Puhle, Hans-Jürgen (1999): Von der Diktatur zur Demokratie: Transformationen, Erfolgsbedingungen, Entwicklungspfade. Wiesbaden: Springer VS.

Merkel, Wolfgang/Lauth, Hans-Joachim (1998): Systemwechsel und Zivilgesellschaft: Welche Zivilgesellschaft braucht die Demokratie? In: Aus Politik und Zeitgeschichte B 6-7/98, pp. 3-12.

Mokre, Monica/Siim, Birte (2013): Conclusion: Intersectionality and the European Public Sphere. In: Siim, Birte/Mokre, Monika (Eds.): Negotiating Gender and Diversity in an Emergent European Public Sphere. Basingstoke/New York: Palgrave Macmillan, pp. 223-230.

Mokre, Monika/Siim, Birte (2013): European Public Spheres and Intersectionality. In: Siim, Birte/Mokre, Monika (Eds.): Negotiating Gender and Diversity in an Emergent European Public Sphere. Basingstoke/New York: Palgrave Macmillan, pp. 22-42.

Molyneux, Maxine (1985): Mobilisation without Emancipation? Women's Interests, States and Revolution in Nicaragua. In: Feminist Studies II, 2.

Molyneux, Maxine (2000): Twentieth-Century State Formations in Latin America. In: Dore, Elizabeth/Molyneux, Martine (Eds.): Hidden Histories of Gender and the State in Latin America. Durham and London: Duke University Press, pp. 33-81.

Molyneux, Maxine (2000a): State, Gender and Institutional Change. The Federatión de Mujeres Cubanas. In: Dore, Elizabeth/Molyneux, Martine (Eds.): Hidden Histories of Gender and the State in Latin America. Durham and London: Duke University Press, pp. 291-321.

Molyneux, Maxine/Razavi, Shara (Eds.) (2002): Gender Justice, Development, and Rights. Oxford: Oxford University Press.

Mommsen, Margareta/Nußberger, Angelika (2008): Das System Putin. München: C.H. Beck.

Montesquieu, Charles (1965) [1748]: Vom Geist der Gesetze. Stuttgart: Reclam.

Mouffe, Chantal (1992): Dimensions of Radical Democracy. London/New York: Verso.

Mueller, Magda/Funk, Nanette (1993): Gender politics and post-communism: Reflections from Eastern Europe and the former Soviet Union. London: Routledge.

Narr, Wolf-Dieter (1994): Wieviel Entwicklung kann sozialwissenschaftliche Theorie ertragen? - Am Exempel: Zivilgesellschaft. In: Das Argument 206, pp. 587-599.

Neumann, Franz (1984) [1942]: Behemoth. Frankfurt am Main: Fischer.

Nève, Dorothée de/Olteanu/Tina (2012): Politische Partizipation jenseits der Konventionen. Leverkusen: Budrich.

Notz, Gisela (2007): Das Museum greift gern auf einsatzfreudige Damen zurück. Bürgerschaftliches Engagement im Bereich von Kultur und Soziokultur. In: Femina Politica 2/2007, pp. 53-61.

Okin, Susan Moller (1998): Gender, the Public, and the Private. In: Landes, Joan B. (Ed.): Feminism, the Public and the Private. Oxford: Oxford University Press, pp. 116-141.

Okin, Susan Moller (2002): Comment on Nancy Rosenblum's 'Feminist Perspectives on Civil Society and Government'. In: Rosenblum, Nancy/Post, Robert (Eds.): Civil Society and Government, Princeton: Princton Univ. Press, pp. 179-186.

Ong, Aikwa (1991): The Gender and Labor Policys of Postmodernity. In: Annual Revoiw of Anthropology, 20, pp. 279-309.

Ostner, Ilona (1997): Familie und Zivilgesellschaft. In: Schmals, Klaus/Heinelt, Hubert (Eds.), Zivile Gesellschaft: Entwicklung, Defizite und Potenziale. Opladen: Leske+Budrich, pp. 369-383.

Pateman, Carole (1988): The Sexual Contract. Stanford: Standford Univ. Press.

Pateman, Carole (1989): The Disorder of Women. Cambridge.

Pauer-Studer, Herlinde (2003): Zivilgesellschaft - Was kann und soll es bedeuten? In: Appel, Margit/Gubitzer, Luise/ Sauer, Birgit (Eds.): Zivilgesellschaft - ein Konzept für Frauen? Frankfurt am Main et al.: Peter Lang, pp. 73-85.

Gender, Civil Society, and Non-Democratic Regimes 69

Penrose, Virginia/Ruppert, Uta (1996): Versuch einer grenzüberschreitenden Verständigung. Eine Einleitung. In: Lemke, Christiane/Penrose, Virginia/ Ruppert, Uta (Eds.): Frauenbewegung und Frauenpolitik in Osteuropa. Frankfurt a.m./New York: Campus, pp. 7-14.

Pető, Andrea/Szapor, Judith (2004): Women and "the alternative public sphere": Toward a new definition of women's activism and the separate spheres in East-Central Europe. In: NORA - Nordic Journal of Feminist and Gender Research 12, 3, pp. 172-181.

Pfaffenholz, Thania (2011): Civil Society and Peacebuilding. A Critical Assessment. London: Lynne Rienner Publishers.

Phillips, Anne (1995): Geschlecht und Demokratie, Hamburg et al.: Rotbuch Verlag.

Phillips, Anne (2002): Does Feminism Need a Conception of Civil Society? In: Chambers, Simone /Kymlicka, Will (Eds.): Alternative conceptions of civil society. Princeton: Princeton Univ. Press, pp. 71-89.

Phillips, Sarah D. (2008): Women's social activism in the new Ukraine: development and the politics of differentiation. Bloomington: Indiana Univ. Press.

Pickel, Susanne (2013): Demokratie, Anokratie, Autokratie und die Verwirklichung der Rechte von Frauen. Wechselbeziehungen zwischen Gender Empowerment, Wertestrukturen und Regimepersistenz. In: Kailitz, Steffen/Köllner, Patrick (Eds.): Autokratien im Vergleich. PVS Sonderheft 47. Baden-Baden: Nomos Verlag, pp. 438-476.

Priller, Eckhard (2011): Dynamik, Struktur und Wandel der Engagementforschung. Rückblick, Tendenzen und Anforderungen. In: Priller, Eckhard/Alscher, Mareike/Dathe, Dietmar/Speth, Rudolf (Eds.): Zivilgagament. Herausforderungen für Gesellschaft, Politik und Wissenschaft. Berlin/Münster: LIT-Verlag, pp. 11-40.

Pristed Nielsen, Helene (2013): Collaborating on Combating Anti-discrimination? Anti-Racist and Gender Equality Organisations in Europe. In: Siim, Birte/Mokre, Monika (Eds.), Negotiating Gender and Diversity in an Emergent European Public Sphere. Basingstoke/New York: Palgrave Macmillan, pp. 179-200.

Rabo, Annika (1996): Gender, state and civil society in Jordan and Syria. In: Hann, Chris/Dunn, Elizabeth (Eds.): Civil society: challenging western models. London: Routledge, pp. 155-178.

Racioppi, Linda/O'Sullivan See, Katherine (1995): Organizing Women before and after the Fall: Women's Politics in the Soviet Union and Post-Soviet Russia. In: Signs 20, 4, pp. 818-850.

Reese, Niklas (2010): „Still Working on it": An Overview on the Current State of Public Activism of Women in the Philippines". In: ASEAS Austrian Journal of South-East Asian Studies 3, 2, pp. 136-150.

Reininger, Belinda M./Rahbar, Mohammad H./Lee, MinJae/Chen, Zhongxue/Alam, Sartaj R./Pope, Jennifer/Adams, Barbara (2013): Social capital and disaster preparedness among low income Mexican Americans in a disaster prone area. In: Social Science & Medicine 83, pp. 50-60.

Rensmann, Lars/Hagemann, Steffen/Funke, Hajo (2011): Autoritarismus und Demokratie. Politische Theorie und Kultur in der globalen Moderne. Schwalbach/Ts.: Wochenschau Verlag.

Reverter-Bañón, Sonia (2006): Civil Society and Gender Equality: A Theoretical Approach. Civil Society Working Papers 24. London.

Richter, James (2002): Evaluating Western Assistance to Russian Women's Organizations. In: Mendelson, Sarah E./Glenn, John K. (Eds.): The Power and Limits of NGOs. New York: Columbia University Press, pp. 54-90.

Rippl, Susanne/Seipel, Christian/Kindervater, Angela (Eds.) (2000): Autoritarismus. Kontroversen und Ansätze der aktuellen Autoritarismusforschung. Opladen: Leske+Budrich.

Ritter, Martina (Ed.) (2001): Zivilgesellschaft und Gender-Politik in Rußland, Frankfurt am Main: Campus.

Ritter, Martina (2008): Die Dynamik von Privatheit und Öffentlichkeit in modernen Gesellschaften. Wiesbaden: Springer VS.

Rolandsen Augustín, Lise (2013): Transnational Collective Mobilisation: Challenges for Women's Movements in Europe. In: Siim, Birte/Mokre, Monika (Eds.): Negotiating Gender and Diversity in an Emergent European Public Sphere. Basingstoke/New York: Palgrave Macmillan, pp. 161-178.

Roth, Roland (2000): Bürgerschaftliches Engagement – Formen, Bedingungen, Perspektiven. In: Zimmer, Annette/Nährlich, Stefan (Eds.): Engagierte Bürgerschaft. Traditionen und Perspektiven. Opladen: Leske+Budrich, pp. 25-48.

Ruhlen, Rebecca N. (2007): South Korean feminist activism: Gender, middle-classness, and public/private discourse in 1990s civil society. Washington: University of Washington.

Ruppert, Uta (1998): Demokratisierung oder Modernisierung von Machtlosigkeit? Geschlechterverhältnisse in den Prozessen gesellschaftlicher Transition in Afrika. In: Kreisky, Eva/Sauer, Birgit (Eds.): Geschlechterverhältnisse im Kontext politischer Transformation. Sonderheft Politische Vierteljahresschrift 28. Opladen: Westdeutscher Verlag, pp. 491-511.

Salmenniemi, Suuvi (2005): Civic Activity – Feminine Activity? Gender, Civil Society and Citizenship in Post-Soviet Russia. In: Sociology 39, 4, pp. 735-753.

Salmenniemi, Suvi (2008): Democratisation and gender in contemporary Russia. London.

Sänger, Eva (2007): Umkämpfte Räume. Zur Funktion von Öffentlichkeit in Theorien der Zivilgesellschaft. In: Femina Politica 16, 2, pp. 18-27.

Sauer, Birgit (1996): Transition zur Demokratie? Die Kategorie „Geschlecht" als Prüfstein für die Zuverlässigkeit von sozialwissenschaftlichen Transformationstheorien. In: Kreisky, Eva (Ed.): Vom patriarchalen Staatssozialismus zur patriarchalen Demokratie. Wien: Verlag für Gesellschaftskritik, pp. 131-168.

Sauer, Birgit (2003): Zivilgesellschaft versus Staat? Geschlechterkritische Anmerkungen zu einer problematischen Dichotomie. In: Appel, Margit/Gubitzer, Luise/Sauer, Birgit (Eds.): Zivilgesellschaft - ein Konzept für Frauen?. Frankfurt am Main et al.: Peter Lang, pp. 117-136.

Sauer, Birgit (2004): Geschlecht und Politik: institutionelle Verhältnisse, Verhinderungen und Chancen. Berlin:WVB.

Sauer, Birgit (2011): Die Allgegenwart der „Androkratie": Feministische Anmerkungen zur „Postdemokratie". In: Aus Politik und Zeitgeschichte 1-2, pp. 32-36.

Saurer, Edith/Lanzinger, Margareth, Frysak, Elisabeth (Eds.) (2006): Women's movements: networks and debates in post-communist countries in the 19th and 20th centuries. Köln: Böhlau Verlag.

Savery, Lynn (2007): Engendering the State. The International Diffusion of Women's Human Rights. New York: Routledge.

Schachtner, Christina (2005): Architektinnen der Zukunft. Lokale Frauenprojekte im Kontext der Globalisierung. München: Oekom Verlag.

Schade, Jeanette (2002): "Zivilgesellschaft" - Eine vielschichtige Debatte, INEF-Report 59. Duisburg.

Schäfer, Rita (2012): Gender und autoritäre Herrschaft in Zimbabwe. In: Femina Politica 21, 1, pp. 86-97.

Schmitt, Britta (1997): Zivilgesellschaft, Frauenpolitik und Frauenbewegung in Russland: von 1917 bis zur Gegenwart. Königstein/Taunus: Helmer.

Schnabl, Christa (2003): (Werte-)Gemeinschaften in der Zivilgesellschaft: Konzepte, Aufgaben und Verortung. In: Margit Appel/Luise Gubitzer/Birgit Sauer (Eds.): Zivilgesellschaft - ein Konzept für Frauen?. Frankfurt am Main et al.: Peter Lang, pp. 87-115.

Schneider, Silke (2004): Civil Society and Gender Justice – Historical and Comparative Perspectives. Interdisziplinäre Tagung vom 9. bis 11. Juli 2004 in Berlin. In: Femina Politica, 13, 2, pp. 154-156.

Schneider, Silke (2010): Verbotener Umgang - Ausländer und Deutsche im Nationalsozialismus. Diskurse um Sexualität, Moral, Wissen und Strafe. Baden-Baden: Nomos Verlag.

Schneider, Silke/Wilde, Gabriele (2012): Autokratie, Demokratie und Geschlecht: Geschlechterverhältnisse in autoritären Regimen. In: Femina Politica 21, 1, pp. 9-16.

Schöning-Kalender, Claudia (1997): Feminismus, Islam, Nation: Frauenbewegungen im Maghreb, in Zentralasien und in der Türkei. Frankfurt am Main: Campus Verlag.

Schwertmann, Philipp (2006): Stiftungen als Förderer der Zivilgesellschaft. Baden-Baden: Nomos.

Sharify-Funk, Meena (2008): Encountering the transnational: women, Islam and the politics of interpretation. Aldershot: Ashgate.

Shigematsu, Setsu (2012): Scream from the shadows: the women's liberation movement in Japan. Minneapolis: Univ. Press.

Sifft, Stefanie/Abels, Gabriele (1999): Demokratie als Projekt. Anmerkungen zur Interdependenz von Staat, Zivilgesellschaft und Geschlechterverhältnissen. In: Abels, Gabriele/Sifft, Stefanie (Eds.): Demokratie als Projekt: feministische Kritik an der Universalisierung einer Herrschaftsform. Frankfurt a.M./New York: Campus, pp. 9-36.

Siim, Birte (2013): Intersections of Gender and Diversity – A European Perspective. In: Siim, Birte/Mokre, Monika (Eds.): Negotiating Gender and Diversity in an Emergent European Public Sphere. Basingstoke/New York: Palgrave Macmillan, pp. 3-21.

Siim, Birte/Mokre, Monika (2013): Negotiating Gender and Diversity in an Emergent European Public Sphere. Basingstoke/New York Palgrave Macmillan.

Silliman, Jael (1999): Expanding Civil Society: Shrinking Political Spaces – The Case of Women's Nongovernmental Organizations. In: Social Politics 6, 1, pp. 23-53.

Sloat, Amanda (2005): The Rebirth of Civil Society. The Growth of Women's NGOs in Central and Eastern Europe. In: Journal of Women's Studies 12, 4, pp. 437-452.

Spendzharova, Aneta B., and Milada Anna Vachudova (2012): Catching Up? Consolidating Liberal Democracy in Bulgaria and Romania after EU Accession. In: West European Politics, 35, pp. 39–58.

Sperling, Valerie (1999): Organizing Women in Contemporary Russia. Cambridge Cambridge University Press.

Squires, Judith (2007): The New Politics of Gender Equality. Basingstoke/New York: Houndsmills.

Stecker, Christina (2007): Ambivalenz der Differenz. Frauen zwischen bürgerschaftlichem Engagement, Erwerbsarbeit und Sozialstaat. In: Femina Politica 16, 2, pp. 41-52.

Stenner, Karen (2005): The Authoritarian Dynamic. Cambridge: Cambridge University Press.

Stenner, Karen (2009): Three Kinds of "Conservatism". In: Psychological Inquiry 20, pp. 142-159.

Stienstra, Deborah (1994): Women's movements and international organizations. Basingstoke: Palgrave Macmillan.

Taylor, Charles (1991): Die Beschwörung der Civil Society. In: Michalski, Krysztof (Ed.): Europa und die Civil Society. Stuttgart: Klett Verlag, pp. 52-81.

The Economist's Intelligence Unite (2011): Democracy Index 2011. https://www.eiu.com/public/topical_report.aspx?campaignid=DemocracyIndex2011 (08.08.2012).

Tocqueville, Alexis de (1987) [1835, 1840]: Über die Demokratie in Amerika. Zürich: Manesse Verlag.

Unterhalter, Elaine/Dutt, Shushmita (2001): Gender, education and women's power: Indian state and civil society intersections in DPEP (District Primary Education Programme) and Mahila Samakhya. In: Compare. A Journal of Comparative and International Education 31, 1, pp 57-73.

Watson, Peggy (1993): Osteuropa: Die lautlose Revolution der Geschlechterverhältnisse. In: Das Argument 202, pp. 659-874.

Watson, Peggy (1995): Zivilgesellschaft und Geschlechterverhältnisse in Osteuropa. In: Das Argument 211, pp. 721-731.

Waylen, Georgina (1999): Demokratisierung, demokratische Konsolidierung und Geschlecht. Überlegungen für eine feministische Analyse. In: Sifft, Stefanie/Abels, Gabriele (Eds.): Demokratie als Projekt: feministische Kritik an der Universalisierung einer Herrschaftsform. Frankfurt a.M./New York: Campus, pp. 37-63.

Waylen, Georgina (2007): Engendering transitions: Women's mobilization, institutions, and gender outcomes. Oxford/New York: Oxford Univ. Press.

Gender, Civil Society, and Non-Democratic Regimes

Weiss, Anita M. (2001): Social development, the empowerment of women, and the expansion of civil society: alternative ways out of the debt and poverty trap. In: The Pakistan development review 40, 4, pp. 401-432.

Wichterich, Christa (1999): Anerkennung, Rechte, Ressourcen. Frauenorganisationen im informellen Sektor in Ländern des Südens. In: PROKLA 117, 4, pp. 535-554.

Wichterich, Christa (2000): Strategische Verschwisterung, multiple Feminismen und die Globalisierung von Frauenbewegungen. In: Lenz, Ilse/Mae, Michiko/Klose, Karin (Eds.), Frauenbewegungen weltweit. Opladen: Leske+Budrich, pp. 257-280.

Wijkström, Filip/Zimmer, Annette (Eds.) (2011): Beyond Membership: Civil Society Organizations in Times of Change. Baden-Baden: Nomos.

Wilde, Gabriele/ Friedrich, Stefanie (Eds.) (2013): Im Blick der Disziplinen: Geschlecht und Geschlechterverhältnisse in der wissenschaftlichen Analyse. Münster: Westfälisches Dampfboot.

Wilde, Gabriele (2001): Das Geschlecht des Rechtsstaats: Herrschaftsstrukturen und Grundrechtspolitik in der deutschen Verfassungstradition. Frankfurt am Main: Campus.

Wilde, Gabriele (2009): Gesellschaftsvertrag – Geschlechtervertrag. In: Ludwig, Gundula/Sauer, Birgit/Wöhl, Stefanie (Eds.): Staat und Geschlecht. Grundlagen und aktuelle Herausforderungen feministischer Staatstheorie. Baden-Baden: Nomos, pp. 31-36.

Wilde, Gabriele (2013): Jenseits von Recht und neoliberaler Ordnung. Zur Integration von Geschlecht in die politikwissenschaftliche Europaforschung. In: Wilde, Gabriele/Friedrich, Stefanie (Eds.): Im Blick der Disziplinen: Geschlecht und Geschlechterverhältnisse in der wissenschaftlichen Analyse. Münster: Westfälisches Dampfboot, pp. 21-54.

Willems, Joachim (2013): Pussy Riots Punk-Gebet. Religion, Recht und Politik in Russland. Berlin: Berlin Univ. Press.

Winker, Gabriele/Degele, Nina (2009): Intersektionalität: Zur Analyse sozialer Ungleichheiten. Bielefeld: transcript.

Young, Iris Marion (1999): State, Civil Society, and Social Justice. In: Shapiro, Ian/Hacker-Cordón, Casiano (Eds.): Democracy's Value. Cambridge: Cambridge Univ. Press, pp. 141-162.

Young, Iris Marion (2000): Inclusion and Democracy. Oxford: Oxford Univ. Press.

Zdravomyslova, Elena (2000): Die Feministinnen der ersten Stunde im heutigen Russland: Ein Porträt vor dem Hintergrund der Bewegung. In: Lenz, Ilse/Mae, Michiko/Klose, Karin (Eds.): Frauenbewegungen weltweit. Aufbrüche, Kontinuitäten, Veränderungen. Opladen: Leske+ Budrich, pp. 51–74.

Zdravomyslova, Elena (2015): Discourse of moral crisis and conservative mobilization in Russia: gender issues. Lecture at the International conference "Gender and Diversity Studies in European perspectives", Jan. 8-10, Rhine-Waal University of Applied Sciences. Kleve.

Zimmer, Annette (2001): NGOs - Verbände im globalen Zeitalter. Inn: Zimmer, Annette/Weßels, Bernhard (Eds.): Verbände und Demokratie in Deutschland. Opladen: Leske+Budrich, pp. 331–365.

Zimmer, Annette (2009): Zivilgesellschaft und Demokratie: Drei Modelle zivilgesellschaftlicher Einbettung. In: Gesellschaft, Wirtschaft, Politik, 3/2009, pp. 397- 406.

Zimmer, Annette (2010): Zivilgesellschaft und Demokratie in Zeiten des gesellschaftlichen Wandels. In: Der moderne Staat, 3, 1, pp. 147 – 163.

Zimmer, Annette (2012a): Die Zivilgesellschaft zwischen Ökonomisierung und Verbetriebswirtschaftlichung. In: Sozialwissenschaften und Berufspraxis, 35, 2, pp. 189-202.

Zimmer, Annette (2012b): Zivilgesellschaft. Ein Leitbild. In: Hradil, Stefan (Ed.): Deutsche Verhältnisse. Eine Sozialkunde. Bonn: Bundeszentrale für politische Bildung, pp. 353-364.

Zimmer, Annette/Krimmer, Holger (2007): Does gender matter? Haupt- und ehrenamtliche Führungskräfte gemeinnütziger Organisationen. In: Femina Politica 16, 2, pp. 62-72.

If Not for Democracy, for What?
Civil Society in Authoritarian Settings

Annette Zimmer

1. Introduction

During the last years, no concept in the social sciences has drawn as much attention in politics and the media as that of civil society. The reasons for this are varied and are closely linked to the rediscovery of civil society due to the third wave of democratization (Huntington 1991). In particular, the dissident movements in Eastern Europe drew on "civil society" as an alternative and democratic societal counter model to Soviet-style authoritarianism (Havel and Keane 1985; Keane 1998; Klein 2001). Since then the concept of civil society has been regarded as a bearer of hope for a renewal of representative democracies in the north as well as a driving force for pushing back corruption and nepotism in young democracies in the south. The emergence of a civil society is seen, above all, as an indicator for societal change toward democracy in countries where authoritarian structures or one-party governments prevail.

However, can civil society fulfill all these expectations? Does the emergence of a civil society, indeed, work as a catalyst for the democratization of state and society? And in terms of gender equality, does civil society also promote a process of emancipation? This paper discusses these issues by introducing civil society as a concept with multiple dimensions and by taking a closer look at civil society actors. Subsequently, different functions of civil society as mentioned in classic works of political theory and philosophy will be presented. Finally, the assumption that civil society and democracy work hand in glove will be questioned and it will be discussed whether civil society organizations can flourish in the "shadows" of an authoritarian state, without preparing the way for democracy.

2. Civil society as a multidimensional concept

2.1 The programmatic, habitual, and area-specific dimension of the concept

Because the term "civil society" is used in a variety of discourses, is colloquially popular, and widely used in media and by the general public, it does not have a commonly acknowledged definition. In German-speaking countries the works of the historian Jürgen Kocka, who contributed considerably to defining the term more concisely, are often referred to (Kocka 2008, 2003, 2002). Kocka lays out a three-dimensional concept and distinguishes between the normative, habitual or behavioristic, and descriptive-analytic components of civil society (Kocka 2003, 31; most recently Lauth 2017: 388f.).

The normative component refers to the programmatic-critical dimension of civil society, giving a theoretical foundation to political and societal participation as well as social justice, which is a central concern for political philosophy and democracy theory (cf. Kocka 2003: 32). From this perspective civil society is "a part of a comprehensive plan or project … , which since the age of the Enlightenment and until today has remained partly incomplete" (Kocka 2003: 33). Thus, civil society stands for a more participative democracy as well as for a critical position regarding the status quo: The term is a synonym for a forward looking program aiming at a continuous enhancement and deepening of democracy, including social justice and gender equality, and has unmistakably a normative as well as a programmatic orientation.

The habitual component of civil society refers to a certain type of social interaction, namely "civilized" interaction in the quite literal sense as peaceful and compromise-oriented interaction. "Civility" is the main characteristic of this society. The political framework is also characterized by "civility" and supports such civilized interaction. It has rules and regulations such as constitutional human and civil rights; it guarantees equality before the law, the right of assembly, and the right to be politically active; it enables the individual to lead a dignified life above the poverty line (Rucht 2009: 88); and, last but not least, it provides equal opportunities in terms of gender mainstreaming.

Civil society in Authoritarian Settings 77

Whereas the normative component of civil society, with its project or programmatic approach, tends to focus on the macro-level of state and society, the habitual component mainly refers to the micro-level. Each individual is requested to show civil virtues and act as a "citoyen," in other words, to disregard individual interests and to reject particularism in favor of the common good. Civil society, in this interpretation, is a synonym for "democracy as a way of life" and provides sense and identity.

Figure 1: Civil society as a concept with multiple dimensions

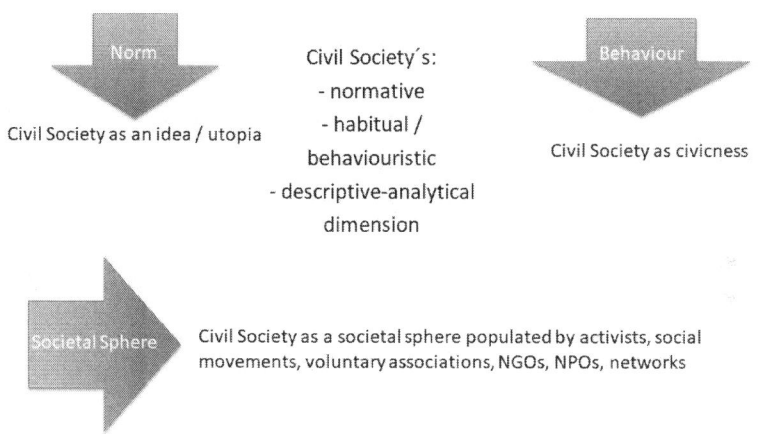

The third dimension of civil society is actor-centered and refers to specifically acting individuals, groups, and organizations. These actors are engaged in associations, networks, informal groups, social relations, and non-governmental organizations (Kocka 2002: 16), which in their totality form the base or infrastructure of civil society. The focus here is on civil society as an expression of societal self-organization. These organizations or groups are proactive and self-organized in a social "sphere or area which, in the case of a modern and differentiated society, lies somewhere between state, economy, and private sphere" (Kocka 2002: 17). Civil society is thus an "intermediate sphere" of societal self-organization. This sphere is structured by a multitude of initiatives, groups, and organizations that "incorporate" the individual into society by bundling their interests and concerns, which are then publicly voiced and promoted in politics and integrated into the state and governmental administration. From this historical and modernization-biased perspective, civil society is the result of processes of societal modernization and functional differentiation. A modern "civil society" emerged from these processes at the beginning of the industrial revolution and still keeps its formative influence today. From this perspective, civil society is a synonym for the "intermediate sphere" of societal self-organization beyond mere family-centered or clan-based organizational structures. The question remains if or to what extent this associational sphere which emerged in modern history and which is often referred to as the "third sector" may contribute to the development as well as the consolidation and deepening of democracy. Only further empirical and contextual research and an analysis of the respective civil society actors, their objectives, and their actions might give satisfactory answers.

2.2 Civil society actors

Unquestionably, civil society shows a very refined actor spectrum. At the center of media and general public attention are the prominent and often charismatic personalities who get involved in civil society movements through word and deed, sometimes even risking their lives, to denounce mismanagement and grievances locally and internationally, to get involved in the resolution of political conflicts, and to become active for the purpose of a fairer and also more democratic society. Nobel Peace laureate Wangari Maathai (2004), the environmental activist and women's rights campaigner from Kenya, or the Chinese human rights activist Liu Xiaobo (2010) come to mind, but equally worth mentioning is the Russian activist group Pussy Riot. In addition to the prominent individuals mentioned above, all those citizens who stand up for their beliefs and protest against grievances and shortcomings are important actors of civil society and hence contribute substantially to public civility.

Other salient actors of civil society are social movements that often emerge when central challenges and social problems are overlooked, not considered, or even consciously ignored by politicians. A classic example of this is the suffragette movement which exerted itself at the beginning of the twentieth century in particular in the USA and in Great Britain with protest actions and demonstrations for women's suffrage. The environmental movement of the 1980s in Germany and worldwide can also be cited in this context. At that time, the demands of environmental activists for sustainable economic and energy policies met with a complete lack of understanding from both parties and trade unions. In the 1970s and 80s, the new women's movement, with spectacular actions and initiatives, put gender equality on the political agenda: the task was to promote gender equality by highlighting gender inequality in both the public sphere and the private sphere of the family. Even civil disobedience was used as a means and the movement contributed considerably to a thorough modernization of societal relations (Gerhard 2008). Findings of the research into civil movements, such as the labor, women's, One World, or *Kinderladen* movements, show that numerous initiatives and organizations spring up in the wake of a civil movement and a kind of civil society movement milieu eventually emerges. These networks, which are based on mutual contacts between individual activists or organizations, might intensify at any time, and in case of, say, an environmental disaster, can be mobilized. The formation of organizations, however, is usually followed by processes of stabilization and institutionalization. The movements' organizations become increasingly detached from their supporting milieu, more professional, and, in order to ensure their existence, increasingly rely on resources other than the voluntary work of sympathizers and activists. The gradual institutionalization and professionalization of social movements is a ubiquitous phenomenon (Joachim 2014). These activist movements successively develop into professionally working organizations, which, while maintaining their original objectives and their public interest orientation, increasingly adopt those structures and processes typical for organizations with a commercial orientation (Zimmer 2014: 173).

Besides individuals and social movements, a civil society comprises "voluntary groups" or associations that unite citizens with a common goal or "merely" for purposes such as socializing, common sporting activities, or to play music. Membership in such voluntary groups is the most common form of civil society activity worldwide. Numerically speaking, civil society as an intermediate social sphere is dominated by such voluntary groups. In Germany alone there are more than 600,000 voluntary associations (Priemer et al. 2017) having the fiscal status of nonprofit organizations with the purpose of the common good. Since the middle of the 1970s, a boom in the foundation of civil society organizations can be observed on a worldwide scale. This "associational revolution" (Salamon 1994) still continues. These organizations distinguish themselves from commercial enterprises or state authorities through a number of structural-specific features. For instance, they generally do not assume tasks of public authority, as it is the case with the police, and their organizational structure and governance is less hierarchical than government agencies. They differ from commercial enterprises inasmuch as they are subject to the "nonprofit constraint," which means that profits are allowed but cannot be distributed to stakeholders; rather, they must be reinvested in line with the organization's commitment to the common good. Multi-functionality is another structural feature of these organizations.

Civil society organizations as voluntary associations evade, at least partially, the functional differentiation of the modern age. They interact with various environments, adopting in each case specific functions. As voluntary associations where like-minded individuals gather under one umbrella, they contribute to the social integration of individuals and groups with their specific concerns and problems into society. The working men's organizations that emerged at the end of the nineteenth century in coal mining communities are a classic example. These organizations, typical for the then-booming industrial regions, substantially contributed to the integration of a newly arrived workforce. Nowadays local immigrant organizations have a similar function, namely the integration of foreign nationals into society while maintaining the customs and traditions of their respective home countries. The emergence of voluntary associations might also be the result of perceived public deficiencies and shortcomings, which are to be relieved or eliminated. Nearly all charitable organizations which provide social services are to be mentioned in this context. Worldwide the overwhelming majority of institutions dealing with social care are rooted in civil society. The existence of many hospitals, orphanages, or institutions for the needy, for childcare, for women's refuge centers, etc., originate from the initiatives of caring citizens. Nowadays these initiatives are usually fully professionalized service providers and social conglomerates that compete with state organizations or profit-oriented companies in the expanding global market for social services.

Figure 2: Multi-functionality of civil society organizations

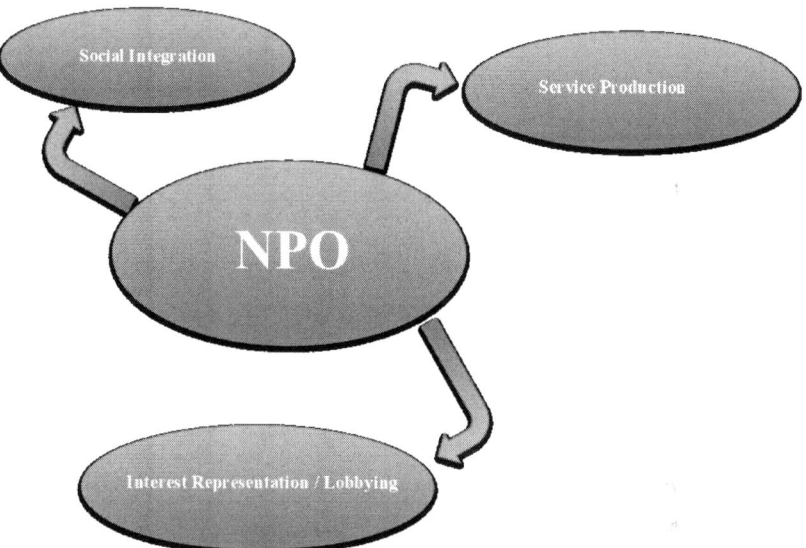

In spite of this market orientation, many of these social service providers still see themselves as lobbyists for their respective clientele. The representation of the interests of members as well as third parties is another common feature of civil society organizations. As outlined above many voluntary associations are established in order to advocate the common goals of their members and to change the governmental and administrative policies that appear to be neglecting certain issues and are not adequately providing related public services or general welfare. Today the initially critical or negative position toward the state has mostly given way to relations based on partnership, which might be described as a "third-party government," where private nonprofit organizations and government agencies cooperate in the provision of a wide spectrum of services (Zimmer 2010).

The question whether and to what extent civil society organizations actually fulfill their objectives, which range from lobbying to societal integration and even to the provision of services for members and/or third parties can only be answered by means of an empirical, context-specific analysis of that particular civil society organization. Retrospectively, however, it appears that many civil society organizations since their foundation have gone through a process of consolidation, institutionalization, and increasing economization and that the initial driving forces behind the emergence of a civil society organization have lost impetus in favor of organizational factors and goals such as ensuring the organization's future and growth. Local sports clubs, for instance, want to maintain their image as member's organizations that facilitate sports activities for everyone, including the young and financially disadvantaged, but competition with alternative sport facilities might cause them to lose sight of their social and civil societal mission in order to secure their own future financially. This gradual shift in priorities can be observed in all established civil society organizations to a certain extent but is most evident in the nonprofit providers of social services who work in close partnership with the state and its agencies in the area of public welfare. Again, whether these organizations form a part of civil society remains to be answered empirically. Thus, it might be concluded that a concise concept of civil society on the meso-level of the organization as well as on the micro-level of activists is problematic in terms of its use in democracy research and particularly for the empirical measuring of democracy (Lauth 2017: 389ff.). In spite of these difficulties, civil society remains an attractive and very compatible concept for the social sciences.

3. Civil society as a subject of the social sciences

Due to its multiple dimensions, the concept of civil society relates to various schools and sub-disciplines of the social sciences. Alongside political philosophy, which analyzes civil society from a societal and democratic-theoretical perspective (Adloff 2005; Klein 2001), research on participation and volunteering (Priller 2011; Vetter and Remer-Bolow 2017) examines empirically the extent, intensity, and forms of civil societal activity covering a wide spectrum of activities and organizations. This strand of research involves documenting civic virtues, from political activities and involvement in sport clubs to the social domain of volunteer work, reading newspapers, and voting in elections; acts of political disobedience such as sit-ins or public protest are also examined. Social capital research, which kicked off with the works of Robert Putnam (1993), also links statements about the existence and intensity of social capital to empirically measurable indicators, namely the existence and density of voluntary associations as well as the frequency and intensity of civil society activity in the form of membership and support of voluntary associations on a regional or national scale. The empirical analysis of the infrastructure of civil society, which involves recording the size and structure of civil society organizations, is a central topic of third sector research (Salamon et al. 2004), which has become increasingly international since the 1990s.[1] The administrative science approach, on the other hand, usually examines the size of a specific country's third or nonprofit sector, its structure, and funding, as well as its coexistence and cooperation with public social service providers; it also asks questions concerning governance and management issues (e.g., Simsa et al. 2013; Zimmer and Hallmann 2015). In this line of thought, the increasing relevance of the civil society sector for the economy and labor market on a worldwide scale is investigated, which differs regionally and nationally depending on the respective political-economic context. Altogether it becomes clear that the importance of nonprofit organizations is increasing worldwide, regardless of the respective political regime (Salamon 1994; Salamon et al. 2004).

In this respect, civil society organizations are also relevant within the framework of policy research. Against the backdrop of the shift from government to governance, and from governmental top-down rule to new non-hierarchical processes in decision-making and policy implementation involving private actors, the importance of civil society organizations and the attention they receive in political science has increased significantly. This is particularly true for the

---

1 Cf. International Society for Third-Sector Research: http://www.istr.org.

social economy and the generation of welfare services in, e.g., hospitals, rehab clinics, preschools, or retirement homes (Zimmer and Paul 2018). However, the increasing importance of civil society organizations as actors in governance arrangements can also be observed in numerous areas of political life and on nearly all political levels. This is true for all local, national, European, or international contexts. An example of the latter might be a non-governmental organization lobbying in New York or Brussels for, e.g., sustainable energy strategies, a certain immigration policy, or gender equality[2] and trying to steer the policy-making in its direction. According to this perspective, civil society research and the traditional research on associations and lobbyism overlap (Zimmer and Speth 2009).

The multidimensional manifestations of civil society as a normative concept and as a public sphere in transition have in recent times come into the focus of gender studies (Schwabenland et al. 2016; Hagemann et al. 2008). In this context, the central question is whether and to what extent civil society promotes emancipation and gender equality or if the opposite is true. Does civil society actually mirror the inequalities and disadvantages of women inherent in society? Even worse, does it further consolidate and sustain these inequalities and disadvantages in a conceptual and de facto sense? Seen positively, more gender equality in politics and in the working environment has been achieved by the women's movement and its protagonists. And the fact that the issue of gender equality is increasingly on the agenda of international organizations and committees can be attributed to worldwide civil society activities mainly by and for women. Basically, feminists view civil society critically: although the natural foundation of civil life is the private sphere, civil society exists in the public sphere and in opposition to the private sphere of the family. The separation between the private and a public sphere is the manifestation of a societal arrangement or construct and its specifics are the result of a societal modernization process accompanied by industrialization. In a traditional bourgeois society, the private sphere, and the family in particular, is the woman's domain, whereas public life including work, the economy, science, and politics is classically assigned to men. In this tradition, women are excluded de facto from

---

2   E.g., The European Women's Lobby: http://www.womenlobby.org/?lang=en

civil society, which exists as a public domain beyond the family. Even if this description no longer applies literally, the question remains and needs to be empirically tested if and to what extent a traditional (civil societal) arrangement lives on and whether civil society is gendered in a way "where a patriarchal set of gender norms regulates participation and behavior" (Seckinelgin 2010: 207). Empirical analyses of civil society organizations and women's involvement in decision-making as well as of their work relationships and career opportunities suggest that traditional behavioral norms and gender stereotypical behavioral patterns persist and prevail. Thus, women are involved above all in their "traditional" domains, namely, the raising of children, education, social issues, and church. Despite the female majority of employees, women with leadership positions in civil society organizations are just as few as women with leadership positions in the economy (Priller and Zimmer 2017). This is to some extent caused by structural factors and to some extent caused by qualified women deciding to remain on a middle management level (Zimmer et al. 2017).

In general, it can be said that civil society actors are the subject of theoretical and empirical analyses from various perspectives of social science. Both sides of the political system, namely the input-side which sets the political agenda and shapes the decision-making processes, as well as the output-side which delivers services partly on order of government agencies, are being examined. The fact that civil society organizations are to a great extent providers of public services is, however, mainly overlooked by political science research, which is rather focused on the nexus between civil society and democracy. Mainstream political research thus limits itself to the analysis of civil society on the input-side of the political system and usually resorts to classical authors of political science and philosophy whose interpretation of civil society is determined by their respective historical context.

4. Functional allocation of civil society from the perspective of political theory and philosophy

Numerous authors agree that civil society and democracy are closely related (Lauth 2017; Adloff 2005; Klein 2001; Cohen and Arato 1995). Reference is made to a set of functions ascribed to civil society. These are in detail:

- the classical communication and public function: civil society provides a forum for the exchange of opinions, deliberation, and decision-making,
- the liberal protective function: civil society constitutes a bulwark against state infringements on economy and privacy,
- and the intermediary function of self-organization, societal integration, and representation of interests (Merkel and Lauth 1998; Lauth 2017: 387).

Civil society as a political community and forum for the exchange of opinions, deliberation, and decision-making has a long tradition dating back to classical antiquity. Its concept of society and politics goes back to the Greek philosopher Aristoteles and his understanding of *politika koinonia* as a self-organized political community and ideal lifestyle of free citizens (Adloff 2005: 17), which concerns itself with state issues. The classical interpretation of civil society in democracy theory literature is criticized for being exclusive (Schmidt 2010: 27f.), as it only included free citizens and thus excluded women, slaves, and tradespeople, who together formed the majority of the town society. Nevertheless, in view of the further development of a civil society concept, since its early beginnings civil society has been associated with public deliberation as a peaceful means for resolving issues and devising strategies as well as with self-determined political action (Adloff 2005: 18).

Both lines of thought – public deliberation as well as the combination of government and society – were subsequently taken up in modern democracy theory by schools of thought using the concept of public deliberation or radical-democratic or radical-republican approaches (Held 2006). According to Jürgen Habermas and his concept of civil society, it has a traditional function which goes back to ancient Greece: civil society is a platform and forum for public deliberation, discourse, and the exchange of opinions, having its core in the field of associations, "which institutionalizes problem-solving discourses on questions of public interest in the public sphere" (Habermas 1992: 443f.).

Civil society is ascribed a different function in the scientific literature commonly referred to as the "L-strand" approach (Adloff 2005: 28), which assumes a plurality of social interests and groups and is based on the idea of opposition, an antagonism, between state and society. The description of civil society as a private sphere and a bulwark against illegitimate and unlawful state infringements that run counter to the social contract is a modern concept that has emerged against the backdrop of a dynamic economic development and the questioning of absolutism with its omnipotent claim to power. In this context "the function of civil society ... is predominantly protective" (Merkel and Lauth 1998: 4) inasmuch as it is to restrict and control absolutist power in both the economy and the private sphere. British contract theorists and moral philosophers of the seventeenth and eighteenth centuries saw civil society as a bulwark against illegitimate state infringements on the one hand and as a social sphere for the unimpeded development of entrepreneurial activities on the other (Schmidt 2007: 114; Adloff 2005: 25). Civil society, in this interpretation, was a project of economic liberalism with the aim of limiting the power of the state, binding government by a guaranteed rule of law, and guaranteeing the freedom of economic action. The state and (civil) society were seen as two opposite spheres, and the role of civil society was to keep the state at bay. From the perspective of democracy theory, civil society is a constitutive component of a "liberal democracy" in the tradition of John Locke and other contract theorists (cf. Adloff 2005: 20; Schmidt 2010: 49ff.), who see the necessity "to define and delimit the sphere of politics carefully, unleash individual energies in civil society, and provide a new balance between the citizen and government underwritten by law and institutions" (Held 2006: 55).

As a consequence, the function of self-organization and therefore of civil society as intermediate sphere which serves the societal integration and the mediation of political interests came into focus. In this respect the empirical analysis and the theoretical legitimation of different configurations of the state became important issues for political philosophy and democracy theory (Adloff 2005: 20f.). But civil society itself also became the subject of empirical and theoretical analyses due to the emergence of numerous public groups and associations in line with industrialization and societal modernization. Given the variety of interests and numerous social groups and concerns in modern society, the question became whether the "bigger picture" would be overlooked, thus sacrificing the greater common good for the pursuance of individual interests. Gender equality had not yet become an issue at that time, despite the fact that central societal issues were discussed in social settings and reading circles mainly hosted by women (Maurer 2001).

Without going into detail about the differences between the various approaches, there are roughly two perspectives of civil society as an intermediary sphere for self-organization and interest mediation as well as for balancing out differing concerns which have prevailed until today and substantially influence discourses on democracy (Klein 2001: 295ff.; Adloff 2005: 37ff.). Whereas the concept of civil society in the tradition of the philosopher Hegel is seen "from above" and regards the state as a guardian of the common good, Alexis de Tocqueville emphasized the variety of voluntary associations that facilitate societal plurality, keep the state at bay, and at the same time have a tempering influence on citizens. Both Hegel and Tocqueville refer in their work to "organized civil society" – namely corporations in Hegel and voluntary associations in Tocqueville – which structures the then new phenomenon of a bourgeois society and enables the pursuit of both particular as well as group interests while bundling public concerns and making them compatible with the common good. However, Hegel and Tocqueville have very different perceptions of how state and civil society interact.

Hegel as the representative of German idealism equates public welfare with the morality that is realized in an (ideal) state. Morality and state are, according to Hegel, inherent parts of "objective spirit" ("das an und für sich Vernünftige" [§258]); however, he is not writing descriptively about a concrete state but rather formulates a normative ideal: If the state is the realization of ethical ideas ("das Sittliche" [§ 249]), it commands a perfect legitimacy based on the rule of law. Bourgeois society, in contrast, is associated with "subjective spirit." It is driven by and dependent on the needs and actions of its members. These differentiations result in a marked distinction between bourgeois civil society and the state. In the Hegelian understanding, the self-organization of citizens in membership organizations titled corporations ("Korporationen" [§250]) fulfills two functions: Firstly, it serves to satisfy citizens' needs and enables them to pursue their own interests. Secondly, the self-organization of citizen or societal corporatism contributes to a process whereby citizens learn to act in line with the state and the ethical life ("das an und für sich Vernünftige") it represents. It follows that in an ideal scenario, the sphere of bourgeois civil society becomes one with that of the state (§ 256) once citizens have sufficiently developed and have embraced reason ("das an und für sich Vernünftige" [§258]) as a basis for their thought and action. Civil society from the Hegelian perspective is thus predominantly a "place of social integration" (Adloff 2005: 35) and offers a supplement as well as alternative to market-driven integration (Adloff 2005: 35; Klein 2001: 302). In contrast "the state ... embodies the moral concept" ("Wirklichkeit der sittlichen Idee" [§ 257]). The functioning of the bourgeois civil society is inconceivable without the state because, on the one hand, the morality embodied in the state needs to exist in order to be conveyed to its citizens. On the other hand, the distinction between state and civil society is necessary in order to allocate the function of satisfying societal needs to civil society, which should be separated from the state sphere. Hence, civil society and state are mutually dependant. However, the state as the enactment of morality is superior to civil society.

A quite different position is held by Tocqueville, for whom voluntary associations fulfill a double function. In a much-cited excerpt from the first volume of his travel journal "Democracy in America," he explains that "Americans of every age, every rank, every spiritual inclination ... continuously unite and pull together" (Tocqueville 1985: 248) in order to take care of the public duties in their self-interest. Tocqueville describes the American understanding of public welfare and civil society, which goes back to the constitutional fathers as well as to the English social contract theorists Locke and Hobbes. Adopting the individualist concepts of the Enlightenment, the common good is no longer seen as objectively feasible or as separated from individual citizens' interests and needs. On the contrary, the common good requires the existence of diverging individual attitudes. The state is kept at a distance thanks to the citizens' self-organization. Voluntary associations, however, are not only a means to promote the establishment of hospitals, gaols, or schools in a practical and pragmatic way; they function at the same time as "schools of democracy" in which civil virtues like tolerance and mutual acceptance are practiced. Civil society is therefore a platform where various citizens' concerns can be put "on the table" to be discussed and questioned. Out of this process arises the possibility to amend a position inasmuch as other views might be heard and understood and one's own standpoint might be critically reflected on. It is this process of change that makes Tocqueville think of civil society as a school of democracy: Under the premise of equality, the most different concerns can be introduced and considered, but when there are contradictions, the concerns must be "toned down" and a compromise must be sought. The channelling effect of such social negotiation processes becomes especially apparent the more different and contradicting positions flow into the discourse. From this process, there arises what is understood as a common good, which guides the state to the (governing) decisions or action it has to take. In this respect, it requires no higher authority for ensuring public welfare since citizens act in the service of the general public driven by enlightened egotism, in their own best interest in order to protect their freedom (Tocqueville 1985: 256) and in order to keep the state at a distance. Numerous voluntary associations of social, economic, or political nature serve this purpose and their plurality and heterogeneity fends off a "despotic majority rule." According to Tocqueville, the common good is neither the objective nor in and of itself reasonable, but rather the result of negotiation processes. Thus, society is a prerequisite of the state, because only here the basis for governmental decision and action can be developed legitimately. A state system requires the existence of a civil society, but the inverse is not true.[3]

This interpretation of civil society as "intermediate sphere" is taken up in the early works of, among others, Karl Marx, who diverge from Hegel, but reflect the ideas of Rousseau. Marx is a radical critic of bourgeois society, which is, in his opinion, dominated by a bourgeois or mercantile class whose adherents have only their individual profit in mind and do not care about the common good. Like Rousseau, Marx puts the "bourgeois" in contrast to the "citoyen" and characterizes the latter as a politically active citizen with great interest in public welfare. For Marx the antagonism between individual interests and the common good can only come to an end through the dissolution of

---

3   My thanks to Roman Paul Turczynski for the in-depth analysis of Tocqueville and Hegel.

the bourgeois civil society and through the emancipation of the citoyen from the bourgeois (Marx 1990). To resolve this situation, both Marx and Rousseau (cf. Adloff 2005: 27) advocate the fundamental repeal of the separation of state and society. However, both authors point toward dangers rendering this solution inappropriate for a modern society with its plurality and heterogeneity, namely the real risk that society and state degenerate into an autocracy if an individual or certain social group that principally negates plurality takes over and declares their specific view as the only true and valid one. In comparative research, this demand to control how citizens think and to follow the interpretation of things as prescribed by a dictator or a ruling clan is generally seen as a distinctive indicator for totalitarian, as opposed to authoritarian, regimes (Linz 2003). The denial of a private sphere and the complete overlapping of the state and (civil) society are typical of totalitarian regimes, in which only one position and opinion is possible, which is expressed through the politics of the leader, be it Hitler, Stalin, Mao, or Kim Jong-Un.

The two differing views of the relation between state and (bourgeois) civil society proposed by Hegel and Tocqueville are reflected in modern democracy theory approaches by pluralists, neo-pluralists, and neo-corporatists. Manfred Schmidt, for instance, makes a distinction between a society- and state-centered version of pluralistic democracy (Schmidt 2010: 210ff.); Robert Dahl takes a society-oriented view, and Ernst Fraenkel a state-centered view. The state-centered variation of pluralistic democracy was elaborated by empirical neo-corporatist research to include the integration and functional allocation of associations in civil society and their role as interface between state and society. In the context of policy making, the state-association relations were examined in different areas, often under the catchphrase "politics against markets" (Esping-Andersen 1985) and with the focus on employers' associations and trade unions as a vehicle for balancing the interests between capital and labor. As a result of the diminishing effectiveness of the "old" unions and federations, Colin Crouch sees a functional realignment toward "new" civil society organizations. This includes, for example, NGOs which represent public concerns worldwide in times of neoliberal and globalized economies and which are often supported by economic actors who are aware of their corporate social responsibility. The nation-state social contract according to John Locke is being replaced by multipolar arrangements in which civil society, in terms of activists and socially responsible enterprises, again plays a central role (Crouch 2011).

While the liberal protective function of civil society is falling by the wayside, civil society as the intermediate sphere for citizens' self-organization, civil engagement, and societal integration is increasingly emphasized along with its traditional role as public communicator. In modern societies a loose link between civil society and the state or governmental administration is presumed, with the implicit assumption that the intermediate functional role of civil society together with its communication and public function promotes – if not immediately, then in the future – a process toward democracy ... Whether this is the case is an empirical question not easily answered: civil society, as a promoter of social integration and driver of public action, can hardly be operationalized; moreover, measuring its impact on democratic development is far from straightforward. On account of the current boom in the number of civil society actors, especially when it comes to NGOs providing social services or are operating in countries with defective democracies or authoritarian political structures, a wide area for empirical investigations has opened up and needs a theory base.

5. Summary and outlook: civil society as part of an imposed model for societal modernization?

The term and the concept of civil society have a long tradition. However, its relationship to democracy as a form of government, as we know it today, has not been continuous. A retrospective analysis (Adloff 2005; Schmidt 2007) reveals that the interest in civil society correlates to the ideas and problems at that time and is thus highly contingent. As indicated above, there is neither a universal conception nor a commonly used definition of civil society. In fact, the different understandings of civil society rather reflect the social and political views prevailing at the time. This is why discussions about civil society and its definition are most lively during times of sociopolitical transition, which might explain the current level of interest in civil society issues in politics, the public sphere, and in the social sciences.

Representative democracies of "The North" follow the civil society tradition of mobilizing citizens to work for the common good; they suggest supporting and complementing the highly professional political apparatus with direct democratic elements and deliberative processes among those who are affected. It is based on an ideal of the classical *societas civilis* as a political community where problems are resolved in a deliberative and consensual manner, and has the objective to at least partly overcome a growing gap between a constitutive or representative political system and (civil) society.

The discourse in countries of "The South," on the other hand, refers to civil society as a catalyst for the development of civic virtues and the establishment of a public sphere beyond clan and/or neo-liberal economic interests of the nouveau riche typical of developing countries. The renaissance of civil society is driven by the hope that civil society organizations with their volunteers might, in the tradition of Tocqueville, strengthen and empower civil self-organization in a community-oriented sense, so that general welfare spending or investment in, for instance, schools, road infrastructure, or hospitals, becomes an expression of enlightened self-interest. In these countries, many hope that civil society as a social domain will contribute to empowering underprivileged social groups, especially women and girls (Schwabenland et al. 2016). And with regard to authoritarian regimes and deficient democracies, at least the hope exists that the emergence of an intermediate sphere of civil society organizations – even if their main objective is to provide social services and they remain part of a corporatist system (Spires 2011) and under state control – might eventually trigger a process, as described by Tocqueville, in which forums to develop civic virtues are established, which, despite the adverse circumstances, develop into schools of democracy.

Generally speaking, it is apparent that research on civil society in authoritarian regimes and defect democracies still largely follows the tradition of Tocqueville. This is why one historical perspective is to a great extent neglected, especially by gender studies (Hagemann et al. 2008): the Hegelian understanding of civil society as a facet of a top-down model of social modernization. Accordingly, the task of civil society organizations is to provide a forum for social integration and a platform to pursue the primarily economic interests of a ruling bourgeoisie, whereas the task of the state is to ensure that conflicts of interest accompanying societal modernization do not get out of hand and endanger public order. In the tradition of Carl Schmitt, this model can be duly described as "authoritarian liberalism." It emphasizes civil society's integrative role and compatibility with market forces. This model of civil society is distinguished by its plurality and heterogeneity and is liberal in the sense of an economic liberalism; the common good in a Hegelian sense is determined and reviewed by the state.

A number of indicators suggest that this subordinate role of civil society supporting state-governed social modernization processes might work out rather successfully. The past German Empire or the current People's Republic of China are exemplary inasmuch as both regimes did or do incorporate civil society organizations into modernization strategies while allowing for a certain level of social plurality, thereby managing social change without, however, running the risk of endangering the power-political status quo (Yuanfeng 2015; Chandra and Wong 2016). From a gender perspective this functional allocation of civil society in an authoritarian environment is interesting inasmuch as civil society certainly remains open for women and may provide them with options and opportunities, e.g., of public engagement or of professional activity. At the same time, the status quo of gender-related societal issues remains principally unquestioned (Hagemann et al. 2008; Teets 2016). Thus statistical evidence of civil society as an area for charitable organizations and voluntary activity shows that civil society might also thrive on a small scale even within an authoritarian framework and might contribute to societal integration and appeasement. Having this in mind, the question whether civil society might contribute to political integration remains unanswered, especially since competing democratic-theoretical attempts to conceptualize civil society are difficult to operationalize and are therefore difficult to capture empirically (Lauth 2017). Hence, the linkage of civil society and democracy is anything but clear, and overestimated expectations of civil society must be warned against. Democracy and civil society might work in tandem, but the emergence of civil society by itself does not necessarily lead to democracy. How civil society works in authoritarian regimes and whether and to what extent an autocratic societal framework might be more of an obstacle to emancipation and thus impede gender equality is a central theme of the chapters of this book.

References

Adloff, Frank (2005): Zivilgesellschaft Theorie und Praxis. Frankfurt: Campus (Campus Studium).
Brandt, Horst D. (2013): Georg Friedrich Wilhelm Hegel: Grundlinien der Philosophie des Rechts. Hamburg: Felix Meiner Verlag.
Chandra, Yato/Wong, Linda (Eds.) (2016): Social Entrepreneurship in the Greater China Region. London/New York: Routledge.
Cohen, Jean. L./Arato, Andrew (1997): Civil Society and Political Theory. Cambridge: MIT Press.
Crouch, Colin (2011): The Strange Non-Death of Neo-Liberalism. Cambridge: Polity Press.
Esping-Andersen, Gosta (1985): Politics against Markets. Princeton: Princeton Univ. Press.
Gerhard, Ute (2008). Frauenbewegung. In: Roth, Roland/Rucht, Dieter (Eds.). Die sozialen Bewegungen in Deutschland seit 1945. Frankfurt: Campus Verlag, pp. 187-217.
Habermas, Jürgen (1992): Faktizität und Geltung. Frankfurt: Suhrkamp Verlag.
Hagemann, Karen/Michel, Sonya/Budde,Gunilla (Eds.) (2008): Civil Society and Gender Justice: Historical and Comparative Perspectives. New York: Berghahn Books.
Havel, Vaclav/Keane, John (Eds.) (1985): The Power of the Powerless: Citizens Against the State in Central Eastern Europe. London: Taylor and Francis.
Held, David (2006): Models of Democracy (Third Edition). Stanford: Stanford Univ. Press.
Huntington, Samuel P. (1991): The Third Wave. Democratization in the Late Twentieth Century. Oklahoma: Univ. of Oklahoma Press.
Joachim, Jutta (2014): NGOs in world politics. In: Baylis, John /Smith, Steve/Owens, Patricia (Eds.): The Globalization of World Politics, Oxford: Oxford Univ. Press, pp. 347-362.
Keane, John (1998): Civil Society: Old Images, New Visions. Stanford: Stanford Univ. Press.
Klein, Ansgar (2001): Der Diskurs der Zivilgesellschaft. Opladen: Leske+Budrich.
Kocka, Jürgen (2002): Das Bürgertum als Träger von Zivilgesellschaft – Traditionslinien, Entwicklungen, Perspektiven, in: Enquete-Kommission 'Zukunft des Bürgerschaftlichen Engagements' Deutscher Bundestag (Ed.): Bürgerschaftliches Engagement und Zivilgesellschaft. Opladen: Leske+Budrich, pp. 15-22.
Kocka, Jürgen (2003): Zivilgesellschaft in historischer Perspektive. In: Forschungsjournal Neue Soziale Bewegungen 16, 2, pp. 29-37.
Kocka, Jürgen (2008): Bürger und Bürgerlichkeit im Wandel. In: Aus Politik und Zeitgeschichte 9-10/08, pp. 3-9.

Lauth, Hans-Joachim (2017): Zivilgesellschaft und die Qualität der Demokratie. In: Croissant, Aurel/Kneip, Sascha/Petring, Alexander (Eds.): Demokratie, Diktatur, Gerechtigkeit. Wiesbaden: Springer VS, pp. 387-408.

Linz, Juan J. (2003): Totalitäre und autoritäre Regime (Ed. by Raimund Krämer). Berlin: Berliner Debatte Wiss.-Verlag.

Marx, Karl (1990): Zur Judenfrage. In: Fetscher, Iring (Ed.): Karl Marx – Friedrich Engels Studienausgabe, Band I Philosophie. Frankfurt: Fischer Verlag, pp. 34-62.

Maurer, Doris (2001): Frauen und Salonkultur – literarische Salons vom 17 bis 20. Jahrhundert. Hagen: FernUni Hagen, https://www.fernuni-hagen.de/imperia/md/content/gleichstellung/heft 36mau.pdf (31.03.2018).

Merkel, Wolfgang/Lauth, Hans-Joachim (1998): Systemwechsel und Zivilgesellschaft: Welche Zivilgesellschaft braucht die Demokratie? In: Aus Politik und Zeitgeschichte 6-7/98, pp. 3-12.

Priemer, Jana/Krimmer, Holger/Labigne, Anael (2017): Vielfalt verstehen. Zusammenhalt stärken. Berlin: Stifterverband/Bertelsmann Stiftung.

Priller, Eckhard (2011): Dynamik, Struktur und Wandel der Engagementforschung: Rückblick, Tendenzen und Anforderungen. In: Priller, Eckhard/Alscher, Mareike/Dathe, Dietmar/Spetz, Rudolf (Eds.): Zivilengagement. Münster: Lit Verlag, pp. 11-40.

Priller, Eckhard/Zimmer, Annette (2017): Hochgeschätzte Beschäftigung in Nonprofit-Organisationen: Wie lange noch? In: Theuvsen, Ludwig/Andeßner, René/Gmür, Markus/Greiling, Dorothea (Eds.): Nonprofit-Organisationen und Nachhaltigkeit, Wiesbaden: Springer Gabler, pp. 387-400.

Putnam, Robert (1993): Making Democracy Work. Princeton: Princeton Univ. Press.

Rucht, Dieter (2009): Von Zivilgesellschaft zu Zivilität: Konzeptuelle Überlegungen und Möglichkeiten der empirischen Analyse. In: Frantz, Christiane/Kolb, Holger (Eds.): Transnationale Zivilgesellschaft in Europa. Münster: Waxmann Verlag, pp. 75-102.

Salamon, Lester M. (1994): The Rise of the Nonprofit Sector. In: Foreign Affairs 73, 4, pp. 109-122.

Salamon, Lester M./Sokolowski, Wojciech and Associates (2004): Global Civil Society: Dimensions of the Nonprofit Sector. Volume 2. Baltimore: Kumarian Press.

Schmidt, Jürgen (2007): Zivilgesellschaft. Bürgerschaftliches Engagement von der Antike bis zur Gegenwart. Texte und Kommentare. Reinbeck bei Hamburg: rowohlts enzyklopädie.

Schmidt, Manfred G. (2010): Demokratietheorien. Eine Einführung. Wiesbaden: VS Verlag.

Schwabenland, Christina/Lange, Chris/Onyx, Jenny/Nakagawa, Sachiko (Eds.) (2016): Women's emancipation and civil society organisations. Challenging or maintaining the status quo? Bristol: Policy Press.

Seckinelgin, Hakan (2010): Civil Society and Gender. In: Anheier, Helmut K./Toepler, Stefan/List, Regina (Eds.): International Encyclopedia of Civil Society. New York: Springer, pp. 205-209.

Simsa, Ruth/Meyer, Michael/Badelt, Christoph (Eds.) (2013): Handbuch der Nonprofit-Organisation. Stuttgart: Schäffer-Poeschel.

Spires, Anthony (2011): Contigent Symbosis and Civil Society in an Authoritarian State: Understanding the Survival of China's Grassroots NGOs. In: American Journal of Sociology 117, 1, pp. 1-45

Teets, Jessica C. (2016): Civil Society under Authoritarianism: The China Model. Cambridge: Cambridge Univ. Press.

Tocqueville de, Alexis (1985): Über die Demokratie in Amerika. Stuttgart: Reclam Verlag.

Vetter, Angelika/Remer-Bollow, Uwe (2017): Bürger und Beteiligung in der Demokratie. Wiesbaden: Springer VS (e-book).

Yuanfeng, Zhang (2015): Dependent Interdependence: The Complicated Dance of Government – Nonprofit Relations in China. In: Voluntas 26, pp. 2395-2423.

Zimmer, Annette (2010): Third Sector-Government Partnerships. In: Taylor, Rupert (Ed.): Third Sector Research. New York: Springer, pp. 201-218.

Zimmer, Annette (2014): Money makes the world go round! Ökonomisierung und die Folgen für NPOs. In: Zimmer, Annette/Simsa, Ruth (Eds.): Forschung zu Zivilgesellschaft, NPOs und Engagement. Wiesbaden: Springer VS, pp. 163-180.

Zimmer, Annette/Hallmann, Thorsten (Eds.) (2015): Nonprofit-Organisationen vor neuen Herausforderungen. Wiesbaden: Springer VS.

Zimmer, Annette/Paul, Franziska (2018): Zur volkswirtschaftlichen Bedeutung der Sozialwirtschaft. In: Arnold, Ulli/Maelicke, Bernd (Eds.): Lehrbuch der Sozialwirtschaft, Baden-Baden: Nomos (forthcoming).

Zimmer, Annette/Priller, Eckhard/Paul, Franziska (2017): Karriere im Nonprofit-Sektor. Arbeitsbedingungen und Aufstiegschancen von Frauen. (Broschüre) Münster (forthcoming).

Zimmer, Annette/Speth, Rudolph (2009): Verbändeforschung. In: Kaina, Viktoria/Römmele, Andrea (Eds.): Politische Soziologie. Ein Studienbuch. Wiesbaden: VS-Verlag, pp. 267-309.

The Authoritarian as Discourse and Practice: a Feminist Post-Structural Approach

Gabriele Wilde

"For the state to function in the way that it does, there must be, between male and female or adult and child, quite specific relations of domination which have their own configuration and relative autonomy." (Foucault 1980: 188)

1. Introduction

Despite worldwide democratization processes (Huntington 1991), autocratic and hybrid regimes are not only the political reality but appear to have increased in the last years. In the present, a quarter of all states, or one-third of the world population, is governed by monarchies, presidential autocracies, family autocracies, and military juntas, as well as by semi-democratic systems, whether authoritarian or deficient; and in several Eastern European and Latin American transformation societies, there exist numerous indications of democratization breakdowns and even the return of authoritarianism.

Besides the obvious constraints of constitutional principles and structures, which often accompany a centralized leadership as it extends state authority, the powerful influence of "the authoritarian" is manifested especially in the societies themselves and has a considerable impact on the constitution of gender orders: It increasingly destroys plurality in the public sphere, manipulates and monopolizes civil society actors, and invokes the family as the nucleus and authentic source of political society; the family becomes the authority of political order, a model, and collective, as well as the location and realm of hard-working, virtuous women (cf. Kreisky and Löffler 2003).

New social power relations do not only appeal to traditional cultural values and norms and reinterpret liberal ideas of freedom and equality (cf. Ranciere

2015), they also involve diverse processes and strategies which hinder the political participation of women. This is especially evident in examples of women holding political office in the autocratic systems of Southeast Asia (cf. Fleschenberg and Hellmann-Rajanayagam 2008): they only have leadership positions when they belong to the political class or are bound by a semi-dynastic context. And the decreased integration of women into the labor market of post-socialist transformational lands is often accompanied by the contradictory increased participation of women in politics and a stronger consideration of women's interests in family, pension, and tax policies (cf. Kreile 2009). Last but not least, because religion serves as a normative framework and reference system in the interdependence of the power of the political regime and the opportunities of women or gender relations – in the form of established but concealed paternalism – it is ascribed a significant role as another intervening variable. But how do authoritarian discourses and cultural, symbolic, and economic practices transform social gender relations? How can the authoritarian be understood in terms of feminist political science?

Understanding the impact of a "renaissance of authoritarianism" (Bank 2009) or "authoritarianism reloaded" (Albrecht and Frankenberger 2010, 2011) on gender relations becomes even more pressing in light of the fact that research on autocracy is still dominated by state formation theory. In such research, the state form of autocracy is ascribed meaning that is just as traditional as it is current. In opposition to the democratic state, all states are conceived as autocratic insofar as "a single person or group of persons, a committee, a junta, or a party governs with uncontrollable power" (Backes 2007: 612). In a definition by Karl Loewenstein (2000: 28), the monopolization of political power is the most important criterion. This criterion directs the attention of what is predominantly comparative politics to the prevailing ruling models and typologies of autocratic systems. By concentrating on the structures and institutions, their basic traits, logics, and maintenance mechanisms, the focus of research on authoritarian regimes until today has been on the institutional securing of authoritarian rule.

But this state- and institution-centered perspective not only neglects the non-institutional mechanisms that secure rule (cf. Köllner 2008: 362) but also overlooks gender relations as the social foundation of authoritarian rule.

Hence, the nexus between women's opportunities and regime context, as well as between the conditions and effective mechanisms, has gone largely unnoticed in mainstream autocracy research. As a consequence, such a perspective, which reduces the political to state institutions, governmental apparatuses, and political decision-making processes, misses not only the specific mechanisms and effects of state policies on the constitution and structure of gender relations but also the processes in which social power relations are established and consolidated in political institutions. As a consequence, the question concerning the constitutive connection between either autocracies or defect democracies and the establishment of gender relations as social power relations has been neither explicitly asked nor systematically researched from a genuine political science, epistemological perspective nor from an empirical-analytic one.

In this chapter, I shall attempt to address this desideratum in political science, namely, in the study of comparative government. I outline a new research perspective in which the domains of non-institutional legitimation strategies and civil society processes are systematically and conceptually included in order to examine the constitutive connection between gender relations as power and domination relations for the functioning, stability, and legitimacy of autocratic systems. Against this background, namely, that gender and gender relations do not refer to a state form but to a form of society in which power and domination relations are categorically established, I introduce an outline of a society-centered analysis (cf. Wilde 2010, 2012b; Graf, Schneider, and Wilde 2017) that takes into consideration the connection between autocracies, as well as hybrid political systems, and the establishment of gender relations as power relations.

In a first step, I examine existing society-centered approaches in political science and show how these approaches, in opposition to state- and institution-centered approaches, formulate an understanding of the political that considers the autocratic regime less in terms of state forms of governing and more in terms of social structures, political institutions, social, cultural, and symbolic practices, and the inscribing of gender and gender relations as the basic organizational principal of autocratic systems.

In a second step, I identify four central areas of study in which social relations as political power and relations of domination are produced and formed:

organized civil society, the public sphere, the family and the private sphere, and the discourse of knowledge.

Based on questions concerning the various inclusion and exclusion mechanisms that are set off by a regime's processes of social equality and inequality, as well as questions concerning the power and domination relations which constitute the regime, a feminist theoretical framework is outlined to scrutinize how gender relations are enlisted by autocracies and to examine systematically their role in power relations.

2. The political as a social power formation

A liberal understanding of the political understands society as the result of the guarantee of rights, state taxation, and institutional decision-making processes. In contrast, society-centered approaches locate the political in society itself and study the conditions and the emergence of politics – democratic as well as authoritarian – in view of social relations and the common acts of persons.

Society-centered approaches in the history of political theory include, for instance, the republican approach of Alexis de Tocqueville (1965); Antonio Gramsci's (1991) concept of hegemony; the Aristotelian understanding of Hannah Arendt (1991, 1993a, 1993b, 1994); the theory of governmentality by Michel Foucault (1980, 2000, 2001); the feminist theory of Carole Pateman (1988, 1994); and the post-structural theory of Chantal Mouffe (2000, 2007, 2008, 2014). These theories are combined here to form a theory of the political that is no longer focused on state institutions or equal legal status for the formation of democratic order. Rather, the diverse, antagonistic quality of society becomes the starting point for deliberation; in this form, sociopolitical forces as the actual source of power come together under a common goal.

The assumption that the instituting of politics is the result of society itself, that is, as Gramsci (1991) makes clear, the result of battles over interpretation which shape certain sociopolitical forces into hegemonic power, is based on an understanding of the political as something other than sovereignty relations or the forms of domination of the political elite. Rather, the focus becomes the diverse forms of power and domination that establish cultural, symbolic, or economic relations as unequal within a society. Power is understood here not only in the sense of Max Weber (1980) as a "chance": a chance "within a social relationship for one to assert his or her own will even against resistance, regardless of what this chance is based on" (28). Society-centered approaches understand and analyze power predominantly in the sense of empowerment and as productive phenomena expressed in the acts of citizens and in the form of discourses (Bargetz et al. 2017).

"*The political* is the instituting authority of *all* order" (Marchart 2017: 3) – the principal aim of society-centered approaches is to understand this meaning of the political; but exactly how society is perceived in view of the basic dimensions of the political, brought out in the examination of following approaches, obviously varies. The topos of political freedom was already conceded great importance in Tocqueville (Wilde 2014c). Tocqueville's freedom was oriented on the ideals of the political society's moral and cognitive self-determination (Tocqueville 1965: 8). This "freedom-constituting sovereignty of a people" is, according to Lars Lamprecht (1990: 523), neither limited to elections nor the sole prerogative of the parliament or even the state. Years later, Arendt (1993a) imputed a similar existential form – one that deals with the political freedom of citizens – to power. And, for Arendt, the leading actor of the political is the moment of acting of the political citizen, not the state. The meaning of social relations for Arendt is determined by her concept of the plural public as the necessary condition for human action and exercising power (cf. Arendt 1993b: 11). According to Arendt, politics emerges "in between and establishes itself as the relation" (Arendt 1993b: 11).

From a feminist perspective, in contrast, gender and gender relations are counted as principles of social organization and governing. These relations are – against the background of structurally separated private and public spheres – politically established, and empower as well as constrain women's freedom to act. Finally, post-structural approaches describe and analyze society along with Foucault (2000, 2001) in terms of contingent power and unequal relations. Society constitutes itself primarily in the form of hegemonic discourse, which emerges because citizens are willing to acknowledge themselves as antagonists with diverse interests and concerns against the background of unequal power positions and to argue and represent their own perspective publicly.

Despite the different meanings of power and domination, these approaches understand civil society as a "power dispositive" in which gender relations "circulate and only function as a chain" (Foucault 2001: 44) in various forms of networks; power is contingent in the sense that it does not function top-down but is produced through political action. Another understanding of the authoritarian emerges with this understanding of the political as a social power formation. When society is understood as a relation that exists through the interaction of manifold power relations, and hence as the effect of political and social power, the authoritarian is manifested as a form of the political in which certain kinds of social power relationships on different levels of social action have stabilized and constitute the political state of societies, their structures, principles of organization, and institutions.

Moreover, the view of the authoritarian as the result of social power relations has methodical and methodological consequences requiring an ascending analysis of power. Examining notions of power, domination, unequal relations, and the economy (Boris 2016) brings about a perspective shift, one which can be studied by feminist research on autocracy (Wilde and Schneider 2012). Based on the assumption that "[t]otalitarianism treats real people as virtual entities" (Žižek 2011: 136), "as a raw material to be transformed" (Serban 2014: 21), the constituting character of the authoritarian can be found in society, in its power relations, and in subject and identity formation, and shifts in gender relations in everyday practices and discourses can be understood as authoritarian politics.

3. The organization of gender power relations in political society: society as the dispositive of power

To examine the connection between autocracies and gender relations from a political science perspective, the direction of analysis must be reversed: To answer the question to answer the question of how politics cause power relationships cause power relationships to stabilize ultimately as relations of power and dominance, we do not search on the level of state institutions or in the decisions of political actors, but look to the social domains in which the social organization of power and domination relations, or to use a notion from Foucault (2000, 2001) "the governing technologies," are at work. In view of the inscription of power relations in civil society, society-centered approaches refer back to different domains in which political organization is at work and where the political establishment of social (gender) relations can be analyzed as power structures empirically, quantitatively or qualitatively.

3.1 Civil society organizations by Alexis de Tocqueville

Tocqueville saw the location for the organization of social relations and their political establishment above all in organized civil society. He unfolded the meaning of associations, cooperations, and volunteer clubs for political society (1965: 127) against the background of a centralized French state, which he described specifically as the form of authoritarianism in modernity. He saw its most important characteristics in the binding of political force to orders and binding legislation – traits which to his mind did not contradict absolutism (cf. Herb and Hidalgo 2005: 105), but, in contrast, led to a centralization of political power. He described the introduction of rational principles into politics in the following way, "The democratic revolution has been effected only in the material parts of society, without that concomitant change in laws, ideas, customs, and manners which was necessary to render such a revolution beneficial" (Tocqueville 1965: 8).

The division between state and society and the transformation of social foundations that Tocqueville described for post-revolutionary France is our first criterion for a society-centered analysis of autocratic systems. For him, the depoliticization of society was manifested above all in the lacking implementation of new possibilities of political participation in the form of civil society associations (Tocqueville 1965: 127), which participate at all levels of the governing institutions and in political decision-making processes.

Tocqueville unfolded the meaning of civil society as a contrast to centralized governing structures in his publication "The Old Regime and the Revolution" (1955). On the other hand, in his debut work *Democracy in America* (1835/1965), he sketched civil society as an indicator of the successful implementation of democracy as "life-form" (127). He recognized in the local self-government of the first settlers of New England – which contributed to training civil society associations in American society significantly – schools of democracy which trained a specific citizen constitution and culture.

According to Tocqueville, civil society represented an effective counterweight to the centralization of political power. For him, civil society became a countermodel to autocratic, authoritarian, and totalitarian forms of governing not least because he saw in this space of political freedom effective restraints against the authoritarian attempts of the state as well as against tyrannical majorities.

In fact, civil society is ascribed an important meaning not only for overcoming power (cf. Zimmer in this volume, 2012) but also for the persistence of power relations. According to Gramsci (1991), civil society organizations – such as philanthropic foundations and religious groups – could contribute to the ideas within a society significantly and in this way stabilize the status quo. As dissident movements in the transformation lands of the former so-called Eastern blocs have shown, civil society can also go against the dominant status quo and can contribute to overcoming relations of domination in the form of protest, social disobedience, and social movements.

3.2 The plural public by Hannah Arendt

In comparison to Tocqueville, Arendt viewed the public sphere as an essential hallmark of the political and as the central domain for the political organization of social (power) relations. Arendt (1994) saw in the existence of public space the defining characteristic of the political and an indication of a free political community. In an Aristotelian understanding, the public is a space of association that binds a person's purpose in a fundamental way to the interaction of many and that requires citizens' judgment and power to act as a result of communicative action (cf. Wilde 2012).

Similar to Tocqueville's development of civil society as a countermodel to the centralization of political power in post-revolutionary France, in her book *The Origins of Totalitarianism* (1962), Arendt saw her concept of the plural public sphere as a countermodel to total domination in fascist and Stalin regimes. Hence, according to Arendt's interpretation, under total domination the political-public agonal space of plural freedom is undermined, and, that is, in the form of a single opinion which is enforced by terror and simultaneously legitimated with reference to a privileged knowledge: the ideology (Rödel et al. 1989: 52). In "Ideology and Terror: A Novel Form of Government" (1962: 460–479), the thirteenth chapter that Arendt added later, she recognized two essential elements of total domination in the destruction of plurality between humans and in the loss of their ability to think and judge. In her understanding, terror as the defining characteristic of total domination destroys "the space between men" (1962: 466), "the living space of freedom" (ibid.)," "freedom as a living political reality" (ibid.)," and "substitutes for the boundaries and channels of communication between individual men a band of iron which ... destroys the plurality of men and makes out of many the One who unfailing will act as though he himself were part of the course of history or nature" (ibid. 465f.).

As the public sphere is the defining characteristic of the political, Arendt outlines the notion of total domination as the "counter-notion of democracy" (Weinert and Mattern 2000: 253; translation GW). The destruction of plurality between humans, which causes them to lose their judgment and the ability to act, marks for Arendt the total limits of the political. This corresponds to a destruction of the public sphere and of what she called "the existence of a right to have rights (and that means to live in a framework where one is judged by actions and options) and a right to belong to some kind of organized community" (Arendt 1962: 296f.).

3.3 The meaning of the private sphere of the family in Carole Pateman

In the work of Carole Pateman, the private sphere of the family becomes the central realm for the political organization of gender relations and their establishment as power and domination relations. In her book *The Sexual Contract* (1988), a key work about the patriarchal history of the state, Pateman considers the function of the private realm – especially in the institutional form of marriage and family – for the meaning and value of citizens' rights: In an examination of contract theory, such as from John Locke, Thomas Hobbes, and Jean-Jacques Rousseau, she recognizes in their depictions of human nature and the natural state two central premises of a logic of socialization – namely, the ideologizing of politics and its restriction to the public sphere – as two essential conditions of patriarchal statehood and domination.

Against the background of the familial private sphere, which feminist approaches view as another important area for fixing gendered power relations (cf. Pateman 1988), attention is given primarily to the question of how and in what form a politicization of privacy or the "familiarisation" of politics is brought about. In addition, using specific identity policies, taken into consideration is the question of how gender relations are constituted, consolidated, and justified as power and domination relations. In connection with Pateman's key assumption that the submission of women in the private sphere is constitutive for the liberal idea and validity of a "public world of civil law, civil freedom and equality, contract and the individual into being" (Pateman 1988: 11), the legitimating function of family and the private sphere for politics must be examined.

In this feminist view, the public sphere can only be a space for political action and political participation if it "diminishes" the sexual contract as a chance for democratic gender relations (cf. Wilde 2009). To "diminish" the sexual contract means to deny the specific living conditions of women as well as sexual asymmetries. It is for this reason that feminists perceive Tocqueville's favored political civil society and Arendt's political public sphere as "masculine" realms in which political freedom is of no use to women. In a political public sphere absent of women, as Anne Phillips makes clear (cf. 2002: 72), democratic relations can only be instituted when the family, or the private sphere, is integrated into a model of civil society and the political public sphere.

3.4 Citizenship as discursive practice by Chantal Mouffe

Citizenship as discursive practice in the work of Chantal Mouffe is the fourth area of investigation in this "inverse" research program. In opposition to a feminist approach, Mouffe believes in abolishing the separation of private and public spheres, "as every attempt to blur the distinction actually opens up a way to a kind of complete control of society by for instance the state," as Ian Angus (1998) noted. Instead of abolishing these spheres by enforcing state regulations, she pleads for the acknowledgment of these different social spheres and the resulting unequal relations in the political sphere. By extending the democratic struggle to all spheres in which relations of domination exist, she recognizes the very condition of possibility for the construction of political identities. For Mouffe, citizenship as discursive practice thus becomes another central domain for the political organization of social relations as political power and domination relations.

In opposition to Arendt, who describes political space as a space of freedom and public discussion, Mouffe sees the political as a sphere of power, conflict, and antagonism. Mouffe's approach, which is developed within the frame of a radical democracy, turns against the dominant post-political concepts of the third way, or the possibility of a universal rational consensus in politics. With reference to current problems such as terrorism, she points to the danger of liberal depoliticization and pleads instead for the antagonistic character of politics. She ultimately seeks to come to terms with the absence of certainty and to acknowledge the element of undecidability (Wilde 2014a).

Mouffe considers this antagonism as constitutive of human society. She recognizes politics as the totality of procedures and institutions and its task is to regulate human interaction and conflict. In her view, political conflict cannot be "neutralized," as liberal authors aim for; moreover, in opposition to a communitarian approach, in plural societies there can be no recourse to substantial values. Rather, Mouffe pleads for the "multiplicity of political spaces" (Laclau and Mouffe 1991: 242), which can be realized by unveiling and discussing all existing power and unequal relations in the political sphere.

4. Toward an analysis of gender dispositive power in autocracies – the construction of gender power relations as an effect of authoritarian and totalitarian politics

With (a) civil society, the (b) public sphere, the (c) politicization of the private sphere, and (d) citizenship as discursive practice, we have named four structural traits or areas of investigation of a feminist post-structural analysis (Wilde 2010; 2014b; Graf, Schneider, and Wilde 2017), which upholds a society-centered vision of democratic gender relations but marks the limits of the political. This framework can be used to analyze the establishment or even the destruction of a political form by means of totalitarian or authoritarian developments (cf. Wagner 2003: 134). Based on this approach, the following research questions become relevant: How is the social construction of gender relations affected by authoritarian and totalitarian policies? What roles do cultural, religious, economic, and social norms play? How and based on which strategies and technologies are these policies implemented and how do they unfold at the social level?

For an analysis of the constitutive connection between autocratic systems and gender relations are the following research perspectives: Based on a republican understanding of civil society (a) as a space to develop social understanding, to discuss normative questions, and for self-organizations in form of social movements and nonprofit organizations like NGOs and NPOs autocratic systems must be examined in terms of the extent to which the political self-organization of gendered subjects is possible or whether the possibilities for political communication and interest in the common action of gendered subjects are inhibited.

Also revealing in this connection is an understanding of the role ascribed to civil society and the extent to which civil society groups actually provide discursive forums in the public sphere – forums established for the sake of a "shared world" (cf. Benhabib 2006) – or whether civil society is composed of selective groups that have been set up strategically by political elites to serve as emissaries between society and the state apparatus and to produce consensus, and, hence, in agreement with Gramsci (1991), belong to the state apparatus. Also playing an important role here are the domains in which NGOs and associations (e.g., religious or women's) are active: their political room for maneuver, their participation in political decision-making and the governing machinery, and the regulation of their access to civil society organizations.

Since civil society comprises a very heterogenous domain of social self-organization, a feminist critical perspective pays particular attention to the emergence, development, and composition of women's movements and organizations. The following conceptual questions should guide research: How much room for maneuver do women's organizations in authoritarian and hybrid regimes have? To what extent are we dealing with homogenous movements? Can the organizations associated with regime movements be distinguished from organizations associated with critical movements? Do the civil society organizations associated with regime movements participate in political decision-making? How close is the movement and its organizations to institutional religion in the respective land, and how are leadership positions obtained in the civil society organizations associated with the women's movement?

Concerning public space as the defining characteristic of the political, in The *Origins of Totalitarianism* Arendt conceives of a plural public sphere to serve as a countermodel to total domination (cf. Wilde 2012). Because Arendt recognizes the central characteristic of totalitarian developments in the destruction of plurality, which is expressed in the "worldlessness" of individuals, she sees civil society as a way to gauge the existence of alternative public spaces (b) (cf. Benhabib 2006). To understand the meaning of Arendt's political thought for the determination of gender relations in autocratic systems, we must examine her central concept of the plural public as the condition for human action and the exercising of power (cf. Arendt 1993a: 227). We must investigate, for instance, the extent to which "public politics disappears" (cf. Rödel et al. 1989: 52) and/or the form in which gendered subjects are given the chance to participate in public political decision-making processes, how gender difference is represented publicly or whether it is made invisible, and whether a single opinion propagates a certain kind of "knowledge" and thus inhibits opinion diversity (cf. Rödel et al. 1989: 52). Also interesting are the effects of the ideologization of the political on gender relations and how strategies of discrimination and self-discipline operate within the frame of these ideologies.

Concerning the investigation of the interdependence of regime and gender relations, it should be empirically investigated whether, the extent to which, and under which conditions women in authoritarian and hybrid systems have access to the public sphere. The social domains of politics, media, economy, and academia are essential for constructing the public sphere in the form of institutionalized specific discourses or meanings of certain social relations. If possible, the relevance, function, and meaning of women in these social domains in authoritarian and hybrid regimes should be investigated quantitatively and qualitatively. Empirically, more precisely, we must understand how women in authoritarian hybrid systems are represented in leadership positions in the economy, politics, media, and academia. What are the values and norms of women in leadership positions, who are thereby in the position to influence domination relations? From out of which relations do female leadership personalities emerge, and how can their professional development be described?

Concerning the separation of public and private spheres (c), we must question how and in which form a politicizing of the private sphere or a familialization of politics takes place and thus establishes, stabilizes, and justifies gender relations as power and domination relations in the form of ideologies and through specific identity politics. In view of the production of gender relations in authoritarian and hybrid regimes, we must analyze the function of legal provisions in the private sphere and their influence on women's position in state and society, the extent politics shapes the private, and the possibilities of women to participate in the public sphere. The following questions have to be focused on: What meaning, role, and function are ascribed to the family and the private sphere in these regimes? How are social and family policies shaped in these regimes? How are the references to religion as normative reference and as institution shaped and distinguished? More precisely, we must consider the legal arrangements in the constitutions, legal texts, and ordinances, as well as the monetary benefits (pension system, family benefits). We can assume the working hypothesis that authoritarian and hybrid systems favor the private sphere in the form of family ideologies and specific identity politics of "motherhood," and then verify or falsify this hypothesis.

Finally, concerning the criterion of discursive practice, we can investigate whether domination relations and gender and structural inequalities are discussed in public discourse, as well as observe the discursive construction of gender and hegemonic subject formation. As criteria for an analysis of authoritarian and totalitarian discourses, Lutgard Lams, Geert Crauwels, and Henrieta Anisoara Șerban (2014) name, "the loss of subjectivity and the Othering of the individual, the cult of personality and mystification of national leaders, the normalization of dominant discourses and demonization of dissonant voices, the artificiality of language (*langue des Bois*), the naturalization of the ideological language" (1–2). In this view, legal and constitutional texts, political programs, and public media discourses should be investigated in terms of their universal values, which are no longer used as weapons in the fight for freedom, equality, and justice but are reinterpreted as instruments for discrimination, exclusion, mistrust, and contempt (Rancière 2015: 42). A further object of research is the question whether, and the extent to which, gender and structural inequalities are subjects of discussion or silenced, and whether a discursive construction of gendered subjects about equality, human rights, and citizenship policies follows: Which gender subject formations can be observed in connection with the regulation of work, disease, poverty, migration, etc.? Discursive construction as well as practices of normalization form the two sides of the authoritarian: by crossing liberal arguments with discourses that are antifeminist, racist, and anti-Muslim, or related to migration and national security, the diverse, plural nature of political society is denied, the democratic strife for the best interpretation is done away with, subjects are put in their place according to "natural," homophobic notions (Hark and Villa 2015), and power relations in line with a conservative value consensus are perpetuated.

5. Conclusion: the authoritarian as hegemonic social power dispositive

Within the framework of a society-centered feminist analysis, a total of four levels of investigation have been identified: the public sphere, civil society, the family and the private sphere, and citizenship as a discursive practice, whereby the authoritarian is conceived as a form of depoliticization, erosion, and establishment of new power relations, and the state is revealed as the central stage for a protectionist, universal, and value-bound politics. The fact that social relations generally become dependent variables of state legitimation and politics in authoritarian discourses and practices is manifested in the establishment of gender relations as power relations above all in light of legitimacy claims and processes, which link rights and political participation with certain ideas of the family, marriage, and equal chances and reject heterogenous social demands with xenophobic, racist, and sexist assertions. The authoritarian increasingly represses attempts to deconstruct the opportunities of women and hegemonic views in public discourses, as well as to construct plural viewpoints and claims in an effort to expand the political room for diverse cultural, public, and civil society practices. At the same time, gender orders are legitimated through principles of economic rationality (the gender-ideological turn) or appeals to national unity. With reference to the notion of a progressive and modernized society, these linguistic constructs are often linked with utopias, alleged traditions, and religious ideals (Lams et al. 2014: 2). In this way, besides the "multiplicity of political space" (Laclau and Mouffe 1991: 242), we are dealing with reductions or enlargements, as role models and practices that appear threatening to the state's "stability" are marginalized: "The consequence is not only a deep chasm between legitimate and illegitimate forms of gender identities, lifestyles, and practices; rather, from a feminist political science perspective, a defining characteristic of the authoritarian turns out to be the reenactment of gender subject and identity constructions and the rejection of particularity and differences" (Graf, Schneider, and Wilde 2017: 84–85).

References

Albrecht, Holger/Frankenberger, Rolf (Eds.) (2010): Autoritarismus Reloaded. Neuere Ansätze und Erkenntnisse der Autokratieforschung. Baden-Baden.
Albrecht, Holger/Frankenberger, Rolf (2011): Die „dunkle Seite" der Macht: Stabilität und Wandel autoritärer Systeme. In: Frankenberger, Rolf/Frech, Siegfried (Eds.): Autoritäre Regime: Herrschaftsmechanismen, Legitimationsstrategien, Persistenz und Wandel. Schwalbach: Wochenschau-Verlag, pp. 17-45.
Arendt, Hannah (1962) [1958]: The Origins of Totalitarism. Cleveland, New York: Schocken books.
Arendt, Hannah (1991): Elemente und Ursprünge totaler Herrschaft. München, Zürich: Piper.
Arendt, Hannah (1993a): Über die Revolution. München, Zürich: Piper.
Arendt, Hannah (1993b): Was ist Politik? Fragmente aus dem Nachlaß. München, Zürich: Piper.
Arendt, Hannah (1994): Vita activa oder Vom tätigen Leben. München, Zürich: Piper.
Backes, Uwe (2007): Was heißt Totalitarismus? Zur Herrschaftscharakteristik eines extremen Autokratie-Typs. In: Stoklosa, Katarzyna/Strübind, Andrea/Besier, Gerhard (Eds.): Glaube - Freiheit - Diktatur in Europa und den USA. Festschrift für Gerhard Besier zum 60. Geburtstag. Göttingen: Vandenhoeck & Ruprecht, pp. 609-625.
Bank, Andre (2009): Die Renaissance des Autoritarismus. Erkenntnisse und Grenzen neuerer Beiträge der Comparative Politics und Nahostforschung. In: Hamburg Review of Social Sciences 4, 1, pp. 10-41.
Bargetz, Brigitte/Lepperhoff, Julia/Ludwig, Gundula/Scheele, Alexandra/Wilde, Gabriele (2017): Geschlechterverhältnisse als Machtverhältnisse. Einleitung. In: Femina Politica 26, 1, pp. 9-23.
Benhabib, Seyla (2006): Denn sie war ein freier Mensch. In: DIE ZEIT, 12.10.2006, Nr. 42.
Boris, Dieter (2016): Populismuskritik ohne Tiefgang. In: Blätter für deutsche und internationale Politik 61, 8, pp. 25-27.
Fleschenberg, Andrea/Hellmann-Rajnayagam, Dagmar (2008): Female Political Power in Asia: Dynasties, Religion, Sacrifices. Some Introductury Remarks. In: Hellmann-Rajnayagam, Dagmar (Eds.): Goddesses, Heroes, Sacrifices: Female Political Power in Asia. Zürich: Lit, pp. 13-27.
Foucault, Michel (1980): Power/Knowledge. Selected Interviews and Other Writings 1972-1977. Edited by Colin Gordon. New York: Pantheon books.

Foucault, Michel (2000): Die Gouvernementalität. In: Bröckling, Ulrich/Krasmann, Susanne/Lemke, Thomas (Eds.): Gouvernementalität der Gegenwart. Studien zur Ökonomisierung des Sozialen. Frankfurt am Main, pp. 41-67

Foucault, Michel (2001): In Verteidigung der Gesellschaft. Frankfurt am Main: Suhrkamp.

Graf, Patricia/Schneider, Silke/Wilde, Gabriele (2017): Geschlechterverhältnisse und die Macht des Autoritären. In: Femina Politica 26, 1, pp.70-88.

Gramsci, Antonio (1991): Gefängnishefte, Bd. 1-10. Berlin/Hamburg: Argument-Verlag.

Hark, Sabine/Villa, Paula-Irene (Eds.) (2015): Anti-Genderismus. Bielefeld: transcript.

Herb, Karlfriedrich/Hidalgo. Oliver (2005): Alexis de Tocqueville. Frankfurt/M, New York: Campus.

Huntington, Samuel (1991): The Third Wave. Democratization in the Late Twentieth Century. Norman: Univ. of Oklahoma Press.

Köllner, Patrick (2008): Autoritäre Regime – Ein Überblick über die jüngere Literatur. In: Zeitschrift für Vergleichende Politikwissenschaft, 2, 2, pp. 351-366.

Kreile, Renate (2009): Transformation und Gender im Nahen Osten. In: Beck, Martin/Harders, Cilja/Jünemann, Annette/Stetter, Stephan (Eds.): Der Nahe Osten im Umbruch: Zwischen Transformation und Autoritarismus. Wiesbaden: Springer, pp. 253-276.

Kreisky, Eva/Löffler, Marion (2003): Staat und Familie: Ideologie und Realität eines Verhältnisses. In: Österreichische Zeitschrift für Politikwissenschaft 32, 4, pp. 375-388.

Laclau, Ernesto/Mouffe, Chantal (1991): Hegemonie und radikale Demokratie. Wien: Passagen-Verlag.

Lams, Lugard/Crauwels, Geert/Şerban, Henrieta Anişoara (Eds.) (2014): Totalitarian and Authoritarian Discourses. A Global and Timeless Phenomenon? Bern: Lang.

Loewenstein, Karl (2000): Verfassungslehre. Tübingen: Mohr.

Marchart, Oliver (2017): Zur Einheit von Theorie und Politik bei Laclau. Einleitung. In: Marchart, Oliver (Ed.): Ordnungen des Politischen. Wiesbaden: Springer, pp. 1-9.

Mouffe, Chantal (2000): The Democratic Paradox. London/New York: Verso

Mouffe, Chantal (2007): Über das Politische. Wider die kosmopolitische Illusion. Frankfurt/M: Suhrkamp.

Mouffe, Chantal (2008): Das demokratische Paradox. Wien: Turia+Kant.

Mouffe, Chantal (2014): Agonistik. Die Welt politisch denken. Wien: Turia+Kant.

Pateman, Carole (1988): The Sexual Contract. Stanford: Standford Univ. Press.

Pateman, Carole (1994): Der Geschlechtervertrag. In: Appelt, Erna/Neyer, Gerda (Eds.): Feministische Politikwissenschaft. Wien: Verlag für Gesellschaftskritik, pp. 73-96.

Phillips, Anne (2002): Does Feminism need a Conception of Civil Society? In: Chambers, Simone and Will Kymlicka (Eds.): Alternative Conceptions of Civil Society. Princeton New Jersey: Princeton University Press, pp. 71-89.

Rancière, Jacques (2015): Die nützlichen Idioten des Front National. In: Candeias, Mario (Ed.): Rechtspopulismus in Europa. Linke Gegenstrategien. Berlin: Rosa-Luxemburg-Stiftung, pp. 42-46.

Rödel, Ulrich/Frankenberg, Günter/Dubiel, Helmut (1989): Die demokratische Frage. Frankfurt/M: Suhrkamp.

Şerban, Henrieta Anişoara (2014): Theoretical Argument. Totalitarian Discourse: The New Snow White/Society in the Discursive Wooden Mirror. In: Lams, Lugard/Crauwels, Geert/Şerban, Henrieta Anişoara (Eds.): Totalitarian and Authoritarian Discourses. A Global and Timeless Phenomenon? Bern: Lang, pp. 15-38.

Tocqueville, Alexis de (1965): Democracy in America. Translated by Henry Reeve. Edited with an Indroduction by Henry Steele Commager. London: Oxford Univ. Press.

Tocqueville, Alexis de (1955): The Old Régime and the French Revolution. Translated by Stuart Gilbert. New York.

Wagner, Peter (2003): Die westliche Demokratie und die Möglichkeit des Totalitarismus. Über die Motive der Gründung und der Zerstörung in „The Origins of Totalitarism". In: Grunenberg, Antonia (Ed.): Totalitäre Herrschaft und republikanische Demokratie. Fünfzig Jahre 'The Origins of Totalitarism' von Hannah Arendt. Frankfurt/M.: Lang, pp. 131-146.

Weber, Max (1980): Wirtschaft und Gesellschaft. Tübingen: Mohr.

Weinert, Viola/Mattern, Jochen (2000): Die Hölle auf Erden. Eine Annäherung an Hannah Arendts Analyse totaler Herrschaft. In: UTOPIE kreativ, 113 (März 2000), pp. 251-263.

Wilde, Gabriele (2009): Gesellschaftsvertrag – Geschlechtervertrag. In: Ludwig, Gundula/Sauer, Birgit/Wöhl, Stefanie (Eds.): Staat und Geschlecht. Grundlagen und aktuelle Herausforderungen feministischer Staatstheorie. Reihe „Staatsverständnisse". Baden-Baden: Nomos, pp. 31-46.

Wilde, Gabriele (2010): Europäische Gleichstellungsnormen: Neoliberale Politik oder postneoliberale Chance für demokratische Geschlechterverhältnisse? In: juridikum. Zeitschrift für Kritik, Recht, Gesellschaft. Gemeinsame Ausgabe mit der Zeitschrift Kritische Justiz. 4/2010, pp. 449-464.

Wilde, Gabriele (2012): Totale Grenzen des Politischen: Die Zerstörung der Öffentlichkeit bei Hannah Arendt. In: Femina Politica 21, 1, pp. 17-29.

Wilde, Gabriele (2014a): Der Kampf um Hegemonie. Potentiale radikaler Demokratie aus Geschlechterperspektive. In: Zeitschrift für Politische Theorie. Themenheft zu Chantal Mouffe 2/2014, pp. 203-216.

Wilde, Gabriele (2014b): Zivilgesellschaftsforschung aus Geschlechterperspektive. Zur Ambivalenz von Begrenzung und Erweiterung eines politischen Handlungsraumes. In: Zimmer, Annette/Simsa, Ruth (Eds.): Quo Vadis? Forschung zu Partizipation, zivilgesellschaftlichen Organisationen und ihrem Management. Wiesbaden: Springer VS, pp. 209-230.

Wilde, Gabriele (2014c): Alexis de Tocqueville Revisited: Between the Centralization of Political Power, Civil Associations, and Gender Politics in the European Union. In: Freise, Matthias/Hallmann, Thorsten (Eds.): Modernizing Democracy. Associations and Associating in the 21st Century. New York: Springer-Verlag, pp. 31-44.

Wilde, Gabriele/Schneider, Silke (2012): Autokratie, Demokratie und Geschlecht: Geschlechterverhältnisse in autoritären Regimen. Einleitung. In: Femina Politica 21, 1, pp. 9-16.

Žižek, Slavoj (2011): Did Somebody Say Totalitarianism? Five Interventions in the (Mis)Use of a Nation. London: Verso.
Zimmer, Annette (2012): Zivilgesellschaft. In: Hradil, Stefan (Ed.): Deutsche Verhältnisse. Eine Sozialkunde. Bonn: Bundeszentrale für politische Bildung, pp. 353-364.

Analyzing the Authoritarian: Post-Structural Framing-Analysis – a Methodological Approach

Isabelle-Christine Panreck

1. Introduction

Classical approaches to authoritarian research that focus on the state and its institutions neglect the social sphere with its manifold, fluid power and dominance relations. Especially in view of the discursive construction of gender and the associated governing technologies, examining only the state and its institutions proves fatal. Feminist theory overcomes this weakness by taking society – in addition to the state – as a central object of analysis (cf. Sauer 2001; Bargetz 2016; for a post-structural perspective, see Mouffe 2013, 2005, and 2000; Laclau and Mouffe 2001). But how can authoritarian governments be understood by feminist political thought? In the course of the current academic controversy about (right-wing) populism, Patricia Graf, Silke Schneider, and Gabriele Wilde have suggested a societal-theoretical expanding of the definition of authoritarianism, beyond the typical fixation on institutions. They state that the authoritarian should be understood "as an action program, which takes up universal values such as equality and justice and reinterprets these values as instruments for discrimination and exploitation by combining them into various discourses and practices" (Graf, Schneider, and Wilde 2017: 70; translation by author).

Despite Wilde's theoretical contribution to the concept of the "authoritarian" for feminist political thought (cf. her chapter in this volume; Graf, Schneider, and Wilde 2017; Obuch et al. 2014; Schneider and Wilde 2012; Wilde 2012), its methodological application in empirical studies is still vague. It is generally accepted that discourse itself should become the center of analysis, and a bottom-up perspective as suggested by Gramsci is preferred (cf. Graf,

Schneider, and Wilde 2017; see also Wilde 2013, 2010; Fraser 1996; Sauer 2001). Nevertheless, the issue of unclarity remains, as discourse becomes a general term instead of an internally consistent paradigm. This paper attempts to close the gap by applying a post-structural framework to the analysis of authoritarian discourses and gender relations, which are viewed here as power and dominance relations. On the one hand, this paper includes Wilde's feminist interpretation of the authoritarian (cf. her chapter in this volume; Graf, Schneider, and Wilde 2017; Obuch et al. 2014; Schneider and Wilde 2012; Wilde 2012); on the other, it employs the well-structured "framing" concept of Robert Entman (2007, 2003, 1993, 1991) and Jörg Matthes (2014, 2007b, 2004) referenced in political communication research.

The combination of these approaches offers three specific advantages for the discursive analysis of societal power and dominance relations. First, framing addresses the need for transparency and clarity, which are often lacking in discourse analyses. Secondly, by applying framing to the concept of authoritarianism, a theoretical analysis is possible in which the entangled nature of power and dominance relations becomes the focus. Thirdly, the combination of these approaches addresses the call of feminist political thought to understand the power and dominance of gender relations as an essential trait of the political (cf. Graf, Schneider, and Wilde 2017: 72; see also Bargetz et al. 2017; Bargetz 2016).

The next section unfolds the three dimensions of the feminist political understanding of the authoritarian, which serves as a basis for the subsequent application of the framing concept. In the following sections, I introduce the post-structural analysis of framing and explain the framing methodology by means of an example, namely, the Serbian invocation of women as "Mother of the Nation" (Friedrich 2012). Finally, a summary is given, which also points out the particular relevance of the concatenation of the different levels of discourse.

2. A feminist theory of the authoritarian

In the current scholarly debate on (right-wing) populism, Graf, Schneider, and Wilde (2017) dispute the fixation on political institutions, which they claim underestimates the dangers of authoritarian tendencies worldwide. Whether in Germany, Chile, or Turkey, the impact of the authoritarian tests the modern understanding of democracy. One particular danger of the authoritarian is its strategy to conflate meanings:

> By conflating liberal argumentation with anti-feminist, racist, anti-Muslim, immigration, and security-related discourses, the diversity and plurality characteristic of political societies are denied; democratic interpretations are replaced with past ideologies; subjects are limited to the "natural" boundaries defined by homophobic ideas; and power structures are perpetuated by the appearance of a conservative consensus of values. (Graf, Schneider, and Wilde 2017: 73; translation by author)

Wilde develops the concept of the authoritarian in terms of democratic theory, referencing ideas on civil society by Alexis de Tocqueville and Antonio Gramsci; Hannah Arendt's republicanism; and Carole Pateman's feminist perspective (cf. Graf, Schneider, and Wilde 2017; Obuch et al. 2014; Schneider and Wilde 2012; Wilde 2014, 2013, 2012, 2010). By linking these ideas, authoritarian tendencies in view of gender and power are revealed in three ways. In terms of an organized civil society, the authoritarian "reinterprets liberal values and norms with the help of various discourses, measures, and practices in a way that limits the self-determination of women in civil society organizations and the general contribution of women's organizations" (Graf, Schneider, and Wilde 2017: 73; translation by author).

The second dimension, namely an acceptance of plurality, is according to Arendt (1989, 1979) a defining characteristic of democratic society. With the destruction of plurality and consequently of the citizens' ability to act freely, state and society begin exhibiting totalitarian traits. Therefore, in the tradition of Arendt, the authoritarian is manifested in the "limitation and de-politicization of the public, which eventually leads to a destruction of societal plurality and to a decrease in citizens' ability to assess and judge" (Graf, Schneider, and Wilde 2017: 74; translation by author). Gender relations are, by means of the construction of family ideology, reduced to traditional gender stereotypes (cf. Graf, Schneider, and Wilde 2017: 74).

The third dimension, in keeping with Pateman, comprises a decidedly feminist critical perspective by questioning the authoritarian (re)definition of liberal heteronormativity in society (Sauer 2001): To what extent are women inhibited in their civic freedom of action and their right to public participation? At this point, the authoritarian is disclosed in the "traditional, conservative model of the family and the discursive construction of dichotomous and homophobic gender roles" (Graf, Schneider, and Wilde 2017: 74; translation by author).

From these three dimensions, Graf, Schneider, and Wilde deduce the characteristics of the authoritarian as "the reenactment of staged constructions of gender and identities that denies their particularity and precludes their differential character" (2017: 84–85; translation by author).

3. Introduction to post-structural framing methodology – fundamental observations

To investigate the authoritarian in this feminist critical theory further, I suggest using the discourse analytical method based on post-structural framing analysis (cf. Panreck 2017: 45–57); this tool uncovers how the authoritarian emerges as a discursive construct and how it redefines and perpetuates gender relations as power structures. Since the metaphorical term "frame" is used across disciplines in sociology, linguistics, economics, political science, and communications, its meaning varies. This paper adopts Chantal Mouffe's (2013, 2000) post-structural interpretation of "frames" and their discursive setting: Frames, on the one hand, are the result of conflicts of interpretation; on the other, they structure such conflicts, thereby redefining power and dominance relations. This understanding of discourse is rooted in the tradition of Michel Foucault, who stressed the productive potential of discourses: They may no longer be interpreted as groups of signs ... but as practices that systematically form the objects of which they speak. Of course, discourses are composed of signs; but what they do is more than use these signs to designate things. It is this *more* that renders them irreducible to the language *(langue)* and to speech. It is this "more" that we must reveal and describe. (Foucault 1972: 49)

Foucault describes the function of discourse which Mouffe elaborates in democratic theory. For Mouffe, the manner of the conflict is decisive: Only after the conflict becomes agonal can it be granted a democratic quality (cf. Mouffe 2013, 2005, 2000).

In this post-structural sense, frames are understood as perspectives which fight within a discourse to be the dominant interpretation and are thus a productive part of the hegemonic conflict. It is assumed that a single perspective is characterized by its particularity and is thus incomplete. To frame, therefore, is to select only one aspect of reality and make it more salient (cf. Matthes 2014, 2007b).

But how can a frame be made transparent? It requires a working definition, such as the one Entman suggested in the early 1990s, which has been widely disseminated in academia: "Framing essentially involves *selection* and *salience*. To frame is to *select some aspects of a perceived reality and make them more salient in a communicating text, in such a way as to promote a particular problem definition, causal interpretation, moral evaluation, and/or treatment recommendation for the item described*" (Entman 1993: 52).

A frame consists of four elements: defining the problem, finding the cause, moral evaluation, and recommended action. The *problem definition* indicates which topic the actors react to with their frames and which aspect they make salient. The process of *causal attribution* starts when they identify the origin of the problem. The *moral evaluation* includes the evaluation of those involved and the consequences of their action. Finally, *recommended treatment* suggests reasonable solutions and their possible effects (cf. Entman 1993: 52; see also Matthes 2007b). Each of the four elements performs an evaluation: Provided they are a reflection of the same fundamental attitude, all elements are linked together consistently and there is a frame. One exception is the *problem definition*, which does not always recommend a certain standpoint. This is why a second evaluation element must be identified in a text. Not every discursive unit contains a frame, though this is rare (cf. Matthes 2007a: 134–139).

Every frame enters into political discourse by means of a strategic actor. Just as for the frame, so is "essentialization" prohibited for the strategic actor. As a subject, the strategic actor is simultaneously an independent and dependent variable of the discourse. In other words, the strategic actor's analysis only provides information about subjects who have become discernible and not about the persons themselves (cf. Foucault 1987: 243). The analysis manifests which groups attain visibility most often in the discourse, and therefore who has the possibility to perpetuate their position in politics. Strategic actors are usually members of the political, civic, or economic elite such as political parties, non-governmental organizations (NGOs), or industrial companies. In view of gender relations in authoritarian regimes, strategic actors' tendencies in the areas of *race, class, and gender* are especially relevant. Whereas democratic (gender) relations are based on the acceptance of particularity and diversity, authoritarian discourses emphasize homogeneity. Communications research refers to this kind of acting as *strategic framing* (cf. Matthes and Kohring 2004: 56). The identification of strategic frames is based on document analysis. The central question is: Which actors introduce their frames into the discourse? Does the conflict of frames reveal diversity and incompleteness or does it contain totalitarian elements?

4. Toolbox of post-structural framing-analysis

The toolbox for capturing frames offers a variety of methods. The usual distinction between qualitative and quantitative methods falls short; rather, framing studies often combine both paradigms. The variation preferred here is based on the analysis of elements according to Entman (and revised by Matthes). The frame is made up, as previously mentioned, of four parts: namely, problem definition, causal attribution, moral evaluation, and recommended action (cf. Entman 1993). Each analysis – in the case of mass media, for example, a newspaper article or in the case of interviews, the transcription – checks for these four elements: The *problem definition* inquires into a theme, which becomes salient through the frame. The *causal attribution* establishes the problem as either personal or situational, i.e., who or what is the cause of the problem. The *recommended action* is correspondingly personal or situational; it is directed toward the future and comprises individual measures or a bundle of measures: What is the solution to the problem? Or, more specifically, who or what can solve the problem? The *explicit evaluation* asks about the problem evaluation. Here, it is less about a dichotomous evaluation of the problem as negative or positive and more about differentiating the gradations, e.g., very positive, quite positive, etc. The degree of gradation also provides information about the extent to which the frame follows an authoritarian logic, since dichotomizations are typical of authoritarian discourse (cf. Graf, Schneider, and Wilde 2017: 74). Subsequently, the most probable evaluation is deduced for each of the four elements. Provided that – apart from the problem definition – all elements uniformly suggest a negative or a positive evaluation, and at least two elements can be clearly identified, a frame can be encoded. Finally, the source of the frame, or the frame's strategic actor, is identified.

5. Frames in authoritarianism research: The case of the Serbian "Mother of the Nation"

The construction and function of frames will be illustrated in the following in an example taken from authoritarianism research. In this example, the frame is deduced from an established body of research. Inductive approaches to framing, which extract the frame from a single text, are also possible. Hybrid approaches extract frames first from a small sample and then apply them to a larger body of text (for a list of advantages and disadvantages of these approaches, see Panreck 2017: 51–54; Matthes 2007b: 65–85).

In the following example of a deductive approach to framing, the findings of Stefanie Friedrich are referenced, who researched the changes in the public image of Serbian women during the disintegration of the state of Yugoslavia and the ensuing civil war (cf. Friedrich 2012). In the course of the Yugoslavian crisis, the conflict concerning the role of women in Yugoslavia escalated. From the various discursive appeals to women, their role as "mother" soon emerged:

> The retraditionalization of gender roles followed ... nationalization and – especially during the civil war – a militarization of gender roles. Men were given above all the role as "brave defenders of the fatherland," whereas women were assigned the role of "Mother of the Nation" whose prime mission was to ensure the survival of the nation by acting as guarantors of biological and cultural reproduction ... Childless women and those standing up for women's reproductive rights were soon labeled "traitors of the fatherland," (Friedrich 2012: 63; translation by author)

It was claimed that the Serbian population would be threatened by marginalization, in comparison to other ethnic groups such as the Kosovo Albanians, due to the lower birth rate. The solution was to provide support for Serbian families with many children (Friedrich 2012: 68–69). In concrete terms, this meant proposals for a pronatalist policy: childless couples would be taxed heavily; families with up to two children would receive tax incentives; and families with up to three children would receive fiscal support. Families with more than three children, which was the case for the majority of ethnic Kosovo Albanian families, would receive no financial support or benefit from tax breaks. In other words, the ethnic Serbian community was the prime benefactor of such policies (cf. Friedrich 2012: 69).

How can the perspective described by Friedrich be formulated as a frame? The discourse about the role of woman comprises various perspectives on women and the different appeals to women. The frame "woman as Mother of the Nation" fulfills the requirement of selectivity by helping a certain aspect to become salient (cf. Table 1). The problem definition (1) focuses on woman's role in society. She is recognized as "mother." But as "Mother of the Nation" she is not only assigned an intra-family role but is also responsible for the preservation of the nation. As casual attribution (2) for the woman's role as "Mother of the Nation" the frame argues not only for the "biological" and "cultural" responsibility of women but also their responsibility for the increase of the Serbian population. Therefore, politics should encourage women to have more children by pursuing a pronatalist population policy privileging ethnic Serbians (3). The explicit evaluation (4) in this example is therefore very positive since the role of mother is revered as fundamental for the preservation of the nation.

Table 1: Example of a frame and the implied fundamental position: "Mother of the Nation." Own representation using the example of Friedrich (2012).

	Problem definition (1)	Causal attribution (2)	Recommended action (3)	Explicit evaluation (4)
Frame element	The woman is the "Mother of the Nation"	Women bear children and thus preserve the population	The reproductive rate should be raised with pronatalistic policies in favor of ethnic Serbians	Very positively: Women are of utmost importance for the nation
Suggested evaluation of the mother role	positively	positively	positively	positively

6. Critical analysis of the discourse

Frames are conflictual. The concrete expression of this conflict elucidates the quality of the discourse and the extent of authoritarian developments. Frames must be gathered, as a first step, before a critical analysis of the discourse in which the frames conflict can be performed (cf. Table 2).

The identification of strategic actors is of central importance. In view of the feminist political approach taken here, the existence of plurality requires a multitude of strategic actors who participate in the discourse. To check this postulate, the strategic actors of the frames must first be identified. Initial indications of possible actor groups which should be involved in the ideal discourse are found in the *Europub Codebook* (cf. Koopmans 2002; see also Koopmans and Statham 1999).

1. The link between frame and strategic framing:
   a. Which strategic actors introduce which frames into the discourse?
   1.1 Example Serbia

b. Which strategic actors introduced the frame "Mother as symbol of the Nation" into the discourse?

In the second step, a critical review of the identified strategic actors is necessary. For Tocqueville (1965), we must question to what extent the strategic actors participate in governmental processes. The critical analysis continues in the tradition of Gramsci (1980): the monopolization of civil society actors by the state is considered. The Serbian example highlights the relevance of the question concerning the distance between state and society: nationalist women's organizations began emerging, thus anchoring the concept of "Mother of the Nation" in public discourse (cf. Friedrich 2012: 70). The fewer civil society actors participating in the struggle for the dominant interpretation, the stronger the authoritarian discourse becomes.

2. Contexts of the actors
   a. Are the actors involved at different levels of the governmental processes (e.g., in the political-juridical system, in associations, in academia, the media, etc.)?
   b. To what extent are actors involved with the state?
2.1 Example Serbia:
   c. In which contexts do the actors act? Do they belong to the political-juridical system (e.g., the executive), civil society (e.g., women's organizations), the scientific community (e.g., university), or the media (e.g., newspaper journalists)?
   d. To what extent is the state involved? Are academic institutions, for example, only an extended arm of the ruling party?

Up to now the frame analysis has been applied to the visibility and participants of a discourse. To understand the authoritarian impact, however, the separation between a visible public sphere and an invisible private sphere must be subject to feminist critique (cf. Sauer 2001; Pateman 1988). Ultimately, the separation of the public and private spheres stabilizes gender power relations and establishes a female subject who is deprived of rights in the political sphere (cf. Wilde 2013: 48).

3. Subject constitution and public and private separation
   a. What is the significance of the separation of the public and private and what impact does it have on gender subjects?
3.1 Example Serbia:

b. To what extent does the frame "Mother of the Nation" foster the public and private separation and what impact does this separation have on Serbian women?

The focus of this analysis so far has been on the actors; Mouffe suggests also looking at the quality of the conflict between the frames and the actors. Most importantly, how do the actors involved in the conflict confront each other? Democratic conflicts are agonal, while authoritarian discourses are antagonistic: Do opposing parties accept other standpoints as legitimate, or does one party try to silence the other, possibly even by questioning the other's right to participate in the discourse itself (cf. Mouffe 2007: 45; Herrmann 2015)? According to Arendt (1989, 1979), discourses that are carried out antagonistically ultimately lead to an eradication of plurality as a characteristic of the public sphere.

Beside the direct ruling of a "ban," authoritarian discourse is also expressed latently through hidden governmental technologies. In this case, the interpretation patterns structuring frames are informative (see also Ritzi 2014: 235; Schäfer 2008; Gerhards and Schäfer 2007). Interpretation patterns ask about the underlying legitimacy of a frame. On which truth is the frame based? Is the frame legitimated by a final justification?

Interpretation patterns without an absolute ground are an indication of high democratic quality. Hence, political interpretation patterns encourage either dealing with controversial issues in the political-juridical system or letting the issue be resolved through the will of the *demos*. In other words, they acknowledge that their own position is only one of many in the struggle to become the dominant interpretation.

By contrast, ethical-social interpretations ground the strategic actors' perspective in view of an abstract ethics lying outside of the democratic strife. The same is true for religious interpretation patterns, which link the position of the frame to a divine truth. "Nature" or "culture" also act as absolute grounds. These kinds of interpretation patterns lay claim to absolute truth and run counter to the logic of open political strife. In view of gender relations in authoritarian regimes, it can be stated: the sooner the frames are based on absolute interpretation patterns, the sooner gender roles are stabilized as repressive power and dominance relations. According to Graf, Schneider, and Wilde (2017), a distinctive feature of contemporary discourse is reinterpretation;

frames based on liberal arguments, which actually fall into the democratic category "political," are misused to legitimate frames that are grounded in authoritarian arguments. A frame analysis must heed this aspect. The deconstruction of these reinterpretations, for instance, can be carried out through an analysis of the linking of discourses. If liberal reasoning always appears in the context of another legitimation – traditional, moral, or biological – this might indicate the concealing function of the liberal argument.

4. Agonal or antagonistic conflict: Opponents or enemies
   a. Direct rule: Are strategic actors banned from the public discourse?
   b. Latent rule: Which interpretation patterns structure and legitimize the frames? Political vs. ethical/moral vs. religious vs. natural vs. cultural/traditional interpretation patterns, etc.
   c. Reinterpretation: In which context does legitimization run parallel to liberal argumentation? Are there attempts to reframe liberal argumentations by contextualizing them with authoritarian argumentations?
4.1 Example Serbia:
   d. Direct rule: Are critics of the frame "Mother of the Nation" granted the right and the opportunity to voice their position in the political discourse?
   e. Latent rule: How is the frame "Mother of the Nation" legitimized? (Recourse to nature and cultural tradition = authoritarian)
   f. Reinterpretation: Do strategic actors link their interpretation patterns (here: recourse to nature and cultural tradition) to liberal arguments (for example, self-determination)?

Finally, an interpretation that combines these four steps enables critical reflection on the function of the subject position "gender" for authoritarian regimes. The question concerning the extent to which the displacing of women as political subjects is constitutive of the authoritarian regime should find special consideration.

Table 2: An ascending frame analysis of the authoritarian. Own representation.

Analysis of steps (ascending order)	Action
Step 1	Guiding question: *Which strategic actors introduce which frames into the discourse?* Extraction of the frames from the text body with the help of the following elements: problem definition, causal attribution, possible solution, explicit evaluation, and the identification of strategic actors
Step 2	Guiding questions: *Do strategic actors act in governmental processes (the political-juridical system, associations, academia, the media, etc.)?* *To what extent are strategic actors involved in state institutions?* Examination of the plurality of the visible strategic actors and their participation in state institutions and governmental processes
Step 3	Guiding question: *What is the function of the public and private separation and what is its impact on the power and domination patterns in gender relations?* Examination of the assignment of strategic actors to the public and private spheres with the help of the gender aspect and its impact on the power and domination patterns concerning women
Step 4	Guiding questions: *Direct rule: Are strategic actors banned from the public discourse?* *Latent rule: Which interpretation patterns structure and legitimize the frames? Political vs. ethical/moral vs. religious vs. natural vs. cultural/traditional interpretation patterns, etc.* *Reinterpretation: In which context do legitimizations stand alongside liberal argumentation? Is there a discursive intertwining with authoritarian legitimizations?* Examine whether the discourse is among opponents (agonal) or enemies (antagonistic). Recourse to direct and latent rule and reinterpretation processes
Conclusion	Interpretation of the results and critical reflection of the subject position of woman and her function in authoritarian regimes

7. Conclusion

A critical analysis of authoritarian regimes should not linger at the institutional level, focusing exclusively on the state. Feminist and post-structural perspectives demand the inclusion of the social sphere, where the main struggle for the "correct" interpretation of societal power and domination relations takes place. This is especially true for the analysis of gender relations in authoritarian regimes. This paper adopted the bottom-up approach of feminist political thought and attempted to apply the discourse-analytic perspective to authoritarian regimes. Wilde's concept of the authoritarian (cf. her paper in this volume; Graf, Schneider, and Wilde 2017; Obuch et al. 2014; Schneider and Wilde 2012; Wilde 2012) was taken up and made productive for the analysis of authoritarian regimes. Discourse is the focus of post-structural framing theory analysis, within which a variety of perspectives, so-called frames, quarrel for the dominant interpretation. In a first step, those frames were extracted from the text body with the help of the transparent framing methodology. In further steps, the power of discourse was emphasized; the analysis of frames disclosed the visibility of actors and the democratic quality of the frame's conflict. The frame "Mother of the Nation" from the Serbian discourse, which portrayed the role of women during the breakdown of Yugoslavia, was analyzed (Friedrich 2012).

Although this contribution focuses on the social level, the institutional level of politics should not be completely neglected. From a post-structural feminist view, however, the institutional analysis is only an approximation. To understand the political, feminist theory must analyze governmental functions of gender relations and the concatenation of discourses, as well as obtain an understanding of the gendered political subject and gender relations as an expression of power and domination relations.

References

Arendt, Hannah (1979): The Origins of Totalitarianism. San Diego, New York, London.
Arendt, Hannah (1989): The Human Condition. Chicago.
Bargetz, Brigitte (2016): Ambivalenzen des Alltags. Neuorientierungen für eine Theorie des Politischen. Bielefeld.
Bargetz, Brigitte et al. (2017): Geschlechterverhältnisse als Machtverhältnisse. In: Femina Politica 26, 1, pp. 11–24.
Entman, Robert M. (1991): Framing U.S. coverage of international news: Contrasts in narratives of the KAL and Iran Air incidents. In: Journal of Communication 41, 4, pp. 6–27.
Entman, Robert M. (1993): Framing: Toward Clarification of a Fractured Paradigm. In: Journal of Communication 43, 4, pp. 51–58.
Entman, Robert M. (2003): Cascading Activation: Contesting the White House's Frama After 9/11. In: Political Communication 20, 4, pp. 415–432.
Entman, Robert M. (2007): Framing Bias: Media in the Distribution of Power. In: Journal of Communication 57, pp. 163–173.
Foucault, Michel (1972): The Archaeology of Knowledge & The Discourse on Language. New York.
Foucault, Michel (1987): Das Subjekt und die Macht. In: Dreyfus, Hubert L./Rabinow, Paul (Eds.): Michel Foucault. Jenseits von Strukturalismus und Hermeneutik. Frankfurt a. M, pp. 241–261.
Fraser, Nancy (1996): Öffentlichkeit neu denken. Ein Beitrag zur Kritik real existierender Demokratie. In: Scheich, Elvira (Ed.): Vermittelte Weiblichkeit. Feministische Wissenschafts- und Gesellschaftstheorie, Hamburg.
Friedrich, Stefanie (2012): Mutter der Nation oder Vaterlandsverräterin? Die politische und religiöse Festschreibung einer militarisierten Frauenrolle in Serbien in den 1990er Jahren. In: Femina Politica 22, 1, pp. 63–72.
Gerhards, Jürgen/Schäfer, Mike S. (2007): Demokratische Internet-Öffentlichkeit? Ein Vergleich der öffentlichen Kommunikation im Internet und in den Printmedien am Beispiel der Humangenomforschung. In: Publizistik 52, 2, pp. 210–228.
Graf, Patricia/Schneider, Silke/Wilde, Gabriele (2017): Geschlechterverhältnisse und die Macht des Autoritären. In: Femina Politica 26, 1, pp. 70–87.
Gramsci, Antonio (1980): Zu Politik, Geschichte und Kultur – Ausgewählte Schriften. Leipzig.
Herrmann, Steffen K. (2015): Politischer Antagonismus und sprachliche Gewalt. In: Hark, Sabine/Villa, Paula-Irene (Eds.): Anti-Generismus. Sexualität und Geschlecht als Schauplätze aktueller politischer Auseinandersetzungen. Bielefeld, pp. 79–92.
Koopmans, Ruud (2002): Codebook for the Analysis of Political Mobilisation and Communication in European Public Spheres. http://europub.wzb.eu/Data/Codebooks%20questionnaires/D2-1-claims-codebook.pdf (27.08.2015).

Koopmans, Ruud/Statham, Paul (1999): Political Claims Analysis: Integrating Protest Event and Public Discourse Approaches. In: Mobilization 4, 2, pp. 203–222.

Laclau, Ernesto/Mouffe, Chantal (2001): Hegemony and Socialist Strategy. Towards a Radical Democratic Politics. London.

Matthes, Jörg (2004): Die Schema-Theorie in der Medienwirkungsforschung: Ein unscharfer Blick in die „Black Box"? In: M&K 52, 4, pp. 545–568.

Matthes, Jörg (2007a): Framing-Effekte. Zum Einfluss der Politikberichterstattung auf die Einstellungen der Rezipienten. München.

Matthes, Jörg (2007b): Framing-Effekte. Zum Einfluss der Politikberichterstattung auf die Einstellungen der Rezipienten. München.

Matthes, Jörg (2014): Framing. Baden-Baden.

Matthes, Jörg/Kohring, Matthias (2004): Die empirische Erfassung von Medien-Frames. In: M&K 52, 1, pp. 56–75.

Mouffe, Chantal (2000): The Democratic Paradox. London.

Mouffe, Chantal (2005): On the Political. Thinking in Action. London.

Mouffe, Chantal (2007): Pluralismus, Dissens und demokratische Staatsbürgerschaft. In: Nonhoff, Martin (Ed.): Diskurs – radikale Demokratie – Hegemonie. Zum politischen Denken von Ernesto Laclau und Chantal Mouffe. Bielefeld, pp. 41–53.

Mouffe, Chantal (2013): Agonistics. Thinking the World Politically. London.

Obuch, Katharina/Sandhaus, Jasmin/Wilde, Gabriele/Zimmer, Annette (2014): Alles verändert sich, damit es bleibt wie es ist. Erste Ergebnisse aus dem Forschungsprojekt „Geschlechterverhältnisse in autoritären und hybriden Regimen" am Fallbeispiel Nicaragua. In: ZEUGS – Working Paper No. 2|2014, pp. 1–9.

Panreck, Isabelle-Christine (2017): Diskurse als Nährboden demokratischer Außenpolitik? Kriegsentscheidungen in der massenmedialen Öffentlichkeit. Baden-Baden.

Pateman, Carole (1988): The Sexual Contract. Stanford.

Ritzi, Claudia (2014): Die Postdemokratisierung politischer Öffentlichkeit. Kritik an zeitgenössischer Demokratie – theoretische Grundlagen und analytische Perspektiven. Wiesbaden.

Sauer, Birgit (2001): Die Asche des Souveräns. Staat und Demokratie in der Geschlechterdebatte. Frankfurt a. M., New York.

Schäfer, Mike S. (2008): Diskurskoalitionen in den Massenmedien. Ein Beitrag zur theoretischen und methodischen Verbindung von Diskursanalyse und Öffentlichkeitssoziologie. In: Kölner Zeitschrift für Soziologie und Sozialpsychologie 60, 2, pp. 367–397.

Schneider, Silke/Wilde, Gabriele (2012): Autokratie, Demokratie und Geschlecht: Geschlechterverhältnisse in autoritären Regimen. Einleitung. In: Femina Politica 21, 1, pp. 9–16.

Tocqueville, Alexis de (1965): Democracy in America. London.

Wilde, Gabriele (2010): Europäische Gleichstellungsnormen: Neoliberale Politik oder postneoliberale Chance für demokratische Geschlechterverhältnisse? In: juridikum. Zeitschrift für Kritik, Recht, Gesellschaft 4, pp. 449–464.

Wilde, Gabriele (2012): Totale Grenzen des Politischen: Die Zerstörung der Öffentlichkeit bei Hannah Arendt. In: Femina Politica 21, 1, pp. 17–28.

Wilde, Gabriele (2013): Jenseits von Recht und neoliberaler Ordnung. Zur Integration von Geschlecht in die politikwissenschaftliche Europaforschung. In: Wilde, Gabriele/Friedrich, Stefanie (Eds.): Im Blick der Disziplinen. Geschlecht und Geschlechterverhältnisse in der wissenschaftlichen Analyse. Münster, pp. 21–54.

Wilde, Gabriele (2014): Der Kampf um Hegemonie. Potentiale radikaler Demokratie aus Geschlechterperspektive. In: Zeitschrift für Politische Theorie 5, 2, pp. 203–216.

Between Militancy and Survival? The Case of the Nicaraguan Women's Movement

Katharina Obuch

1. Introduction

Since the revival of civil society research in the 1980s, women's movements worldwide have gained attention for their promotion of societal modernization, dismantling of traditional gender roles, and fight for inclusive democracy. Women's organizations fulfill various functions including agenda setting, state control, and the representation of interests or service provision. However, hardly any attention has been given to the women's activists and organizations operating in "hybrid" regimes. A hybrid regime refers to formerly transitional states that combine formal democratic structures with autocratic legacies in their political liberties, civil rights, and rule of law (Croissant 2002: 32). Accordingly, any discussion of women's movements in these regimes is highly controversial. Not only are we dealing with difficult political contexts – countries with little or no former democratic experience and at least partially authoritarian governments limiting civic action by restricting public space and civil liberties – but many of these regimes are characterized by macho and patriarchal societies, which are reflected in gender-related inequality and violence.

In Nicaragua – the country under study – democratic structures are still struggling to consolidate despite the glorious start of democratization with the Sandinista Revolution of 1979. A small political elite has been alternating in power, and the current President, Daniel Ortega, is being accused of fostering an autocratic backlash and enforcing political polarization – not least through his ambiguous attitude toward civil society.

In an attempt to narrow the existing research gap on civil society and gender in hybrid regimes, this chapter critically examines the Nicaraguan women's movement and its share in the modernization and democratization of gender relations in Nicaragua. Which challenges does the movement face and how does it influence a transformation of the present gender order? Is the movement truly a pioneer of inclusive democracy, or might it actually contribute to the continuation of traditional gender roles?

The study is based on a literature survey and interviews conducted with women's activists and civil society experts in Nicaragua.[1] The chapter starts with a brief introduction of the state of the art on hybrid regimes, gender, and civil society. The case of Nicaragua is subsequently introduced, and its classification as a hybrid regime and the present gender order are discussed. The main part presents the findings on the women's movement and the challenges it faces. It concludes with a typology of Nicaraguan women's organizations according to their potential to challenge the existing gender order.

2. Regime-hybridity, gender relations, and civil society

2.1 Hybrid regimes and gender

The Arab spring and further uprisings against autocratic leaders worldwide have recently inspired societal and scholarly discourse about the proliferation of democracy – in conjunction with the worldwide euphoria provoked by the "third wave of democratization" (Huntington 1993) in the 1970s and 1980s. Nonetheless, empiricism shows that once former autocratic leaders are overthrown, only few countries take steps toward democratic consolidation. Instead of a worldwide triumph of democracy, democratic indices show a

---

[1] I conducted thirty-two interviews in Nicaragua for my Ph.D. thesis (2011–2016). A more detailed analysis is presented in my book *Civil Society Organizations in the Hybrid Regime of Nicaragua: Challenging or Maintaining the Status Quo?* (Obuch 2017).

spread of transitional or mixed regimes (see Freedom House, Democracy Index). Most of these regimes combine former democratic structures with significant deficits of political liberty, civil rights, or the rule of law (Croissant 2002: 32). More precisely, the formal democratic institutions such as political parties, regular elections, and high courts are forced to coexist with the existing clientelism, patrimonial structures, and often-omnipotent executive. These autocratic legacies limit civil society's scope of action, e.g., they restrict public space or the liberties of association and opinion.

In democratization studies, these hybrid regimes have recently turned into a proliferating area of study (see Diamond 2002; Gilbert and Mohseni 2011; Morlino 2009). Experts agree that many of these regimes seem to be stuck in "some middle hybrid terrain" (Karl 1995: 73) between an authoritarian past and the anticipated democratic future. Hybrid regimes stand out for their hybrid democratic nature, socioeconomic difficulties, a lack of former democratic experience, and their apparently astonishing stability and persistence. Moreover, findings suggest that regime-hybridity tends to manifest itself within gender relations as well. Formal improvements such as participation, quotas, and women's rights may stand vis-à-vis a re-traditionalization of gender roles and the persistence of stereotypes in societal discourse and in the public and private spheres (Obuch et al. 2013).

2.2 Civil society in hybrid regimes

Since its revival in the 1980s, the concept of civil society has become an unchallenged model, strengthening democracy, justice, and civic participation. Civil society discourse has been closely linked to the notion of democracy, and it is generally acknowledged as contributing to the longevity and depth of political regimes (Zinecker 2011: 6; Pollack 2003: 53). At the same time most experts agree that civil society – including associations, foundations, trade unions, NGOs, or individual activists – actually depends on a democratic context to fully live up to its potential (Foley and Edwards 1996; Kocka 2004: 71).

The values and tasks of civil society have been discussed and classified in various ways (see Pollack 2003; Wnuk-Lipinski 2009). In order to determine its role in political regimes, a distinction must first be made concerning its function. On the one hand, civil society is said to play a major role in agenda setting, citizen information, citizen representation, and in the fight for minority rights; it enforces the democratic-participatory strength of society. On the other, it is seen as fulfilling an integrating and intermediary function: it disburdens the state, enforces institutional trust, and creates and deepens the bonds between the state and its citizens (Anheier, Priller, and Zimmer 2000; Pollack 2003; Warren 2011).

But what about civil society in hybrid regimes? There are far fewer findings on the functions and roles of civil society in non-democratic settings. Though the traditional, neo-Tocquevillian understanding of civil society views it as "schools of democracy" and as a forum for democratic spirit (Tocqueville 1985), critics point to the limits of civil society actors under autocratic rule and emphasize their integrative and bonding effect on a regime.

First of all, civil society is usually seen as a hope for democratization – whether as a space of preservation and flourishing of democratic thought within autocratic societies or as a direct source of protest and insurrection against autocratic leaders. Empiricism has proved the importance of social movements and resistance groups for the initiation of democratic transitions in many Latin American countries, the collapse of communism in Eastern Europe (Wnuk-Lipinski 2009), and the recent "Facebook" revolutions in North Africa (Stepan and Linz 2013). And women's movements and organizations are attributed an important role in particular for their fight for democratic power relations and integral democracy – from the Madres de Plaza de Mayo in Argentina (see Femenía and Gil 1987) to women's organizations in the Eastern European resistance movements (Einhorn and Sever 2003).

At the same time, some scholars draw on historical experiences from the Weimar Republic and National Socialism (Berman 1997; Koshar 1987) or findings from contemporary illiberal states to paint a much different picture. They point to the risks connected to civil society: namely, its stabilizing effects on political regimes no matter their shade; the integrative impact of associations; and the dangerous dynamics of organized masses in non-democratic contexts (Bernhard and Karacok 2007; Kaldor and Kostovicova 2008; Tusalem 2007; Diamond 1994). Taken together, these diverse approaches bring to light that civil society, despite its various virtues and achievements, as summarized by Zinecker (2011), is neither "bound to a democratic setting" nor "always good, charitable and pro-democratic."

3. The case: Nicaragua

3.1 The hybrid regime of Nicaragua

Nicaragua's democratization process starts with the Sandinista Revolution in 1979, which overthrew the forty-year-long dictatorship of Anastasio Somoza and his family dynasty. The following period of Sandinista rule (1979–1990) was marked by the introduction of formal democratic structures: elections were established in 1984, a constitution was adopted in 1987, political participation was encouraged, and interests were organized (Reiber 2009: 282). Nevertheless, the Sandinistas had their own understanding of democracy and participation, one which is not completely compatible with today's understanding of liberal democracy (Merkel 2010: 219). Moreover, many of their achievements, such as educational and land reform or the successful literacy campaign, were soon challenged or overshadowed by the emerging civil war. In 1990, peace negotiations and the following elections gave rise to a neoliberal era in which the institutionalization of democracy that started during the Sandinista Revolution was advanced by means of constitutional reform, the formation of political parties, and the establishment of democratic elections in 1996, 2000, and 2006. Nonetheless, social inequality increased, the gap between the rich and the poor widened, and a debate about the social foundations of democracy was initiated. Corruption and quarrels among the liberal-conservative coalition and pacts among the political elite further contributed to the discontent of the population (Reiber 2009; Schobel and Elsemann 2008).

In the 2006 elections former revolutionist Daniel Ortega, still the leader of the Sandinista party Sardinista National Liberation Front (FSLN), took advantage of the disunity of the political right, the general discontent and mistrust among the population, and changes in the electoral law. His presidency (reelection in 2011 and 2016) is characterized by ambiguous developments: positive innovations and improvements of social justice and equality have been accompanied by setbacks in other areas, such as democratic governance and the rule of law (Schnipkoweit and Schützhofer 2008: 6). On the one hand, social programs like *Hambre Cero* (Zero Hunger) and Ortega's self-presentation as president of the poor eventually succeeded in addressing large parts of the population living on less than two dollars a day, who had been disregarded and impoverished during preceding governments. On the other, we find electoral fraud, suspended balance of power in favor of a superior executive branch, and questionable coalescence of state institutions with party structures. Indeed, his "government of reconciliation and national unity" has led to increasing political polarization, with critics accusing Ortega of leading the country back to autocracy (Colburn 2012; Gómez Pomeri 2012).

According to the criteria outlined above, Nicaragua, despite its singularity, can be classified as a hybrid regime. It shares characteristics with many other third-wave countries: its nearly complete lack of previous democratic experience, the failure of the democratic system to reduce the high level of socioeconomic inequality, and an ambiguous regime character, i.e., formal democratic institutions are accompanied by a weak rule of law and deficient civil rights and political liberties.

3.2 A mirror of regime-hybridity: gender roles in Nicaragua

The interdependencies of regime-hybridity and the present gender order in Nicaragua can best be illustrated by considering the following issues: the traditional, historical, and cultural legacies affecting the everyday life of women, the disputable degree of female participation in politics and society as a whole, and the present government's ambiguous attitude toward gender relations.

3.2.1. Historical and cultural legacies

Nicaraguan society is deeply marked by machismo and paternalistic structures; the traditional "caudillismo" – in the sense of dominant, non-democratic, and male leadership – still shapes the country's political culture (representative of women's organization, interview 1). In public opinion, women are still bound to their traditional role as mothers, while men are seen as heads of the household and breadwinners. But such assumptions run counter to social reality. In Nicaragua a third of all women are single parents, either due to economic reasons such as high numbers of work-related migration or to the simple irresponsibility of many men. Moreover, current surveys reveal that women – traditionally responsible for managing the household – are more concerned with economic issues and suffer from food insecurity far more than men, probably due to their traditional economic dependence (Booth and Seligson 2012: 219ff.). Nicaraguan women suffer most from the country's widespread poverty (almost one-third of all Nicaraguans live below poverty line [*World Factbook* 2015]), social inequality, and lack of education. Socioeconomic reasons and the absence of family planning (and contraceptives) are still preventing the majority of women from living a self-determined life. There is a high rate of child pregnancy, as nearly 30% of all women between the ages of fifteen and nineteen are already mothers, and mothers and children lack quality medical attention, adequate nutrition, and social insurance (CENIDH 2013: 116).

These conservative traits of Nicaraguan society are reinforced by the power of the Church. The majority of the population consider themselves devout believers, even though Nicaraguan clerics and church leaders stand out for their decidedly unprogressive agenda. Their highly conservative approach is evident in their successful commitment to the prohibition and penalization of "therapeutic" abortion in 2006 and in their fight against Law 779 (Law against Violence against Women) (civil society expert from civil society organization [CSO], interview 2). Antifeminist thought is indeed strongly supported by a good number of the population, including many women, and it manifests itself in various ultraconservative groups and congregations, who draw support from their disaffirmation of the Sandinista Revolution and claim to defend the country from cultural imperialism (i.e., feminism brought by outsiders). They promote ultraconservative, unprogressive values and traditional gender roles and relations. Compared to the women's movement, they are little in terms of number but quite influential in shaping state policy (Kampwirth 2006: 92; Pizarro 2003).

What is more, a predominant experience in the lives of many Nicaraguan women is violence. Central America is known for its high rates of violence against women, recently gaining notoriety for a large number of so-called femicides (see Bruneau, Dammert, and Skinner 2011; Prieto-Carrón, Thompson, and MacDonald 2007). Although Nicaragua seems to be one of the less affected countries when compared to its northern neighbors, violence against women in the form of murder, sexual abuse, or domestic violence remains a major problem. According to the World Health Organization, more than two-thirds of all women between the ages of fifteen and forty-nine reported having suffered physical or sexual violence at least once (*The Nicaragua Dispatch* 2012). According to the Latin American Public Opinion Project (LAPOP), home is the most dangerous place for Nicaraguan women, as 78% of all registered aggressions take place here (CENIDH 2013: 113). Meanwhile, the quantity of unsolved cases including femicides reflects a climate of insecurity, mistrust, and especially impunity (CENIDH 2013: 114). Worryingly, this climate is reproduced by many women themselves, as there is a widespread tendency to simply typify aggressions by husbands, sons, or other familiars as mere *faltas* (mistakes). This is illustrated by surveys in which 70% of women reporting violence say it occurred at home but tend not to consider it a crime (Booth and Seligson 2012: 229).

3.2.2. Participation

Nicaraguan women's participation in society and the political sphere is especially influenced by their primary role as caretakers: they are mothers in charge of the family and childrearing. Nicaraguan women are only slightly less socially involved than men, but their engagement is mostly concentrated on church and school-related groups (Booth and Seligson 2012: 244ff.). While the organization of women is high at the community level, they have difficulties reaching official positions within political parties or becoming leaders of mixed organizations (representative of women's organization, interview 1). By contrast, there is a strong women's movement, and 7.6% of all women declare being active in a women's organization (Booth and Seligson 2012: 247). Socioeconomic vulnerability affects women's ability to participate and get involved outside their homes. Women tend to be less informed, more distrustful, and less self-confident – features which do not facilitate political participation and civic engagement (Booth and Seligson 2012: 251).

In an interview about the existence of different political cultures for men and women in Nicaragua, one Nicaraguan political sociologist emphasizes the specific obstacles faced by women in his country when trying to become politically active. When spontaneously asked to participate in a communal meeting, women were much more opposed to the idea than their male counterparts. They worried about their personal security ("How will I get there and get home later?"), their reputation ("What will others think of me coming home alone at night?"), and neglecting their family ("Who will take care of the family while I am away?") (civil society expert [CSO], interview 2).

These obstacles are reflected in the argument of one women's activist, who states that Nicaraguan women participating in civil society have to "triplicate their power and energy" (representative of women's organization, interview 6). A growing number of women are expected to work outside the home while still caring for their household and children. This leaves them with very little time to become politically engaged citizens – the little time that they otherwise would have had for themselves and recreation (representative of women's organization, interview 6).

When it comes to women's participation in the political sphere, Nicaragua again paints an ambiguous picture, which is also expressed in the discussion about Violeta Chamorro, one of the country's ex-presidents (1990–1996). Though the former experience of a female president generally translates positively in view of female political leaders (Booth and Seligson 2012: 234), her election campaign reduced her to her role as the wife of former revolutionist

Pedro Joaquin Chamorro; moreover, her self-produced image as "wife, widow and mother" (Kampwirth 2006: 78) reflects a traditionalist, rather unprogressive thinking. Similarly, the current government takes pride in its promotion of women, e.g., the introduction of gender quotas (half of the country's mayors are now women) (CENIDH 2013, 120) or the increasing percentage of women in party political posts. Nonetheless, as we will see in the next section, there is a widespread allegation that in practice these achievements are undermined by vertical power structures and the factual subordination of women.

3.2.3 The government's discourse

As we have seen in the two previous sections, the tenuous role of women in Nicaraguan society can be traced back to several traditional as well as socio-economic legacies. And this tenuous role is still reflected in the present government's discourse and attitude toward women and gender relations. Since its electoral victory in 2006, the governing party FSLN has revived its official revolutionary discourse on the role and importance of women in Nicaraguan society. It has created many social programs to benefit women in particular, most of them from the rather poor and rural areas (Kampwirth 2011: 15). Moreover, the party introduced gender quotas and has a high share of FSLN women delegates in parliament and ministries (Kampwirth 2011: 19). The outstanding role of Nicaragua's First Lady Rosario Murillo should also be mentioned, who is sometimes said to informally hold even more power than President Ortega himself; she is quoted by party loyals to emphasize the government's progressiveness.

Nonetheless, many accuse the present government of actually retaining its ambiguous attitude toward women, which was expressed during the revolution, by hiding its real interests behind official rates and quotas: "Although officially it seems as if there was equal participation, in the decision-making process, women keep their role of subordination to the orders of the party" (representative of women's organization, interview 1). Indeed, in 2006 the Sandinista delegates demonstrated how easily they agreed on sacrificing women's rights for party interests. In the face of upcoming elections and following a pact with the Catholic Church, they supported the prohibition of therapeutic abortion against tremendous mobilizations and resistance of the women's movement (CENIDH 2013: 118).

To critics, the government's true colors become obvious in its traditionalist discourse on the motherly role and sexual or reproductive rights, which is especially reflected in Murillo's esoteric discourse. In daily messages to the people she demonizes feminism and feminist activists as agents of an imperialist power (Oettler 2010: 56), while praising the protection of women's traditional roles and their responsibilities as mothers and devoted wives.

Even harsher controversy exists about President Ortega himself, who was accused of sexual assault and rape by his stepdaughter Zoilamérica in 1998 and has since successfully managed to avoid prosecution and punishment. The incident has turned into a delicate issue for all those trying to fight against gender-related violence and misogyny within Nicaraguan society. Moreover, it has been a starting point for the final break of a huge part of the women's movement from the Sandinista party.

The contradiction between the official discourse and societal reality (CENIDH 2013, 110) has therefore been demonstrated on several occasions. For example, the handling of the long-awaited Law 779, which theoretically constitutes an improvement of women's rights but up to now has remained without adequate budget, has been criticized for its lack of or delay in implementation (CENIDH 2013: 112), and it has suffered from several attempts by Sandinista delegates to revoke important aspects. One women's activist summarized the problems that arise from the government's unprogressive discourse and ambiguous attitude in the following way:

If still the President, the First Lady, the Minister of Education, so to say top level decision-makers, keep sending out the message that everything happens by the will of God, that men are the heads of family, that the cohesion/unity of a family is most important no matter the cost, that you do not wash your dirty laundry in public ... these messages resound in the media, in the schools, in the hospitals ... so that we are talking to a brick wall. (Representative of women's organization, interview 6)

4. The Nicaraguan women's movement

4.1 Evolution

The evolution of the Nicaraguan women's movement has been closely linked to the development of civil society in Nicaragua in general. Moreover, Nicaraguan women's organizations are often seen as a vanguard of civic agency and moral authority (civil society expert [CSO], interview 8).

Although the first feminist ideas and writings date back to the 1930s, the real development of an organized women's movement took place in the 1970s as part of a broader civic movement during the growing resistance against the Somoza dictatorship (Cuadra and Jiménez 2011: 12). The enduring dynasty provoked resistance within diverse parts of the population including peasants, workers, and students. The dynasty also affected women in their specific areas (family and economy) due to the increasing costs of living and the imminent political persecution of their sons and husbands (representative of women's organization, interview 5). Over time, women became an essential part of the movement, which finally overthrew Somoza in 1979, and they played a major part in the following revolution. According to several sources, up to an estimated 30% of all Sandinista combatants were women (Kampwirth 2011: 4), while others served as volunteers in health brigades or the national alphabetization campaign (Hamlin and Quirós Visquez 2013: 6). The Sandinista's mass organization of the population is historically seen as a starting point for the development of Nicaraguan civil society and feminist organizing (civil society expert and donor, interview 7; Kampwirth 2006: 76) – without which feminism wouldn't have evolved the way it did in Nicaragua (Kampwirth 2011: 4). All parts of the population started organizing. Women under Sandinista rule were organized in mass organizations or became secretaries in various labor unions (representative of women's organization, interview 6). Such organizing processes fostered popular participation but were restricted by their vertical style and the requested loyalty to the governing party (Borchgrevink 2006: 7).

Nonetheless, the differences between the government's attitude toward gender relations and the postulations of the critical women's activists soon became obvious. The different expectations not only led to a struggle between the emerging women's movement and the Sandinista government but also laid the foundation for the division of the women's movement into a moderate, rather party-loyal wing and a new feminist opposition (Kampwirth 2011: 5ff.). While the government's priority was to win the ongoing civil war against the US-financed counter-revolutionists and to provide for the soldiers, women did not want to put aside their interests in improving female health care, including their fight for the right to abortion (representative of women's organization, interview 3). The conservative male view on the issue represented by many of the governing elite – i.e., the revolution needs to replace the casualties and the revolutionary task of women was to give birth to revolutionists – naturally challenged the ideas of many women's activists (Hamlin and Quirós Visquez 2011: 8). Women's attempts to translate the revolution's objectives universally, i.e., equality and liberation of society in the private sphere and in the sphere of gender relations, as well as the demand to be recognized for their contribution to the revolution, were met with harsh disapproval by their male party colleagues (representative of women's organization, interview 3).

When the Sandinista party was voted out of office in 1990, new challenges and opportunities eventuated for the civil society sector in general and for the women's movement in particular. First of all, there was a "boom" in terms of the number and diversity of CSOs for several reasons: the end of the civil war and the further development of democratic structures promoted the freedom of public space and guaranteed liberties conducive to civic action. Second, the former government employees needed to create new jobs, which they found in the emerging civil society sector. Third, they were met with a wave of international solidarity, which – in the era of a worldwide increase and irrevocable belief in NGOs – was reflected in financial aid specifically directed toward the construction of civil society (civil society expert and donor, interview 7).

Nonetheless, challenges were inevitable; the loss of the former Sandinista party structures meant that even party-loyal organizations had to redefine and seek autonomization. This process reached its peak in 1998 with the accusations of Ortega's stepdaughter Zoilamérica. In 2006, the prohibition of therapeutic abortion demonstrated the FSLN's renouncement of women's support, which led to the development of autonomous women's organizations that were ever more critical of traditional party colleagues and FSLN politics (Kampwirth 2011: 11).

Up until today, the women's movement has maintained its role as an outstanding actor within Nicaraguan civil society (representative of women's organization, interview 6). It gains strength from its historical significance and persistence, in opposition to the contemporary variety of short-lived projects and initiatives in other areas. It stands out for its historical capability to fight (representative of women's organization, interviews 1 and 3) and it is characterized by its diversity in terms of organizational form (from movement to NGO), topics of interest, and target groups (e.g., indigenous women, rural women, sexually abused women, lesbians, etc.). A high level of controversy still surrounds its working instruments (from service provision and practical assistance to political lobbying) and class. Many women's activists claim that the women's movement is not bound to the universities or academia in general. Instead, it is and should be made up of women from rural areas and the working class, as well as housewives, who tend to be less visible or even disappear behind their professional combatants (representative of women's organization, interview 3).[2]

4.2 Challenges and limits

Despite its historical strength and international reputation, the Nicaraguan women's movement now faces a series of unique challenges effectuated by the hybrid regime.

---

[2] For a more detailed overview of the evolution of the Nicaraguan women's movement and feminism in Nicaragua, see also Collinson and Broadbent (1990), Isbester (2001), Kampwirth (2004), Luciak (2001), and Randall (1994). For a summary of the development of Nicaraguan civil society in general, see García Palacios and Ullua Morales (2010) and Serra Vázquez (2007, 2011).

4.2.1 Women's organizations and the state

Since its return to power, the current Nicaraguan government has tried to close or control public space, make it impossible for most parts of civil society to exert influence, and denied all kinds of dialogue (representative of women's organization, interview 3). Especially affected have been the self-appointed "autonomous" groups such as Movimiento Autónomo de Mujeres (MAM), which emphasizes independence from party political structures. The government uses different strategies to control the movement, from direct repression over co-optation to substituting them with organizations that are loyal to the government.

To legitimize its course of action, the Ortega government is spreading a demonizing discourse on civil society. CSOs – in particular disagreeable Nicaraguan organizations and international NGOs – are presented as targets of outside interference and agents of imperialist powers trying to take autocratic control of the country (civil society expert [CSO], interview 8). In this context, adversarial women's groups (i.e., the groups that explicitly criticize the Ortega government) have become a major target; they are accused, repressed, and condemned as the "incarnation of the evil" (Oettler 2010: 52). When asked about governmental repression, women's activists reported having their houses searched, being intimidated on the phone, prosecuted, criminalized, and accused of being "abortistas" and laundering money (Hamlin and Quirós Viquez 2011: 17). Even more effective seem to be what many women's activists have called attempts to "suffocate" them: the government constructed administrative barriers and harassed the organizations and individual feminist leaders (representative of women's organization, interview 1). For instance, attempts have been made to reduce the movement's resources by pressuring international donors and cooperation partners (representative of women's organization, interview 1). The government not only exacerbates the general flow of money by foreign donors or development agencies, but also pressures donors to stop giving money to certain organizations and to finance only the projects that have been approved (representative of women's organization, interview 1).

Regarding the strategy of co-optation, the government has made many attempts to attach women to party structures via social programs and controlled participation at the community level. And some of the traditional FSLN-loyal organizations, such as the famous Movimiento de Mujeres Nicaragüenses "Luisa Amanda Espinoza" (AMNLAE), which struggled for independence during opposition years, have rapidly returned under the party's thumb with the FSLN's return to power (representative of women's organization, interview 3). A vivid example of the government's intention to substitute or dispute present feminist organizations was the high-profile launching of a new countermovement called "Blanca Arauz" (named after the wife of party eponym Augusto César Sandino) in 2008. Nonetheless, this attempt to create alternative participation structures rapidly failed when the new movement – probably due to a missing proper agenda – soon sank into oblivion (representative of women's organization, interview 1). Altogether, these tense relations with the present government have made the self-proclaimed autonomous and feminist women's organizations the most belligerent advocate of civic action and democracy in Nicaragua, as well as more vulnerable than ever before.

4.2.2. Dependency on international cooperation

For Nicaraguan civil society and the women's movement, international cooperation has played a major role as a primary source of funding and support since the first solidarity movements in the 1980s. The support of various bilateral, multilateral, and private donors has been of immeasurable value for the development of the Nicaraguan CSO sector. Nonetheless, international support has its pitfalls; it has evoked criticism concerning the risk of artificial professionalization and project dependency, supposed post-colonialist interference and influence, and, last but not least, its promotion of a completely dependent CSO sector incapable of financial self-sustainment.

In addition to the difficult political situation and the restriction of public space, the withdrawal of international cooperation in the last years has posed a significant challenge to the CSO sector. Although the withdrawal of many European and American developmental organizations is connected to widespread confusion about the Ortega government's course and dismissive attitude, it is also due to the economic crisis in Europe and a general shift of interests to other regions such as North Africa (civil society expert [CSO], interview 2). All in all, a shortage of funds has led to the closure of several European embassies, a shrinking staff, the reduction of projects, and a careful selection of partner organizations based on political considerations. When asked to evaluate the consequences of the diminution of international cooperation, several women's activists lamented the "lack of commitment" (representative of women's organization, interview 3) to their organizations and criticized the donors for maintaining an unassertive attitude and buckling in the face of an autocratic government instead of supporting opposition forces (representative of women's organization, interview 3).

Dependence on international donors not only leads to substantial problems in times of dwindling funds but also affects the CSO sector as a whole. Many members of the women's movement have criticized the pressure of NGOization and required bureaucracy since the very beginning, in fear of sacrificing the historically diverse, open, non-hierarchical character of their movement to artificial, externally headed organizations. The conversion to NGO has forced many organizations to respond to multiple actors (national and foreign governments, international organizations, donors) (representative of women's organization, interview 6), which puts them at risk for losing sight of their original objectives. Also, many have developed highly professional yet elitist bodies, which are dissociated from their grassroots members. Last, critics claim that external funding has led to an artificial inflation in the sector with hundreds of small organizations springing up like mushrooms. These new CSOs tend to be highly dependent on the acquisition of projects and find it extremely difficult to develop a proper profile, which makes them even more vulnerable in times of reduced funding (civil society expert [CSO], interview 9).

In conclusion, the increasing withdrawal of international cooperation since 2007 has made the women's movement vulnerable: due to the absence of self-sustainability, there has been a general decline in organizations. Correspondingly, many activists state that the major challenge for the future will be to secure survival without international cooperation (civil society expert and donor, interview 7).

4.2.3. *Internal fragmentation*

A third challenge for the Nicaraguan women's movement is closely linked to the former ones, namely, the risk of internal fragmentation. Though the movement has been diverse and heterogeneous since its beginning, the persisting hybrid democratic structures have generated internal quarrels and competition, which endanger the movement's internal cohesion and historical strength (Oettler 2010: 54). Increased disunity seems to go beyond former struggles about priorities and can be traced back to several causes.

First, even though the movement has always been supported by diverse members, especially in terms of education and origin (representative of women's organization, interview 5), this has become particularly problematic in the current setting. Despite the movement's pride in their activists from all classes of society, today's most prominent leaders seem to belong to a small intellectual group, or a tiny middle class, whose representativeness for the majority of Nicaraguan women is highly questionable. Second, the pressure for NGOization and professionalization by international donors has caused disagreement about organizational forms and endangered the original character of the movement, as well as intensified competition for diminishing funding (representative of women's organization, interview 6). The most significant factor provoking internal quarrels and disunity, nevertheless, is the division along political lines or the different attitudes toward the present political context. Traditional Sandinista organizations adhering to the revolution as a legitimation for the present government can be seen alongside radical feminist networks protesting Ortega's presidency. Therefore, the movement seems to have been divided into different wings, which are defined not only by their disparate origins and working fields but also in view of their presumably conflictive impact on the existing gender order. The following section presents these findings in the form of a threefold typology, which are also summarized in Table 1.

4.3 Nicaraguan women's organizations and the present gender order: a typology

4.3.1 The "feminists"

The most salient wing of the Nicaraguan women's movement today consists of the self-proclaimed "autonomous" organizations gathered around the MAM and the feminist movement. Most of these groups have their roots in the revolution, but slowly alienated themselves from the Sandinista party due to disagreements about the role of women in the revolution (representative of women's organization, interview 3). Later, in the 1990s, the autonomization process was pushed forward and the "feminists" developed with a proper profile as fighting for women's rights and the modernization of a patriarchic, macho society. This wing is made up of feminist intellectuals, mostly highly educated women from the tiny Nicaraguan middle class. They gather together as individual activists or in groups in informal networks and organizations; they only seldom dispose of legal personality out of fear of losing their movement character or because it is downright impossible due to their contentious relationship with the government (representative of women's organization, interview 1).

An activist summarized their progressive agenda as the promotion of "equity and democracy, from a feminist perspective" (representative of women's organization, interview 1). The fostering of democracy is a central objective, as Nicaraguan feminists believe that their ideas are most likely to be realized in a democratic environment (representative of women's organization, interview 1). They fight for women's rights, some of which are highly controversial among Nicaraguans, like the right to therapeutic abortion, and they speak against the persisting machismo within the population and the political culture. They focus on cultural values and societal structures. In practice, they organize public debates, promote feminist education, host programs for leadership formation, and foster political mobilization for women's rights (representative of women's organization, interview 1).

As stated above, these groups have developed into the most critical and offensive opponents of the present government, and have thus become a target of repression and persecution (civil society expert [CSO], interview 2). As they expand their claims to the reconstitution of democracy, they are – in light of the decline of other political parties – the closest thing to political opposition for the present government. Faced with, in their words, an "unbearable" president, they have time and again not only clashed with the government but also with the more moderate divisions of the movement. Furthermore, they suffer most from the ongoing withdrawal and reservation of international donors. To avoid open confrontation, such donors tend to adapt their selection criteria and areas of interest to the government's will, even at the risk of reproducing and reinforcing governmental repression mechanisms (representative of women's organization, interview 3).

4.3.2 The "partisans"

A second wing of the movement is made up of CSOs characterized by their uncritical loyalty and closeness to the governing FSLN party, such as the historical organization AMNLAE as well other less prominent groups. These party-loyal organizations also have their roots in the revolution, which they see as the basis for the emancipation of women, but they never freed themselves from their Sandinista origin.

AMNLAE was founded during the fight against Somoza in the 1970s and became by far the strongest women's organization in the 1980s. It played a key role in "challenging traditional authority" (Kampwirth 2006: 76) and representing women's interests in the revolution. Nevertheless, with the revolution proceeding, their party loyalty began to impede their "ability to challenge gender inequality" (Kampwirth 2006: 76; Kampwirth 2011: 8). New movements and critical groups formed in response; they did not want to postpone their interests in favor of the supposed superior interests of the revolution (representative of women's organization, interview 3). The organization's uncritical support of the Sandinista government's idea of the organization of women – i.e., women should take over the duties of the men who have went off to war (representative of women's organization, interview 5) and concentrate on service provision – clashed with other, more progressive parts of the movement which continue until today.

Distancing themselves from the controversial term "civil society," AMNLAE and other government loyal CSOs refer to themselves as "social" organizations, thus emphasizing their focus on the population at large and local matters. Their work is focused on service provision and assistance to women in different fields, for example, with the upkeep of women's houses, medical attention, or workshops teaching them new skills. Their work tends to be based on rather traditional female images, as they support women in their work as mothers and homemakers, which often clashes with the feminist-wing ideology. The attitude of these organizations was fittingly summarized by one of their own activists: "Women are not interested in arguing, they want to resolve their problems, don't they?" (representative of women's organization, interview 5). Still, their complete loyalty to the present government is manifested in their restraint and subordination to the proper agenda when it comes to party political interests.

With Ortega's return to power in 2006, this part of the movement was quickly co-opted and reintegrated into FSLN party structures (representative of women's organization, interview 3), which transformed many CSOs into "satellite" groups of the present government (civil society expert and donor, interview 7). Consequently, these groups support, more or less, government policies or at least lack the autonomy to question or take a stand against potentially disagreeable or misogynous policies (representative of women's organization, interview 1). When asked about their motivation, they claimed that they needed the government in order to influence public policies (representative of women's organization, interview 1), and that they gain power via their closeness to a political party (representative of women's organization, interview 3), but admitted that they cannot revolt in the way their feminist counterparts do (representative of women's organization, interview 5). Many participants have indeed managed to achieve political posts as mayors or vice mayors due to their party membership. Still, it is highly questionable whether this official participation in the present regime context translates into real power to shape gender policies.

4.3.3 The "service providers"

A third group can also be made out, which has more or less successfully refrained from the political sphere and concentrates on service provision and assistance preferably in the fields of health and education. This wing of the movement has its roots in the boom of CSOs in the 1990s or later and includes international NGOs and their local counterparts. Most of them dispose of a legal personality and status as an NGO or at least cooperate with one officially registered organization in order to receive financial support from international cooperation. Their agenda is focused on the improvement of the living conditions and economic status of women. Such organizations work in the fields of medical attention or education; they aim to empower women financially via college credits or technical skills formation, among others. Their objective is restricted to providing practical and financial help for targeted groups, e.g., sexually abused women, women in rural areas, or single mothers. They focus directly on improving women's economic and social status while refraining from political involvement.

The "service providers" tend to avoid political interference and choose to work in rather less controversial fields. By improving the living standards of women, they believe the ensuing economic empowerment and modernization will foster a long-term transformation of the traditional gender order. Nonetheless, this type of organization risks letting the state off the hook and could even be said to support the present regime in the short run by disburdening it of its core function and preventing protest.

Table 1: Typology of women's organizations in Nicaragua

Types	Members / origin	Relation to government	Agenda	Role within regime
Feminists	Critical feminist Nicaraguan elite; movement character – intellectuals, activists; middle class women, distanced from population at large	Strongest critics (political opposition) of the present regime; target of criticism and persecution	Foster intellectual debates on rights, education, equality; fighting for democracy and a democratic gender order	Challenge the present regime and its gender order
Partisans	Traditional party-loyal mass organizations	Loyal to the FSLN party, subordinate their objectives to the government's agenda	More or less support the present government's traditional female images and lack a proper agenda	Reinforce the present regime and its gender order
Service providers	Internationally funded NGOs, in cooperation with local community organizations	Depoliticized, attempt to avoid struggle with government; disburden the state of its responsibilities	Project-oriented service provision and emergency assistance mainly in the fields of health and education; improving women's living conditions	Support bottom-up modernization of gender relations: but tolerate the present regime

Source: author

5. Conclusion

This chapter scrutinized the Nicaraguan women's movement and its contribution to societal modernization and democratization in the hybrid regime of Nicaragua. The research interest was built on the theoretical premises that, first of all, regime-hybridity is also manifested on the level of gender as a sphere of important societal power relations. Second, it is grounded in the idea that women's organizations can have a crucial share in the rupture of these hybrid democratic structures on the level of gender, if not within the political regime itself. However, the findings indicate that the Nicaraguan women's movement first and foremost faces a diverse set of challenges related to the present political context. These range from an omnipotent government trying to restrict, weaken, and shape civil society according to its own will and a historical dependency on international cooperation to an increasing internal disunity vis-à-vis the political regime.

The persisting regime hybridity seems to have led to a threefold division of the movement. First, there is the remaining belligerent, small feminist elite movement, which maintains its traditional role as a pioneer of democracy and gender equity. This wing has become increasingly isolated through the government's repression, the lack of international support, and their increasing distance from the population at large. The second division includes a set of organizations traditionally loyal to the Sandinista party that have been co-opted by the current president. They support the government's traditional image of women and seem to lack a proper agenda to foster societal change. The third group consists of professional NGOs and their local partner organizations, which are supported by international donors. These more than ever tend to focus on emergency action and service provision, mostly in the less controversial fields of health and education. Their agenda focuses on the long-term improvement of women's living conditions and societal modernization. Nevertheless, by doing so, they risk – at least in the short-term – tolerating current hybrid regime structures instead of challenging them and the traditional gender order.

As a whole, the hybrid regime context in Nicaragua seems to be weakening the historically strong women's movement by enforcing political polarization, fragmentation, and a shift toward less conflictive areas of interest. The different actors gathered under the movement have failed to develop a common strategy vis-à-vis the increasingly autocratic tendencies, and their disunity is maintained by intense economic competition for declining funding. The movement's belligerent tradition seems to be at stake due to a shift toward service provision and depoliticization within many organizations – at the expense of commitment to real societal change and the transformation of gender relations. Because women's organizations are focusing more and more on the concrete living conditions and long-term economic development of women, they risk losing sight of their feminist political agenda. At the same time, political repression and the loss of international support seem to mostly affect those still willing to fight, leaving the whole sector caught in a trap between "militancy and the struggle for survival" (representative of women's organization, interview 6).

References

Anheier, Helmut/Priller, Eckhardt/Zimmer, Annette (2000): Zur zivilgesellschaftlichen Dimension des Dritten Sektors. In: Zur Zukunft der Demokratie. Herausforderungen im Zeitalter der Globalisierung. Edited by Hans-Dieter Klingemann and Friedhelm Neidhardt. Berlin: Edition Sigma.

Berman, Sheri (1997): Civil Society and the Collapse of the Weimar Republic. In: World Politics 49, 3, pp. 401–429.

Bernhard, Michael/Karakoc, Ekrem (2007): Civil Society and the Legacies of Dictatorship. In: World Politics 95, 4, pp. 539–567.

Bob, Clifford (2011): Civil and Uncivil Society. In: The Oxford Handbook of Civil Society. Edited by Michael Edwards. Oxford: Oxford University Press.

Booth, John A./Seligson, Mitchell A. (2013): Political Culture of Democracy in Nicaragua and the Americas, 2012: Towards Equality of Opportunity. Nashville: Vanderbilt University Press.

Borchgrevink, Axel (2006): A Study of Civil Society in Nicaragua. Norwegian Institute of International Affairs, no. 699.

Bruneau, Thomas/Dammert, Lucía/Skinner, Elizabeth (2011): Maras: Gang Violence and Security in Central America. Austin: University of Texas Press.

Centro Nicaragüense de Derechos Humanos (CENIDH) (2013): Derechos Humanos en Nicaragua 2012. Managua: CENIDH.

Chambers, Simone/Kopstein, Jeffrey (2001): Bad Civil Society. In: Political Theory 29, 6, pp. 837–865.

Colburn, Forrest D. (2012): Nicaragua, Forlorn. In: World Policy Journal 29, 1, pp. 91–100.

Collinson, Helen/Broadbent, Lucinda (1990): Women and Revolution in Nicaragua. London: Zed Books.

Croissant, Aurel (2002): Von der Transition zur defekten Demokratie. Demokratische Entwicklung in den Philippinen, Südkorea und Thailand. Wiesbaden: VS Verlag.

Cuadra, Elvira/Jiménez, Juana (2011): El movimiento de mujeres y la lucha por sus derechos en Nicaragua. Movimientos sociales y ciudadanía en Centroamérica. Managua: CINCO.

Diamond, Larry (1994): Rethinking Civil Society. Toward Democratic Consolidation. In: Journal of Democracy 5, 3, pp. 4–17.
Diamond, Larry (2002): Thinking about Hybrid Regimes. Elections without Democracy. In: Journal of Democracy 13, 2, pp. 21–35.
Einhorn, Barbara/Sever, Charlotte (2003): Gender and Civil Society in Central and Eastern Europe. In: International Feminist Journal of Politics 5, 2, pp. 163–190.
Femenía, Nora Amalia/Ariel Gil, Carlos (1987): Argentina's Mothers of Plaza de Mayo: The Mourning Process from Junta to Democracy. In: Feminist Studies 13, 1, pp. 9–18.
Foley, Michael W/Edwards, Bob (1996): The Paradox of Civil Society. In: Journal of Democracy 7, 3, pp. 38–52.
García Palacios, Omar A./Ullua Morales, Chantal A. (2010): Las relaciones del gobierno de Nicaragua y la sociedad civil. Helsinki: Kepa's Working Papers no. 32.
Gilbert, Leah/Mohseni, Payam (2011): Beyond Authoritarianism: The Conceptualization of Hybrid Regimes. In: Studies in Comparative International Development 46, pp. 270–97.
Gómez Pomeri, Ricardo (2012): Nicaragua zwischen Absolutismus und Demokratie. Wiesbaden: VS Verlag.
Hamlin Zúniga, María/ Quirós Viquez, Ana (2013): Las mujeres en la historia de Nicaragua y sus relaciones con el poder y el Estado. Managua, Nicaragua: XII Congreso Latinoamericano de Medicina Social y Salud Colectiva "Crísis, aceleración y despojo en el capitalismo global. Avances y retrocesos en la lucha por la salud y la universalización de derechos."
Huntington, Samuel P. (1993): The Third Wave: Democratization in the Late Twentieth Century. Norman: University of Oklahoma Press.
Isbester, Katherine (2001): Still Fighting. The Nicaraguan Women's Movement 1977–2000. Pittsburgh: University of Pittsburgh Press.
Kaldor, Mary/Kostovicova, Denisa (2008): Global Civil Society and Illiberal Regimes. In: Global Civil Society 2007/8: Communicative Power and Democracy. Edited by Martin Albrow, Helmut K. Anheier, Marlies Glasius, Monroe E. Price, and Mary Kaldor. Los Angeles: Sage
Kampwirth, Karen (2004): Feminism and the Legacy of Revolution: Nicaragua, El Salvador, Chiapas. Athens: Ohio University Press.
Kampwirth, Karen (2006): Resisting the Feminist Threat: Antifeminist Politics in Post- Sandinista Nicaragua. In: NWSA Journal 18, 2, pp. 73–100.
Kampwirth, Karen (2011): Latin America's new Left and the Politics of Gender. Lessons from Nicaragua. New York: Springer.
Karl, Terry Lynn (1995): The Hybrid Regimes of Central America. In: Journal of Democracy 6, 3, pp. 72–86
Kocka, Jürgen (2004): Civil Society from a Historical Perspective. In: European Review 12, 1, pp. 65–79.
Koshar, Rudy (1987): From Stammtisch to Party: Nazi Joiners and the Contradictions of Grass Roots Fascism in Weimar Germany. In: The Journal of Modern History 59, 1, pp. 1–24.

Luciak, Ilja A. (2001): After the Revolution: Gender and Democracy in El Salvador, Nicaragua, and Guatemala. Baltimore: Johns Hopkins University Press.
Merkel, Wolfgang (2010): Systemtransformation. Eine Einführung in die Theorie und Empirie der Transformationsforschung. Wiesbaden: VS Verlag.
Morlino, Leonardo (2009): Are there hybrid Regimes? Or are they just an optical illusion? In: European Political Science Review 1, 2, pp. 273–296.
Murphy, Jonathan (2011): The Dark Side. In: Third Sector Research. Edited by Rupert Taylor. New York: Springer.
Obuch, Katharina/Sandhaus, Jasmin/Wilde, Gabriele/Zimmer, Annette (2013): Alles verändert sich, damit es bleibt, wie es ist. In: Journal Netzwerk Frauen- und Geschlechterforschung NRW 33, pp. 48–53.
Obuch, Katharina (2017): Civil Society Organizations in the Hybrid Regime of Nicaragua: Challenging or Maintaining the Status Quo? Baden-Baden: Nomos.
Oettler, Anika (2010): Die Regierung im Konflikt mit der Frauenbewegung. In: Der neue Sandinismus in Nicaragua. Autoritärer Selbstbedienungsstaat oder neues Entwicklungsmodell? Edited by Ivo Schnipkoweit and Timm B. Schützhofer. Universität Kassel: OneWorld Perspectives.
Pizarro, Ana Maria (2003): We Urgently Need a Secular State for the Sake of Women's Health. In: Envio 266 (Sept. 2003), pp. 29–38.
Pollack, Detlef (2003): Zivilgesellschaft und Staat in der Demokratie. In: Forschungsjournal Neue Soziale Bewegungen 16, 2, pp. 46–58.
Prieto-Carrón, Marina/Thomson, Marilyn/MacDonald, Mandy (2007): No More Killings! Women Respond to Femicides in Central America. In: Gender and Development 15, 1, pp. 25–40.
Randall, Margaret (1994): Sandino's Daughters Revisited: Feminism in Nicaragua. New Brunswick, NJ: Rutgers University Press.
Reiber, Tatjana (2009): Demokratieförderung und Friedenskonsolidierung. Die Nachkriegsgesellschaften von Guatemala, El Salvador und Nicaragua. Wiesbaden: VS Verlag.
Roth, Roland (2003: Die dunklen Seiten der Zivilgesellschaft. In: Forschungsjournal Neue Soziale Bewegungen 16, 2, pp. 59–73.
Schobel, Kurt/Elsemann, Nina (2008): Das politische System Nicaraguas. In: Die politischen Systeme in Nord- und Lateinamerika. Edited by Klaus Stüwe and Stefan Rinke. Wiesbaden: VS-Verlag.
Schnipkoweit, Ivo/Schützhofer, Timm B. (2008): Editorial. In: Der neue Sandinismus in Nicaragua. Autoritärer Selbstbedienungsstaat oder neues Entwicklungsmodell? Edited by Ivo Schnipkoweit and Timm Schützhofer. Universität Kassel: OneWorld Perspectives.
Serra Vázquez, Luis (2007): La Sociedad Civil Nicaragüense. Sus organizaciones y sus relaciones con el estado. Managua: Centro de Análisis Socio-Cultural Universidad Centroamericana.
Serra Vázquez, Luis (2011): Civil Society Index for Nicaragua. Restrictions and the Politicization of Civic Space. Challenges for Civil Society in Nicaragua. Managua: RNDDL/CIVICUS.

Stepan, Alfred/Linz, Juan (2013): Democratization Theory and the 'Arab Spring.' In: Journal of Democracy 24, 2, pp. 15–30.

Tocqueville, Alexis de (1985): Über die Demokratie in Amerika. Stuttgart: Reclam.

Tusalem, Rollin F. (2007): A Boon or a Bane? The Role of Civil Society in Third- and Fourth-Wave Democracies. In: International Political Science Review 28, 3, pp. 361–386.

Warren, Mark E. (2011): Civil Society and Democracy. In: The Oxford Handbook of Civil Society. Edited by Michael Edwards. Oxford: Oxford University Press.

Wnuk-Lipinsky, Edmund (2009): Civil Society and Democratization. In: The Oxford Handbook of Political Behavior. Edited by Russel Dalton and Hans-Dieter Klingemann. Oxford: Oxford University Press.

Zinecker, Heidrun (2011): Civil Society in Developing Countries – Conceptual Considerations. In: Journal of Conflictology 2, 1, pp. 1–18.

The Tunisian Constitution between Democratic Claim and Constitutional Reality

Gabriele Wilde and Jasmin Sandhaus

1. Introduction

Thirty-seven months after the beginning of the so-called Arab Spring, a good three years after the self-immolation of Mohamed Bouazisi on December 17, 2010, the new Constitution of Tunisia was adopted on January 26, 2014 with a vast majority, 200 votes in favor out of a total of 216 votes cast (12 against, 4 abstentions) (see Ostry 2014: 1).

The Constitution is divided into a preamble and 149 articles, which regulate and formulate the essential questions regarding the form of government, the national identity, and the role of women, strictly put, all the required and necessary statements about the political framework that identifies Tunisia as a constitutionally established civil and republican state.

Is Tunisia therefore on the way to a democratic political society? The question arises primarily in connection with the finding that constitutional texts are no more and no less than written ideas and intentions about the way policy should be made and with what content, and in which form political decisions should be made. Accordingly constitutions mainly provide information about the political objectives, but not about the reality of written policy. Therefore, in order to be able to make statements about potential of the Tunisian Constitution for democratic gender relations (Hergenhan 2015), it is necessary at this point to question the constitutional reality and its social and political conditions.

A research project on gender relations in authoritarian and hybrid regimes carried out at the Centre for European Gender Studies (ZEUGS) at the University of Münster dealt with the question of the function of gender relations for the stability and legitimacy of autocracies. The guiding research in this context is an understanding of autocracies as political systems in which the distribution of political influence and agency among the citizens is prevented and egalitarian gender relations are considered destabilizing for the political system.

Based on this view the chapter reflects – after a presentation of the essential content of the Constitution – Tunisia's democratic potential on three different levels: In the first step, the development process of the Constitution and the actors who appear in the political public sphere are viewed: How is political power distributed, who participates in the constitutional process, and which political actors determined the work of the constituent assembly?

In the second step, the participation of the civil society organizations is examined: How are civil society actors and groups integrated in the political process? To what extent do they represent pluralistic ideas and opinions? And to what extent were they involved in the public political discourse and decision-making and in what form?

Then, in the third step, the Constitution's contents are illuminated: What conceptions and meanings of equality, freedom, and justice form the normative framework for political decisions in the future? What views on gender differences and gender relations are reflected in the respective articles of the Constitution? To what extent are traditional values reflected in these views? What ideas remain excluded? What are the gaps and missing pieces? From there, the challenges are outlined that arise on the basis of the recognition of democratic politics in Tunisia.

2. Key content of the Constitution

The preamble and the first article do indeed define Islam as the state religion; at the same time, in opposition to that demanded by the Ennahda, Sharia was not incorporated in the Constitution as the legal foundation (see Antonakis-Nashif 2013: 3). Rather, the emphasis of the republic as the valid form of political organization indicates the significant role that was explicitly granted in the Constitution (see Ostry 201: 2f.) to universally applicable human rights:

Tunisian Constitution between Claim and Reality 167

"In the name of God, the All-merciful, the very merciful, we represent Tunisian people, members of the Constituent National Assembly, elected due to the revolution of dignity, freedom, and justice ...

With the aim of building a participatory-democratic republican regime in which the state will be civil and based on institutions, in which the sovereignty belongs to the people ..., thanks to the principle of division of power ... in which the right to organize is established on the principles of pluralism, neutrality of the administration, good governance, and free elections as the cornerstone of political competition, in which the exercise of power is based on the respect for human rights and freedoms, the supremacy of rights, the independence of the judiciary, justice, and equality in rights and duties of the citizens, as well as within all social classes and regions ...

In consideration of the dignity of humankind, that the cultural and civilization-determined belonging to the nation, which emerges from the national unity, which is based on the middle class, brotherhood and solidarity ...

We, in the name of the people, by the grace of God, create the following Constitution."[1]

The first two articles of the Constitution possess eternal character and cannot be changed (see Ostry 2014: 2f.). With that said, the serious endeavor of the political actors became undoubtedly clear: to create a framework for Tunisian society that corresponds to the traditional cultural foundations, as well as the democratic demands placed on modern societies; in Article 1 and 2 of the Constitution the text states:

"Tunisia is a free state, independent and sovereign, Islam is its religion, Arabic its language, and the Republic its order. These articles may not be altered." (Article 1)

"Tunisia is a country with civilian character, based on citizenship, the will of the people and the supremacy of rights. These articles may not be altered." (Article 2)

Furthermore, the role and the independence of Parliament were strengthened: "The people exercise the legislative power through their representatives in the

---

[1] So far there are no authorized translations of the Tunisian constitutional text formulated in the Arabic language. All quoted passages were translated on the basis of the French constitutional text (http://www.tunisie-constitution.org/fr) by Alexia Duten, Research Assistant at the Institute for Political Science at the University of Münster, into the German language and then, for the purpose of this English edition, translated by Joseph Rodriguez, an independent translator, from German into English.

'Assembly of the Representatives of the People' or by referendum" (Article 50). From now on the Parliament itself has the formal right to bring forth legislative initiatives as well as to monitor government action and to decide on the state budget.[2]

The offices of the president and the prime minister have been retained. While the prime minister of the executive stands in the head position, the president has a relatively strong position, which goes beyond purely representative functions. Elected directly by the people, he has policy-making power in the area of foreign policy as well as in security issues, can declare a state of emergency, and can call a no-confidence vote against the government:

> "Laws can be initiated by a proposal of at least ten lawmakers or by draft legislation proposed by the president or the head of government.
>
> The head of government is responsible for the introduction of draft legislation that pertains to the ratification of treaties and the budget proposal. These bills are to be treated as a priority." (Article 62).

Even the independence of the judicial branch was secured on several points. Although the "Ennahda" spoke out against it, for the first time in Tunisian history the legality of the laws is examined by a constitutional court (see Article 120).

The division between the executive and judicial authorities will also finally be ensured in that, for example, the judges are no longer nominated by the minister of justice, but rather by a new "High Council of the Judiciary" (Article 112) and are appointed by the president (see Ostry 2014: 5):

> "The judges are appointed by an enactment of the president, in accordance with regulations of the High Council of the Judiciary.
>
> The appointment to the high judicial offices is carried out by order of the president after consultation from the head of government and is based on an exclusive list that is presented by the High Council of the Judiciary. The law determines the high judicial offices" (Article 106).

In addition to the articles on freedom of opinion, thought, expression, information and publication (Article 20), and freedom of religion (Article 6), the formal ruling for women's equality in Article 20 can be rated as a milestone

---

2   See Article 50 and 62 of the Tunisian constitution.

for an Arab country. Moreover, the intention to promote equal opportunity for women and to guarantee an equal representation in elected bodies seems progressive in regional comparison (see Antonakis-Nashif 2013: 4).

3. The distribution of political power in the constitution-making process

Since the fall of Ben Ali on January 14, 2011, Tunisia has without question taken consistent steps toward a democratic system. This is already demonstrated by the fact that political actors succeeded in October 2011 – only nine months later – to carry out legitimate, free, and open elections for a constitutional assembly (see Preysing 2013: 54).

For many this alone serves as an indication of the democratic transition in Tunisia, and the publicness of the electoral process, which was overseen by 180 European election monitors (see MOEU 2011: 4), and leaves no doubt about the serious intentions of political actors to constitute Tunisia as a civil and democratic state. In this regard, especially in the initial stage, "a struggle for legitimacy and political direction" defines the political reality (Preysing 2013: 49; translated by authors). The need for stability was accompanied by an exploration of the most diverse political movements and led to the development of numerous institutions.

One of the most important was undoubtedly the formation of a National Council for the Protection of the Revolution (*Conseil National de protection de la revolution* [CNPR]). This establishment, which was founded on February 11, 2011 and was composed of representatives from a total of 28 political parties and civil society organizations, explicitly called for collaboration in the political formation of Tunisia's future (see ICG 2011: 13; Paciello 2011: 15; Zemni 2014: 11).[3]

---

3   The following 28 organizations participated in the CNPR: 1. Le Conseil National des Avocats, 2. L'Union Générale Tunisienne du Travail (UGTT), 3. Forum démocratique pour le travail et les libertés, 4. Parti Communiste des ouvriers de Tunisie, 5. Le Courant Baa'siste ,6. Ennahdha, 7. Le Mouvement du Peuple, 8. Le Mouvement des Patriotes Démocrates, 9.

With this aspiration the CNPR ultimately proved to be a driving force toward the first transitional government Ghannouchi and successfully set up speedy elections to the constitutional assembly, the *Assemblée Nationale Constituante* (ANC). The importance of this organization was demonstrated not at least by the fact that only a month later it became a part of the "High Authority for Achievment of the Goals of the Revolution,Political Reforms and Democratic Transition". From that point in time this designated organization, also known as "High Authority," acted as a kind of steering committee which prepared the election laws that were finally enacted on May 10, 2011 by the transitional government (see Zemni 2014: 6f.).

Crucial to the new law regarding election to the constitutional assembly was that in addition to the conditions for a proportional (in ratio) right to vote and a (gender) equal representation of electoral candidates, members of the former Tunisian unity party of Bourguiba and Ben Ali, the *Rassemblement constitutionelle démocratique* (RCD), were excluded (see Zemni 2014: 6). There were no further restrictions – they apparently wanted to give the pluralistic groups and diverse political movements the opportunity to participate, which ultimately led to the admission of a total of 77 political parties in the election for the constitutional assembly on October 23, 2011. Given this high number of parties, about half of which made it in the ANC, it was quite surprising for many that the Islamist party Ennahda won the elections with 42% of votes. This party, which under Ben Ali was prohibited in 1989, together with the social-liberal party *Congrès pour la Republique* (CPR) and the center-left party

---

Le Mouvement Baa's, 10. Association internationale pour le Soutien aux Prisonniers Politiques, 11. Ligue de la Gauche Travailliste, 12. Le Congrès pour la République, 13. Le Mouvement Unioniste Progressiste, 14. Le Parti du Travail Patriotique et Démocratique, 15. Associa- tion des Magistrats Tunisiens, 16. Union des Diplômés Chômeurs, 17. Organisation Liberté et Équité, 18. Parti de Tunisie Verte, 19. Syndicat National des journalistes Tunisiens, 20. L'Amicale Nationale des Anciens Combattants, 21. Le Courant Réformateur pour le Développement, 22. Union Générale des Étudiants Tunisiens, 23. Le parti Populaire pour la liberté et le Progrès, 24. Gauche Indépendante, 25. Centre Tunisien pour l'indépendance des Magistrats et des Avocats, 26. Les Patriotes Démocra-tes, 27. Ligue des Écrivains Libres, 28. L'Association Tunisienne de Lutte contre la Torture (cf. Chaker o.J.: 7).

Ettakatol formed the transitional government in the form of a troika (see Loetzer 2012: 13).[4]

A look at the final composition of the ANC further shows that traditional political parties and movements predominated: On the one hand in the form of parties that already existed under Ben Ali, such as the *Ettakatol* and the CPR, which together with the *Ennahda* formed the leadership, or the Party of Democratic Socialists (*Mouvement des Démocrates Socialiste* [MDS]); on the other with newly founded parties by political actors who were close to the old regime, such as the *Al Aridha* party founded by Mohamed Hashim Hamdi. New reformist parties were merely the PDM – the modern Democrats – an electoral alliance with which the center-left and secular *Ettajdid* party, which was established in 2007 and had emerged from the former communist Party, also associated itself, and the patriotic Democrats (MPD) – a Marxist-Arab national party, whose Secretary General Chokri Belaïd was murdered (see Loetzer 2012: 8ff.). The democratic party (PDP) can be seen as another reformist, secularly aligned party, which under Ben Ali was exposed to the strongest restrictions and still counted as the biggest competitor of Ennahda before the election of the ANC (see Loetzer 2012: 7).

Despite the election law requirement to fill the electoral ballots equally with both sexes, the inclusion of women in the ANC corresponded to rather traditional ideas. The predetermined parity was only implemented by one party, *Al Qotb,* and insufficiently at that, while other parties granted women a distinctly weaker position (see Dalmasso and Cavatorta 2013: 236).

One reason for this is clearly that the parity principle did not pertain to the candidates or the ranks on the ballot lists. As a result, 93% of the chief positions on the list were filled by men, while women mostly occupied the lower ranks (see Tunisia Live 2011b). In the end a total of 49 out of 217 seats in the ANC

---

4   The Islamist party Ennahda (Al Nahda), which received 42% of the votes in the elections, shared the leadership of the ANC with the social-liberal, secular Congrès pour la Republique (CPR), which was founded in 2001, prohibited in 2002, and legalized after the revolution, and received 13.4% of votes. The third party in the leadership is the secular-oriented, center-left party Ettakatol. Also known as Forum démocratique pour le travail et les libertés (FDTL), this party, already founded in 1994 and legalized since 2002, received 9.2% of votes.

were filled by women, 42 of them were members of the Ennahda, one of whom later became vice-president of the ANC (see NDI 2012: 8).

The most important Tunisian women's organization, *Association Tunisienne des Femmes Démocrates* (ATFD), founded in 1989, was denied participation in the ANC, although it was involved in the "High Authority" (see ICG 2011: 27). In the end, the proportion of women in the ANC was 22.7%, about the same as under Ben Ali (see Joline 2012: 14). The results of the distribution of political power among the "former, traditional, and male" actors are ultimately shown by their enormous influence on the drafting of a constitution. From a total of six commissions that were formed for the respective constitutional main points, the Ennahda took over the chair in three commissions, indeed that of the "Preamble," of the "Bill of Rights," and of the "Regional Authorities," while the social liberal CPR, the Ettakatol, and the democratic PDP, each with one chair, split the main points regarding the arrangement of "legislative and executive powers" of the "justice system" and the "constitutional bodies" (see Pickard 2012: 2).

4. The participation of civil society organizations in the Tunisian constitutional process

In a general sense the involvement of civil society organizations in the political process is seen as an indication of democratic structures. By the middle of the twentieth century, however, the Italian politician Antonio Gramsci (1991) pointed out the importance of investigating the closeness of civil society organizations to government parties and the government system. In his analysis of the great influence and success of National Socialism in Germany and Italy, he drew particular attention to the significant role civil organizations played in the implementation of the national socialist ideology. Beside the question of which civil society actors participated in the Tunisian constitutional process, Gramsci's approach leads particularly to the question of the way in which they take part, that is, whether the respective organizations act in more of a consensus-producing manner in accordance with the ruling forces or actually represent a political countervailing power.

In Tunisia it was generally the case that the participation of the civil society in the constitutional process took place rather informally, especially in the form of demonstrations and protest campaigns that exerted influence on the course of the constitutional process, the decisions, and reforms (see Antonakis-Nashif 2013: 1). The mobilization of the civilian public occurred through social media such as Twitter and Facebook, to which at least one-third of the population had access (see Penner-Angrist 2013: 548f.). They undoubtedly contributed to bringing "the struggle for the wording in the draft of the constitution to the streets" – as Anna Antonakis-Nashif (2013: 3; translated by authors) formulated in her report on the legitimacy and constitutional crisis in Tunisia.[5]

An institutional inclusion of civil society organizations in the constituent process however was very limited; there is at best the discourse from a "cautious" inclusion of portions of civil society (Preysing 2013: 49). This took place particularly within the framework of the CNPR and with its inclusion in the "High Authority," in which, in addition to the parties, unions, and associations, representatives of regional groupings of the women and youth movement and families of martyrs were involved (see Paciello 2011: 15; Zemni 2014: 11).

5. Union Générale Tunisienne du Travail (UGTT)

In addition to the social networks and the participation of various civil society organizations, above all Tunisia's leading union, the *Union Générale Tunisienne du Travail* (UGTT), counts as the main actor of organized civil society

---

5 An example of this is the action by Selma Mabrouk, a member of the Commission for Rights and Freedoms in the ANC, who left the Ettakatol after the first decision regarding the complementary clause and published the wording of the controversial Article 28 on her Facebook page, even before it was officially announced, and thereby mobilized civil society actors. Because of this, a limitation of gender equality in the second draft of the constitution was able to be prevented (see Antonakis-Nashif 2013: 3).

(see Yousfi 2013: 23).[6] It not only contributed significantly to the spread of the demonstrations and the ever-increasing pressure on the people in political power, but it also played a leading role in the institutionalization of the ANC and was the initiator for the convening of the National Dialogue Forums, which ultimately led to the passage of the constitution (see Antonakis-Nashif 2013: 4).

The organization of the three National Dialogue Forums was a reaction to the ANC's lack of progress in the drafting of the Constitution. In addition, the civilian population and political opposition also criticized the draft bills of individual articles in the Constitution. Three crucial incidents in particular threatened the constituent process: First was the entrenchment of the complementarity of the sexes in the constitution demanded by the Ennahda, which means that women are not to be considered equal but merely complementary to men (see Marks 2013: 237). Furthermore the two murders of the opposition politicians Chokri Belaid and Mohamed Brahmi paralyzed the work of the ANC (see Khalil 2013: 7). All the National Dialogue Forums were organized from a quartet, to which, besides the UGTT, three other civil society organizations belonged: the employers' association UTICA *(Union Tunisienne de l'Industrie, du Commerce et de l'Artisanat)*, the Tunisian human rights league LTDH *(Ligue tunisienne des droits de l'homme)*, and the bar association (see Omri 2013).

The first National Dialogue Forum initiated the quartet in October 2012, after the ATFD and large parts of the population protested vehemently against the Ennahda's adherence to traditional role models (see Zeghal 2013: 270). This meeting between the represented parties in Parliament and the four civil society actors was, however, boycotted by the Ennahda and the CPR (see Antonakis-Nashif 2013: 4).

A second Dialogue Forum was convened by the interim President Moncef Mazourki on April 14, 2013 in response to the political stagnation after the murder of Belaid. The fact that the strongest party in the ANC, the Ennahda,

---

6   The UGTT was founded in 1946 and was the only union in Tunisia until the fall of Ben Ali. It is managed in the form of an executive council and currently includes 500,000 to 600,000 members. Abdessalem Jerad was Secretary General until after the fall of Ben Ali. Acting Secretary General is Houcine Abassi.

officially condemned the murder, but could not free itself from the numerous allegations of being entangled in the crime, made the collaboration in the constituent assembly considerably more difficult (see Khali 2013: 7). It may be the reason why the UGTT did not participate in this second forum.

The third and decisive National Dialogue Forum was convened on October 25, 2013. Preceding these talks had been the second murder of Brahmi, which triggered violent riots again and led to 60 out of the 217 delegates giving up their work in the ANC, whereupon Mohammed Ben Jaffar, the current president of the ANC, completely suspended the work in the ANC on August 6, 2013 until September (see Antonakis-Nashif 2013: 4ff.). Subsequently, the UGTT called for the establishment of a new technocratic government under the leadership of Medi Jomaâ in order to continue the constitutional process. Indeed, the vote was boycotted by 11 of the 21 participants, according to press reports in the media, because they assessed Jomaâ as being close to the Ennahda (see taz 2013). Surprisingly, the Ennahda approved the proposal and on January 9, 2014 turned over the responsibility of government in favor of a technocratic cabinet. This included 22 ministers and 7 secretaries of state, whose seats were limited to the preparation of the parliamentary and presidential elections, while at the same time a reelection was ruled out from the outset. This promised an acceleration of the negotiations free from partisan antagonisms and political struggle (see Ostry 2014: 6f.).

The dominant role that the UGTT played as political actor within the constitutional process, both in the media and in the scientific literature, is seen as indisputable (see Omri 2013; Ostry 2014: 6); its role as a democratic actor, however, remains questionable.

The UGTT exemplifies the fundamental ambivalence in the struggle for political power and political interests. Thus, a civil society organization can only exercise influence when it combines the interests and demands of the civilian population, but at the same time involves itself in the conditions of the political apparatus of power in order to bring about something with its initiatives. This ambivalence becomes particularly clear in autocratic regimes, and during the time of Bourguiba und Ben Ali it brought about the success story of the UGTT, founded in 1946, the only trade union permitted until the fall of Ben Ali. While the leadership level of the member-greatest and largest trade union with its nearly 600,000 organizers can definitely be described as infiltrated by the respective dictators and close to the regime, regional levels, such as the federations for health, the postal system, education, as well as various local sub-organizations were able to maintain their independence as far as possible (see Bellin 1995: 130; Yousfi 2013: 24f.).

This entrenched inconsistency in the UGTT also continued in the role that it took during the revolution. In this regard, it represents a conflicting nature like no other civil society organization. Its endeavor to be recognized by both those in political power and civil society also pushed the UGTT within the scope of the constitutional process into an ambivalent political power game: As a *political actor* always close to the regime, the UGTT was the only civil society organization whose members as independent agents in the ANC codetermined the discourse of the Constitution without being institutionally incorporated as legitimate and elected political actors.

As the *civil society* actor with the most members, however, the UGTT is considered an informal critic of the work in the ANC and created an alternative political stage with the National Dialogue Forums, on which political actors and civil society should perform together, but without granting the various civil society groups formalized, transparent, and fair access. The National Dialogue Forums hence developed as the central place for political discussions, while the work of other civil society groups and women's organizations has been marginalized. This becomes very clear by the suppression of their role in the constitutional process in both the media coverage and in the scientific literature (see Omri 2013).

As the *voice of civil society*, the UGTT fueled the protests of the civil population, called for a general strike on April 14, 2011 (see ICG 2011: 6), and pooled their diverse interests in the framework of dialogue forums without actually making the results discussed in the forum binding for the political actors. As an independent civil society member of the ANC, the UGTT's initiatives alone are therefore considered to be quite formative in nature.

And, finally, the UGTT entered the struggle for credibility as a *democratic actor* vehemently for gender equality and the promotion of equal opportunity in the Constitution and considered this as a basic structure for a modern Tunisia. In contrast, these principles in its own organizational structure, as well as in the National Committee of Women's Workers, which represents the interests of women who to date work predominantly in the informal sector, in the textile industry, or in health and education fields (see Solidarity Center 2013), have not been implemented. A plan is indeed in place to introduce a quota for women in elected bodies, but whether this also applies to the executive council of the highly centralistic organized UGTT (see Yousfi 2013), in which so far no women are to be found, although they represent 48% of the members, remains to be seen (see Solidarity Center 2013). Ultimately, this is also dependent on the political implementation of the equality rights for women that were determined in the Constitution.

6. Effects of the Tunisian constitution for democratic gender relations

The Tunisian constitution formulates an abundance of equality and liberty rights that expressly and explicitly take into account gender equality and equal opportunities for women. The formal equality of women takes place in Article 20:

> "The citizens (male and female) are equal in their rights and obligations. They are equal before the law without any discrimination. The state guarantees citizens freedom and individual and collective rights. It ensures the conditions necessary for a humane life."

Additionally, Article 45 ascribes further rights to women:

> "The State strives to protect the rights of women, to support them and improve them. The State guarantees equal opportunity between women and men, in order to fulfill different responsibilities in all domains. The State acts to ensure parity between women and men in elected assemblies.
>
> The State takes the necessary measures to eradicate violence against women. Moreover, the State declares it is willing to promote equal opportunity for women by ensuring equal representation within elected bodies."

Progress also means equality in the right of inheritance, which appears in Article 20. Men have had the advantage on this issue since the independence, despite progressive women's rights, and were entitled to a significantly larger part of the inheritance (see Weber 2001: 24f.).

Without question the new constitution can contribute to an "empowerment" of women, especially in peripheral regions where the way of life is strongly oriented toward traditions and therefore traditional gender roles have manifested to a greater degree. Nevertheless, the constitutional expert Salwa Hamrouni makes a clear and dramatic assessment in an interview with the *Deutsche Welle* when she states: "This is a schizophrenic constitution which contains one thing and its opposite, so that everyone is satisfied in the end" (see DW 2014; translated by authors). What is interesting is that despite the increased appreciation of the role of women, the Constitution also retains the family as the central authority of society (see Ostry 2014: 2ff.). Pertaining to the family Article 7 states: "The family is the essential core of society and the State should provide for its protection."

In her book on gender contract, the British political scientist Carole Pateman (1988) has called attention to the way in which the establishment of separate rights for the private family sphere limits the validity of public equal rights for women.

The risk of the constitutional protection of the family contributing to the establishment of unequal gender relations emerges in particular with the divorce law and in the context of the special protection of life in Article 21: "The right to life is sacred, only in extreme cases, which are regulated by law, can it be compromised." This article can restrict women's right to self-determination – as the German abortion debate in the 1980s and 1990s, for example, made clear (see Wilde 2001). More aggravating for Tunisian women is that in the future a constitutional court will verify the validity of the basic civil rights and liberties, but at the same time there will be no possibility to appeal on a constitutional issue (see Ostry 2014: 2–5). It is also problematic that the constitution contains no anti-discrimination law – so there is no explicit legal protection against unequal treatment for Tunisian women to date, such as in the labor market. Political regulations are not provided with regard to equality or against discrimination and exclusion.

The consequences that can arise for egalitarian gender relations have already been shown in connection with the Code du Statut Personell (CSP) under

Ben Ali. Unlike Bourguiba, who first and foremost reformed the traditional family structure with the introduction of CSP and improved the status of women through the abolishment of polygamy and the possibility of divorce (see Weber 2001: 24f.), Ben Ali used women's rights and politics regarding women as a political-strategical struggle against Islam. The promotion of women, strengthening of women's rights, and the establishment of the ATFD and their participation in the World Conference on Women in 1995 were measures that served primarily to weaken the Ennahda and its support among the populace and distract from its repressive politics toward the West (see Weber 2001: 35f.). Actually the strengthening of women's rights did not change the social position of women decisively. Even though Ben Ali filled central and high-ranking positions with women, such as vice-president of the parliament or as political advisor (see Brand 1998: 242), this hardly led to the formation of gender-equitable, egalitarian, and alternative public spheres. The progressive women's rights have contributed to an increased visibility of women in the Tunisian public sphere, but neither their role nor their image has changed. The greatest cause of this is Ben Ali's neoliberal economic policy, which impelled women to increase their responsibility for the family and their dependence on men (see Murphy 2003: 183f.). The confirmation of the power relationships in the family by the CSP, which attributed a superior position to men in accordance with Islamic law and put the family under the control of the state (see Sadiqi 2008: 460), counteracted the public role of women as actors with equal rights. Women had to reckon with harassment if they moved about in public or used public transport (see Murphy 2003: 183), without having the rights to be able to take legal steps against this discrimination and unequal treatment.

Even the increasing number and visibility of women's organizations in the public realm had little or no impact on their capacity to act or their transformative potential, because the women's organizations were either close to the government and therefore to its policies, were funded directly by the cultural affairs or women's ministry, or were heavily restricted by the repression of Ben Ali (see Murphy 2003: 186). The public space still remained a male-dominated sphere, whose access often remained closed to women, for instance, party meetings that took place on premises only accessible to men (see

Kandiyoti 2011; Kerrou and Najar 2009). The women's organizations that appeared on a public level, like the *Club d'Etude sur la Condition des Femmes,* were often exposed to hostilities from the government, but also from men and the media, since they violated the traditional conventions (see Weber 2001).

This little recourse by the CSP illustrates the consequences that arise when different rules and rights apply to women in the public domain than in the private family domain. At the same time the politically-strategical expansion of women's rights under Ben Ali shows that formal equality rights in the Tunisian Constitution are indeed a necessary but not sufficient condition for democratic gender relations. This is also pointed out in the Gender Gap Report of the World Economic Forum, which indeed grants Tunisia a high rank among the Arab States, 108 out of 135, but simultaneously documents that in reality the formal gender equality in the Constitution has still not been implemented (see Bertelsmann Stiftung 2014). This ultimately requires political measures and reforms that enable women to take action against discrimination. Only with this empowerment, as the philosopher Hannah Arendt (1991: 462) put it, will women be granted the right to have rights.

7. Challenges for future Tunisian politics – a conclusion

The Tunisian Constitution draft reflects, on the one hand, the political conflicts that characterized the ANC and the entire country after the escape of Ben Ali, and, on the other, documents the attempt to reach a collaboratively supported solution as quickly as possible. A redistribution of power or even greater transparency, however, it is not.

Without a doubt numerous demands of a variety of political parties, civil society groups, and those of the demonstrating populace streamed into the constitutional text. Nevertheless, the former, old, familiar, and male political actors had and still have the final word. This concerns both the political power structure and the enormous influence of the UGTT as the dominant civil society organization. It deals with a phenomenon that can also be observed in other transitional societies, for example, in Egypt, Afghanistan, Hungary, and currently in the Ukraine. To revert back to the experiences of the familiar, established groupings with their power games and integrate them into the new system is not fundamentally wrong; however, at the same time there is a great danger that the reforms will be defeated by traditional conceptions and remain connected to a political culture that, instead of taking plurality, diversity, and the difference between citizens into account, aims toward a prescribed homogeneity and shies away from democratic conflict.

Therefore, measured against the postulate of a just distribution of political power to act, it cannot be said that the Constitution came about in a democratic fashion. Nevertheless, it exhibits all the features of a political framework that are necessary for a democratic reality. Whether this opportunity is seized, however, depends on several factors.

Many have made the economic development of the country the priority. Without question, subsidies and opening the country to foreign companies and investors are important prerequisites for consolidating the treasury depleted by Ben Ali's clan and thereby combatting the high unemployment and poverty. In contrast, others see a condition for democratic development and reform in the policies of education, health, gender equality, and social matters in the free and open elections. That alone, however, will not suffice to justify Tunisia as a democratic society. This requires, as the Belgian political scientist Chantal Mouffe (2007; 2000) maintains, radical democratic structures of a discursive public that are open to all civil society and political actors. For this, it is essential to have a strong parliament that does not ignore social pluralism and is ready to handle the conflicts that arise in the face of differing views of justice, equal opportunities for participation, and individual self-determination. In our view, this is the most important and urgent democratic challenge that the Tunisian society has to face in the near term, if it is to become what it wants to be: a democratic society.

References

Antonakis-Nashif, Anna (2013): Legitimitäts- und Verfassungskrise in Tunesien. Zuspitzung durch politische Morde und die Entwicklungen in Tunesien. SWP-Aktuell, 49. http://www.swp-berlin.org/fileadmin/contents/products/aktuell/2013A49_atk.pdf (13.02.2018)

Arendt, Hannah (1991): Elemente und Ursprünge totaler Herrschaft. München/Zürich: Piper.

Bellin, Eva (2005): Civil Society in Formation: Tunisia. In: Norton, A. R. (Ed.): Civil Society in the Middle East. Leiden: Brill, pp. 120-147

Bertelsmann Stiftung (2014): Das letzte demokratische Ausrufezeichen – Faktencheck Tunesien. http://www.bertelsmann-stiftung.de/cps/rde/xchg/bst/hs.xsl/nachrichten_121408.htm. (13.02.2018)

Brand, Laurie (1998): Women, the state, and political liberalization: Middle Eastern and North African experiences. New York: Columbia University Press.

Chaker, Houki (o.J.): Les conseils pour la protection de la revolution.

Dalmasso, E./Cavatorta, F. (2013): Democracy, Civil Liberties and the Role of Religion after the Arab Awakening: Constitutional Reforms in Tunisia and Morrocco. Mediterranean Politics, 18, 2, pp. 225-241.

Deutsche Welle (2014): Tunesiens widersprüchliche Verfassung. http://www.dw.de/tunesiens-widerspruechliche-verfassung/a-17385867. (13.02.2018)

Hergenhahn, Jutta (2015): Geschlechterdemokratie in der postrevolutionären Verfassung Tunesiens. In: Femina Politica 24, 1, pp. 65-72.

International Crisis Group (2011): Popular Protest in North Africa and the Middle East (IV): Tunisia's Way. Middle East/North Africa Report No. 106.

Joline, Courtney (2012): Women in Post Revolutionary Tunisia: Political Inclusion and Prospects for the Future. ISP Collection.

Kailitz, Steffen/Köllner, Patrick (2013): Autokratien im Vergleich. Politische Vierteljahresschrift, Sonderheft 47.

Kandiyoti, Deniz (2011): Promise and peril: women and the 'Arab spring'. http://www.opendemocracy.net/5050/deniz-kandiyoti/promise-and-peril-women-and-arab-spring. (13.02.2018)

Kerrou, Mohamed/Najar, Sihein (2009): Recherche action sur la participation politique des femmes au niveau local en Tunisie, UN-INSTRAW.

Khalil, Lydia (2013): Trends in a tumultuous Region. Middle East after the Arab Awakening. ASPI Strategic Insights (64). https://www.aspi.org.au/publications/strategic-insights-64-trends-in-a-tumultuous-region-middle-east-after-the-arab-awakening/SI64_MiddleEast.pdf

Loetzer, Klaus (2012): Tunesien und die erste islamistisch geführte Regierung in Nordafrika. KAS Auslandsinformationen 3. http://www.kas.de/wf/doc/kas_30490-544-1-30.pdf?120315175758. (13.02.2018)

Marks, Monica (2013): Women's Rights before and after the Revolution. In: Gana, Nouri (Ed.): The Making of the Tunisian Revolution. Contexts, Architects, Prospects. Edinburgh: Univ. Press, pp. 224-251.

Mission d'Observation Electorale de l'Union européene (2012): Rapport final: Election d'Assemblé Nationale Constituante 23rd Octobre 2011. Brüssel. http://www.eueom.eu/files/pressreleases/english/rapport-final-moe-ue-tunisie-2011_fr.pdf. (13.02. 2018)

Mouffe, Chantal (2000): The Democratic Paradox. London/New York: Verso.

Mouffe, Chantal (2007): Über das Politische. Wider die kosmopolitische Illusion. Frankfurt a.M.: Suhrkamp.

Murphy, Emma (2003): Women in Tunisia: Between State Feminism and Economic Reform. In: Doumato, Eleanor/Posusney, Marsha (Eds.): Women and globalization in the Arab Middle East: gender, economy, and society, Boulder: Lynne Rienner, pp. 169–194.

National Democratic Institute (2012): Tunisia's National Constituent Assembly. Gender Assessment.

Omri, Mohamed-Salah (2013): Trade Unions and the construction of a specifically Tunisian protest configuration. http://www.opendemocracy.net/mohamed-salah-omri/trade-unions-and-construction-of-specifically-tunisian-protest-configuration. (13.02.2018)

Ostry, Hardy (2013): Konfiszierte Revolution. Tunesien zwei Jahre nach dem Sturz Ben Alis. KAS Länderbericht. http://www.kas.de/wf/doc/kas_33276-1522-1-30.pdf?130124155932. (13.02. 2018)

Ostry, Hardy (2014): Neue Verfassung für Tunesien tritt in Kraft. Unikat und Kompromiss zugleich. KAS Länderbericht. https://www.kas.de/wf/doc/kas_36837-1522-1-30.pdf. (13.02. 2018)

Paciello, Maria Cristina (2011): Changes and Challenges of political transition. MEDPRO Technical Report No.3. Brüssel. http://www.medpro-foresight.eu/system/files/MEDPROTRNo 20WPPacielloonTunisia.pdf. (13.02.2018)

Pateman, Carol (1988): The Sexual Contract. Cambridge: Polity Press.

Penner Angrist, Michele (2013): Understanding the Success of Mass Civic Protest in Tunisia. The Middle East Journal 67, 4, pp. 547-564.

Pickard, Duncan (2012): Lessons from Constitution-Making in Tunisia. Atlantic Council Issue Brief. http://www.atlanticcouncil.org/images/files/publication_pdfs/403/mec121213tunisia.pdf. (13.02.2018)

Preysing, Domenica (2013): Tunesien: Vorreiter des Aufbruchs, Vorbild des Wandels? In: Jünemann, Annette/Zorob, Anja (Eds.): Arabellions. Zur Vielfalt von Protest und Revolte im Nahen Osten und Nordafrika. Wiesbaden: Springer VS, pp. 43-66.

Sadiqi, Fatima (2008): Facing Challenges and Pioneering Feminist and Gender Studies: Women in Post- Colonial and Today's Maghrib. In: African and Asian Studies 7, 4, pp. 447-470.

Solidarity Center (2011): Keine Frau im neuen Vorstand der UGTT. http://www.solidaritycenter.org/Files/Tunisia.EnglishFinal.bug.pdf; http://survey.ituc-csi.org/Keine- Frau-im-neuen-Vorstand-der.html?lang=en (13.02.2018)

Taz (2013): Neuer Premierminister in Tunesien. Ohne Parteibuch, ohne Begeisterung. http://www.taz.de/!129418/. (13.02.2018)

Tunesische Verfassung (2014): http://www.tunisia-live.net/2011/10/28/women-status-in-the-constituent-assembly/ (non-authorized translation) (13.02.2018)

Tunisia Live (2011a): UGTT elects new Executive Bureau. http://www.tunisia-live.net/2011/12/29/ugtt-elects-new-executive-bureau/. (13.02.2018)

Tunisia Live (2011b): Women's Status in the Constituent Assembly. http://www.tunisia-live.net/2011/10/28/women-status-in-the-constituent-assembly/. (13.02.2018)

Weber, Anne F. (2001): Staatsfeminismus und autonome Frauenbewegung in Tunesien. Hamburg: Deutsches Orient-Institut.

Wilde, Gabriele/Schneider, Silke (2012): Autokratie, Demokratie und Geschlecht: Geschlechterverhältnisse in autoritären Regimen. In: Femina Politica 21, 1, pp. 9-16.

Wilde, Gabriele (2001): Das Geschlecht des Rechtsstaats: Herrschaftsstrukturen und Grundrechtspolitik in der deutschen Verfassungstradition. Frankfurt am Main: Campus-Verlag.

Yousfi, Hèla (2013): UGTT at the Heart of a troubled Political Transition. In: Puschra, Werner/ Burke, Sara (Eds.): The Future We The People Need. Voices from New Social Movements in North Africa, Middle East, Europe & North America Friedrich-Ebert-Stiftung. International Policy Analysis, pp. 23-28.

Zeghal, Malika (2013): Competing Ways of Life: Islamism, Secularism, and Public Order in the Tunisian Transition. In: Constellations 20, 2, pp. 254-274.

Zemni, Sami (2014): The Extraordinary Politics of the Tunisian Revolution: The Process of Constitution Making. In: Mediterranean Politics 20, 1, pp. 1-17.

"I'm here too, Girlfriend ... ": Reclaiming Public Spaces for the Gendering of Civil Society in Turkey

Joyce Marie Mushaben

1. Introduction

Headed by religious conservative Prime Minister Recip Tayyip Erdoğan (Justice and Development Party [AKP]), the Turkish government took a repressive, hard-line approach to many societal protests linked to the Gezi Park occupation of May 2013. Although Turkey has experienced many ups and downs involving the rule of law, the latest wave of excessive state force has been inflicted by the very party credited with constitutional-legal reforms that were to pave the way for its admission to the European Union. Then, as now, Erdoğan sought to blame the unrest on extremist "others" intent on destroying the "indivisible unity" of the nation. Ironically, his highly charged rhetorical efforts to divide and conquer the protestors while consolidating his own "50%" base produced the opposite effect. Visiting Istanbul at the height of the Gezi protests in June 2013, Germany's Green Party leader Cem Özdemir expressed surprise at the motley assortment of students, Kurds, Alevis, atheists, Muslims, leftists, secularists, nationalists, environmentalists, human rights activists, and even soccer teams sharing intense conversations between waves of teargas, water cannons, and police beatings. He concluded, "One almost has to congratulate Erdoğan. Because of him, people have come together here who would normally be at each other's throats" (Hürriyet Daily News 2013).

Turkey has encountered many potholes along its long road to democracy since 1959, but a renewed application for EU membership submitted by Prime Minister Turgut Özal in 1987 granted it access to many externally funded initiatives focusing on gender equality, minority rights, and civil society formation through the 1990s. EU rules mandating cooperation among conflicting groups have profoundly affected not only the country's ties to the outside world but also internal societal relationships. Satisfied that it had solved "the Women's Question" with Kemalist reforms granting females the right to vote, run for office, and engage in paid labor in the 1920s, the Turkish state exhibited little tolerance for real-existing societal differences along ethnic, religious, and ideological lines. Throughout the 1980s and 1990s, appeals to Turkish nationalism regularly pitted secularist-feminists against Kurdish women and female religious groups over issues ranging from headscarves to honor killings, preventing a united gender-rights front. Paradoxically, the military coup of 1980, as well as the election of the "Islamic" Justice and Welfare Party (AKP) in 2002, opened new avenues for civil society collaboration among equality advocates of all sorts, even as more young women began to practice *hejab*, legalized in 2008. This study examines the changing nature of female participation in Turkish civil society, as well as the changing relations among once antagonistic women's groups, attributable not only to processes of Europeanization but also to generational change, new educational opportunity structures, and the rapid diffusion of new communication technologies.

Three factors appear to have played a crucial role in "building bridges" among once antagonistic societal forces in Turkey as of the 1990s. The first involves *demographic change*, coupled with the rapid expansion of higher educational opportunity along "Bologna" lines.[1] As of 2012, the population numbered roughly 76 million, 43% of whom are under 24; nearly half were born after the 1980 coup that produced a brutal crackdown on right-wing and leftist parties. By 2009, the share of young women and men attending higher educational institutions had risen to 32.6% and 33.4%, respectively (Ruthenberg et al. 2012: 4). Although per capita GDP has more than doubled ($10,800), 18% live below the poverty line; youth unemployment exceeds 20% (Steinvort 2013). Given Turkey's expanding economy, younger cohorts can be expected to trigger a "revolution of rising expectations."

---

1   The Bologna process requires EU member-states to align undergraduate and graduate degree programs to foster mutual recognition of professional qualifications across national boundaries, facilitating the "free movement" of labor.

Gendering of Civil Society in Turkey 187

The second element centers on *EU conditionality*, coupled with new forms of cross-cutting cooperation introduced by a wide variety of international and local NGOs. Turkey's blossoming *project culture* has triggered the professionalization of civic activism, the emergence of new political groups, the reshuffling of societal strata, and the forging of collaborative relationships among once adversarial associations (Kuzmanovic 2010). Surveys indicate that while millions are losing faith in the ever more authoritarian AKP, they are simultaneously gaining confidence in their own ability to reshape the country, as manifested in the mushrooming of post-Gezi "park fora," comparable to European "citizen initiatives" of the 1980s.

The third factor driving democratization in Turkey pertains to the growing assertiveness of women themselves, even in Anatolia and the Kurdish regions, where females encounter collective stereotypes portraying them as backward, religious, uneducated, or, even worse, as "barefoot and pregnant." Reflecting the experience of equality activists in other hybrid states, Turkish women quickly learned to leverage support from international institutions to shame, blame, and otherwise motivate their own leaders to undertake constitutional and statutory reforms. By depoliticizing and externalizing their demands, they ironically opened the doors to women's groups whose lifestyles are generally at odds with their own but whose needs are also shifting due to the neo-liberal economic policies of their own party, the AKP.

Globalization and EU accession processes have reconfigured Turkey's socioeconomic landscape since the 1990s; the latter has laid the foundation for a genuine civil society, core elements of which manifested themselves through the Gezi park protests. I begin with a review of major reforms adopted in response to *EU conditionality*, before and after the AKP assumed power in 2002. While 2005 brought a marked slowdown in top-down efforts to meet *acquis* requirements, one also observes an internalization of EU norms and values from below, characterized by Nick Manning as "cognitive Europeanization" (Manning 2007: 497). I illustrate this with a treatment of changing relations among women's groups operating outside the formal EU negotiation process. I conclude with thoughts on the gendering of public space embodied by the Gezi Park demonstrations and women's special role in driving "generational change." We commence with legal reforms set in motion by Turkey's desire to join the EU, an entity Western feminists themselves long rejected as "a rich man's industrialist club" (Valance and Davies 1986) – until they grasped its extraordinary potential for enhancing gender equality across the member states (Abels and Mushaben 2012).

2. Necessary but not sufficient: EU conditionality

The 2013 protests that began as a tree-saving exercise in Gezi Park mirror social movement trends witnessed on other continents (Mushaben 2014). Compounding various globalization pressures are the countless legal, democratic, and socioeconomic demands Turkey must meet in order to become a full-fledged EU member. Resting on thousands of pages of regulations, directives, and court verdicts known as the *acquis communautaire*, EU conditionality entails a multi-stage negotiation process. Turkey's association with the Community dates back to 1959; it was the only state to acquire full membership in the Customs Union in 1995, well before the CEE countries were accorded candidacy status. Repeated military interventions (1960, 1971, 1980, 1997, 2007) triggered intermittent tensions, but its repeated applications for membership could not be rejected outright, based on the 1963 Ankara Agreement.

The 1999 Helsinki Summit and Council approval of Turkey's *National Program for Adoption of the Acquis* (2001) opened the door to formal negotiations in 2004. The EU extended candidate status in October 2005, hinting that Turkey could complete the process by 2014. A tripartite coalition consisting of the Democratic Left Party (DSP), the Nationalist Action Party (MHP), and the Motherhood Party (ANAP) initiated the first of many reforms, starting with thirty-plus amendments to the postcoup Constitution of 1982. The most nationalist of the three, the MHP, opposed minority rights and elimination of the death penalty; it supported active suppression of Kurdish terrorists and rejected moves by other groups against "the indivisible unity of the state."

A constitutional amendment obliging the state to advance equality, along with a new Civil Code (2001), accorded women the same rights as men regarding divorce and child custody. The government's willingness to promote "a

Gendering of Civil Society in Turkey 189

reform package dealing with extremely sensitive issues while a party that has the most radical views on these was a coalition partner" came as a surprise even to EU officials (Müftüler-Baç 2005). In December 2002, the Commission ruled that Turkey had fulfilled the "basic" Copenhagen Criteria, leading to further financial assistance. Despite the EU's 1996 adoption of gender mainstreaming, neither the Commission nor the Council noted Turkey's problems with violence against women in early evaluations: The 2003 Progress Report devoted only two paragraphs to honor crimes and violence, compared to thirteen pages on minority rights. The Commission did not stress gender inequality as a significant obstacle until 2004, later exploited to justify member-state *Turcoscepticism* over "cultural differences" (Müftüler-Baç 2005; Canan-Sokullu 2001). It is thus not surprising that the AKP "tends to interpret gender equality issues as a mere box-ticking exercise in compliance with the EU accession agenda" (Dedeoglu 2012: 274).

A successor to the outlawed *Refah* (Welfare) Party, the Justice and Development Party (AKP) quickly recognized "democratization" as a vehicle for pursuing a religious agenda. Elected in 2002, it used "minority" and "human rights" discourse to advance its own understanding of religious freedom, e.g., women's right to *hejab* at state universities.[2] Reaping the benefits of earlier economic restructuring, the AKP adopted six more EU-impelled reform packages between 2003 and 2004. Focusing on "good governance" and institutional capacity-building, the first encountered little resistance; it liberalized laws on freedom of speech, cultural expression, and association. The second extended political, cultural, and welfare rights to Kurds, comprising roughly 18% (13.3 million) of the population.[3]

The AKP moreover reduced the military's formidable control over security-related decision-making and financial and civilian affairs via the Council of Higher Education, the Communication High Council, and the Supreme Board

---

[2] A 2008 law revoked a constitutional ban on religious symbols, especially Muslim headscarf use in public spaces (e.g., at universities), framed as a question of fundamental individual freedom. See Göçek (1999) and Hancock (2008).

[3] The 1982 Constitution contained no references to minority rights beyond Article 42, which barred any language but Turkish as a "mother tongue"; as ethnic groups, Kurds, Kirmanchis, Zazas, and others were "non-existent."

of Radio and Television (Özal 2012). Penal Code revisions eliminated the death penalty in 2005. Judicial reforms made it harder to ban political parties, outlawed torture and repealed Article 8 of the Anti-Terror Law, used to imprison journalists for "crimes against the indivisible unity" of the Republic.[4] The Turkish state adopted nine constitutional reform packages between October 2001 and June 2004. Given the deep cleavages between modernizers and reactionaries, the proactive response to EU conditionality was nothing short of "remarkable" (Müftüler-Baç 2005: 28). Progress slowed considerably after 2005, however, leading the Commission to recommend a suspension of negotiations by late 2006.

The AKP's gender policy record has been quite mixed, becoming less woman-friendly since its 2011 reelection. Early Civil and Penal Code revisions granted women and men the "same" rights to marital property, but subsequent welfare reforms reinforced the family as the focus of women's existence, undercutting other types of economic security. The 2003 Labor Law banned sexual harassment and discrimination based on marital status but offered no support structures to reduce the "double burden." Companies employing over 150 women are supposed to establish day care facilities, but now firms deliberately limit the number of women they hire (Dedeoglu 2012: 283).

In 2004, women rallied against an AKP bill to reinstate a sexist adultery law (Ilkkaracan 2004). The 2005 Penal Code criminalized domestic violence, marital rape, and genital examinations ("virginity tests") undertaken without a prosecutor's consent but denied consent-rights to women themselves.[5] Lawmakers amended Article 10 of the Constitution to read: *Women and men are equal. The state has the responsibility to ensure the implementation of these rights.* In 2010, however, the AKP added: *Measures for children, the elderly, the disabled, widows of injured and martyred soldiers and officers, and war veterans should not be regarded* [as] *against the principle of equality.* Some eighty women's organizations opposed the addition, which reframed women as persons in need of "special protection." Curiously, the state does not supply

---

4   With limited effect: see Alemdar, as well as Amnesty International (2012).
5   The law had previously made distinctions between "virgin" and "non-virgin" victims when sentencing males for offenses against women's bodily integrity (e.g., abduction, rape, child abuse, abortion, pornography, prostitution, and adultery).

Gendering of Civil Society in Turkey 191

special protection where it is really needed: domestic violence is most pervasive in the rural east and southeastern regions. The 2005 Law on Municipalities requires areas with more than 50,000 residents to open women's shelters; by 2009, only 19 of 244 municipalities had complied, offering 54 shelters for 40 million women (Coşar and Yeğenoğlu 2011: 563).

The AKP's willing embrace of neoliberalism, actively promoted by the IMF and EU actors, has altered the interface between its nationalist and religious aspirations. Erdoğan openly blames modern welfare state policies (reducing female dependence on men) as well as feminist efforts to secure women's individual rights "for the increasing dissolution of the ... rationalised nuclear family." He disparages feminists as "instigators of moral corruption" for "playing against nature and ... disrupting the natural order of the family" (Coşar and Yeğenoğlu 2011: 560). Under the 2003 Labor Law and the 2008 Law on Social Security and General Health Insurance, married women are to engage in flexible, part-time or home-based work. The government even drew up a "Daily Working Plan of the Working Woman" according to which female laborers, simultaneously exhorted by Erdoğan to produce at least three children each, are expected to submit to an exhaustive daily schedule in order to incorporate domestic affairs into the workday, amounting to over 15 hours in total. Under this time schedule, women are expected to wake up and clean the house in ten minutes (06:00–06:10), to do "personal cleanup" and "to rest" for 30 minutes after work (18:30–19:00), to ensure that dinner finishes in 15 minutes (19:30–19:45), to prepare dinner for the next evening in an hour (20:15–21:15), and to tidy rooms in 15 minutes. Only after that are they given time for personal work and rest (Coşar and Yeğenoğlu 2011: 566).

Accounting for 52% of the population, women comprise 24% of Turkey's paid labor force. Although it ranked third-last among OECD states (2010) in higher educational enrollments, the share of women attending tertiary institutions rose to 32.6% (Ruthenberg et al. 2012: 4). Female labor force participation nonetheless *declined* from 72% in 1955, to 28% in 1988 (shrinking agricultural sector), to 22% in 2008. Two-thirds of working women hold jobs not covered by the social security system (Dedeoglu 2012: 277–78; Munin 2011). Whereas single, divorced, or widowed women could previously access health care through their employed fathers, dependent daughters now only enjoy this option until age 25, well before they enjoy secure labor market status. They now face stigmatizing means tests. Roughly 36% of all citizens lack health care coverage, despite the AKP's introduction of a green card system for the poor, largely covering Kurds (Kilic 2008: 491). Despite its *National Action Plan for Gender Quality, 2008–2013*, the AKP defines poverty as a problem of development rather than as the result of discrimination.

Women have much to gain from EU membership, which will bring *equal treatment, positive action,* and *gender mainstreaming* to bear on Turkish employment policies. Although EU conditionality jump-started democratic reforms, its promise of full membership has been losing credibility, halting reform processes (Avci and Çarkoğlu 2011). Awarded the European Parliament's Sakharov Prize in 1995, Leyla Zana nonetheless argued that once-jailed activists like herself "would rather be imprisoned in a Turkey negotiating with the EU than one that was not" (Müftüler-Baç 2005: 16–30). Erdoğan's reaction to Gezi Park protests rested on an erroneous belief that he could reassert control over a new generation by invoking his own "religious" authority and appealing to parents to call their children home. Neither group is about to comply.

Meeting with leaders of women's associations to promote his "Democratic Opening for the Kurdish Issue," Erdoğan categorically declared in July 2010, "Women and men cannot be equal. They are complementary. I do not believe in women–men equality. I am for equality of opportunity."[6] The Prime Minister attributes both Islamic "holiness" and nationalistic solidarity to Turkey "as naturally constituted, historically fixed states of being." As one Gezi protestor noted, "The whole world knows that it's about more than just a park and police brutality. The government's list of sins is long." A thirty-three-year-old artist likewise declared, "When it comes to women, the prime minister talks about our bodies as if they belonged to him. ... He dictates to us how many children we should have and he wants to ban abortions, and yet he does nothing against the so-called honor killings, and against the daily acts of violence against women."[7]

---

6   Quoted in Coşar and Yeğenoğlu (2011: 566).
7   The Prime Minister also wants to ban caesarian section operations. Quoted in Steinvort (2013).

Younger women are more sensitive to predatory practices against the environment, destruction of old neighborhoods, unregulated capitalism, the intimidation of minorities, the arrest of journalists, prohibitions on alcohol sales (but not in profitable tourist areas), "and even kissing in public."[8] Thus, the push for gender equality in Turkey has developed a dynamic of its own. It is not only the usual feminist suspects who want more effective participatory venues but also the group who party officials insisted "have not been and will never be enslaved to feminist ideology": female AKP parliamentarians and Islamist women.[9]

3. The fallacy of "one-size-fits-all" feminism: women's mobilization in Turkey

While Western feminists have long criticized "white male theoretical canons" and historical norms classifying women's needs as "special interests," they also display hegemonic tendencies relative to non-western gender movements. As Gundrun Axeli Knapp cautions, "fast travelling concepts" like *intersectionality* ("race, gender class, et cetera") are quickly "abstracted from their epistemological premises, and stripped of their concretion, context and history" by scholars more interested in global theories than in local practices (Knapp 2005: 254). Imposing its own ideational paradigms, academic feminism often judges women's movements elsewhere as less advanced, despite their equally long "history of bargaining with patriarchy" (Knapp 2005: 557). This trend has been reinforced by the NGOization of gender campaigns, allowing international donors to dictate the definitions, indicators, and timetables applied to *equality*. Lacking relevant language skills, I have tried to overcome this ideational gap

---

8 Erdoğan even referred to Atatürk, an avid *raki* drinker, as a "drunk." He insists that the national drink is *ayran* (yogurt), but most Turks would probably opt for çay (tea). See Blaser (2013).

9 The full quote reads: "We do not support the conflict that is created by feminist thought between women and men. The women of [AKP] have not been and never will be enslaved to feminist ideology." Fırat, cited in Cosar and Yeğenoğlu (2011: 564).

by drawing almost exclusively on the works of Turkish scholars writing in English or German.

According to Deniz Kandiyoti, feminist movements in Turkey had no choice but to recognize nationalism as "the leading idiom through which issues pertaining to women's position in society" had to be articulated for many decades (Kandiyoti 2010: 166). Dating back to 1923, Atatürk and his Republican successors insisted on a mono-cultural framework for Turkish identity that denied legitimacy to but could not prevent violent clashes among single-cleavage groups, defined in terms of right vs. left, secular vs. religious, or majority culture vs. ethnic minorities. Paradoxically, the 1980 coup opened a window of opportunity for paradigmatic shifts in consciousness and strategy among women's organizations. Saime Ozcurumez and Feyda Sayan Cengiz stress that the "structural shock" inflicted by the military's ban on all right/left associations and parties reconfigured the institutional setting that had long dictated how women's groups were required to act to ensure their own survival within the system (Ozcurumez and Sayan-Cengiz 2011).

The bottom line, as Gül Aldikaçti Marshall notes, is that the societal awakening that has given rise to summers of discontent in Istanbul, Ankara, Izmir, and beyond owes less to "European modernizers leading recalcitrant Turks out of ignorance and obscurity ... through top-down political reforms" than to women reclaiming their agency based on a self-empowering civil society (Necati Polat, cited by Johansson-Nogués and Jonasson 2011: 114.). In contrast to the country's established political and bureaucratic elites, Turkish women were ready, willing, and able to advance once the EU opened the door to democratic transformation: "They knew what they wanted and what had to be done to accomplish their aims ... The long-term discursive struggle that marked the 1980s and 1990s allowed feminists to develop agendas and tactics that they could use when the time was right in the 2000s," despite occasional steps backward under the dominant AKP (Marshall 2013: 12).

The Progressive Women's Association, for example, was created under orders from the Turkish Communist Party (TCP) in 1975; comprising a TCP auxiliary, its 20,000 female members had to frame their demands for legal, political, and educational equality in terms of class, secularism, and Kemalism. The military's shutdown of preexisting partisan and civil society associations after 1980 "opened up space" for a new wave of feminists to articulate particularistic demands, "emancipated if still unliberated" from a "national good" that ignored the private sphere and everyday life (Kandiyotin 1987). Wary of attracting political attention during the repressive postcoup years, women convened consciousness-raising sessions under the guise of tea parties, then in the form of charity foundations. Successfully lobbying for Turkish ratification of the Convention on the Elimination of All Forms of Discrimination Against Women (CEDAW) in 1986, they established information centers, gender studies programs, and feminist journals, then moved on to domestic violence and other issues linked to *women's rights as human rights.*

The human rights master-frame, deriving from state ratification of CEDAW and the Beijing Action Platform, supplied international and national legitimacy; it handed equality activists a crucial instrument for identifying shared problems and sources of oppression, e.g., a strong state that persistently claims it represents "the best interests of the people despite the people" (Arat 1999: 378). Individual female activists functioned as effective brokers, capable of constructing bridges and steering reconciliation among mutually hostile organizations. They utilized confidence-building techniques to meliorate suspicion and mistrust, cultivating a willingness to dialogue (Negron-Gonzales 2012). The early 1990s saw a shift from formal to substantive equality demands. The mere existence of competing and conflicting groups helped to pluralize public space and open alternative venues for women's democratic mobilization (Arat 1999: 371).

Military moves that crushed the right, the left, and religious parties after 1980 created an associational vacuum that women were able to fill because their activities, e.g., lobbying for CEDAW, were "deemed politically insignificant" (Arat 1999: 374). Building on Yesim Arat's categorizations, I delineate five distinct groups who are coming together on some fronts, their major ideological differences notwithstanding.

4. The "Saturday Mothers"

Roughly 300 mothers first assembled in the central district of Galatasaray, Istanbul, on May 27, 1995, to protest a lack of information about relatives who had "disappeared" in police custody. Reconvening every Saturday, they relied on their silence and maternal roles to legitimate demands for individual rights. State officials claimed that the missing were in prison or off fighting with the Kurdistan Workers' Party (PKK) in East Anatolia. Engaged in a violent campaign against the PKK, they waited until summer 1996 to try to shame the Saturday protestors by gathering "Friday mothers" to stand at the grave sites of sons killed fighting the militants. Persistence among the former attracted media attention, as well as recognition from Amnesty International and the International Human Rights Association: In 1996 the European Parliament accorded the Saturday Mothers the Carl von Ossietzky Medal.

The General Directorate of Security sent a van called the "Mobile Center to Search for Lost People," but women refused to "register" the names of missing relatives. On September 6, 1998, the state deployed its police forces, declared their protests illegal, and took several mothers into custody. As Arat argued, Turkey's longest civilian protest to date, lasting 173 weeks, conveyed the lesson that "mothers no more belong (sic) to the house, but to the streets." This lesson would be taken up again in summer 2013 (Arat 1999: 376).

5. Kemalist women and secular feminists

Like the women formerly associated with the TCP, Kemalists were constrained by the nationalist paradigm, with its absolute commitment to secularism and republicanism. As the self-appointed modernization agent, the Republic's claim that women and men enjoyed the same constitutional rights rendered equality activists dependent on the state; the former blocked earlier efforts to create a Women's People Party in 1923 as well as an autonomous Union of Turkish Women (1935). "State feminism" has trapped these activists in a double bind: public *qua* constitutional rights to education, employment, and

Gendering of Civil Society in Turkey 197

political participation have not transformed deeply embedded gender expectations that women remain completely responsible for children and household management.

Kemalist feminists proved quite resistant to forging alliances with Islamist women. Secularists actively opposed the Welfare Party-True Path coalition headed by the first female Prime Minister, Tansu Çiller, who had courted the female vote but ruled, in her own words, "like a man."[10] Usually urban, well-educated, and professionally engaged, these equality advocates are well connected to NGOs, having rallied 51 of them for a Women's Walk against Sharia in 1997. Another 80 NGOs protested the 2008 Social Security Law for promoting maternal roles and ignoring unpaid household labor. They took vehement stands against Muslim headscarves, seeing them as the thin-edge-of-the-wedge for propagating patriarchal religious values through AKP and Gülen infiltrated bureaucracies, educational institutions, and civil society structures (Arat 2010).

Some fears were well-founded: Sunni-oriented religious instruction is now required in public schools, while relations between gender "state machinery" and women's groups seriously deteriorated under the AKP. The Directorate General on the Status and Problems of Women (KSSGM) was established in 1990 to monitor CEDAW requirements. Chronically understaffed and underfunded, the Directorate is little inclined to cooperate with feminist groups. In 2007, for example, Director Nimet Cubukcu received faxes from 54 secular advocacy groups condemning her "backward, discriminatory behavior." Contrary to CEDAW expectations, the AKP has combined or transferred various KSSGM functions to other agencies responsible for children, the elderly, the disabled, and the veterans' relatives.

Since 1997, civil society associations have nonetheless collaborated in drawing up "shadow reports," offering critical correctives to state submissions to the UN Committee on Status of Women. Participating organizations include the Federation of Women Associations of Turkey, founded in 1976. This organization pulls together entities such as The Association for Researching and

---

10 Feminists accused Çiller of providing proof that "no one dies because of lies." See Arat (1998).

Examining Women's Social Life; the Turkish Women's Council; Turkish University Women; associations involving Ankara Women's Health, Women Artists, and Ankara's Business and Professional Women; others center on Ankara Women Painters, the Protection of Women's Rights, the Çamlıca Girl Schools, and Cooperation with Village Teachers. Both UN and EU officials rely heavily on these shadow reports, realizing that the Turkish government "has had a tendency to frame every legislative change as a complete and fully satisfactory improvement of women's rights" (Marshall 2013: 129). Other groups, like the Equality Watch Committee, Women for Women's Human Rights/New Ways, Purple Roof, the Women's Solidarity Foundation, Flying Broom, and the Women's Centre (KAMER) engage in lobbying the state. According to Feride Acar, Gülbanu Altunok, and Elif Gözdaşoğlu-Küçükalioğlu (2008: 33–34), most, unfortunately, "do not take intersectionality into account."

In 2004 a consortium of women's civil society organizations applied for and attained formal membership in the European Women's Lobby, even before Turkey acquired EU–candidate status. Attempts to build "solidarity beyond borders" creates tensions, however, between entities big and "professional" enough to secure grants and those that are not. "Lobbying and advocacy [have] become the territory of those who can come to be known as experts," ignoring those pursuing repetitive field work on a voluntary basis, more typical of religiously motivated women (Kuzmanovic 2010; Hassan 2011; Negron-Gonzales 2012).

6. Islamist women and "feminists of faith"

Women mobilizing on behalf of their own religious rights were also constrained for decades by "non-fraternization" rules vis-á-vis secularist organizations. Muslims began campaigning against headscarf bans on university campuses enforced by the Commission of Higher Education after 1987. New forms of activism split this segment into strict conservatives who want to "serve society" in accordance with traditional religious dictates and reformists seeking leadership opportunities, and/or women-friendlier interpretations of religious texts (Hassan 2011). Describing herself as "a feminist with faith," lawyer Sibel Eraslan has urged women to recognize that "neither husbands nor state authorities have legitimate authority over them: there is no deity over 'them' but God." Another lawyer, Zeynep Sen, rejects feminism as a Western ideology, yet used UN Development Program platforms to lobby for international aid to Muslims in Bosnia and Chechnya (Arat 1999: 379).

Following a long "history of hostility," Islamist rights leaders linked to Milli Görüs founded Mazlum Der in 1991, hoping to pursue communication with a human rights organization (IHD) dominated by Kurdish nationalists and leftists (Negron-Gonzales 2012: 417–18). The number of Islamic HR-entities surged after the 1997 crackdown on religious activists and politicians (known as the post-modern putsch), giving rise to a network of national bodies with grassroots branches.[11] Mindful of the 1993 Sivas Massacre of Alevis by Sunni radicals, Mazlum Der recognized the need to struggle on behalf of all oppressed groups as an Islamic duty, beginning with Kurds long subject to arbitrary arrest, torture, and forced evacuations. This reorientation supplied a new mantra along the lines of, "We have suffered from this Kemalist ideological state and its associated military as much as you Kurds have" (Yavuz and Özcan 2006: 109).

Outlawed in 1997, the Welfare Party (WP) and its successors began to mobilize women; female membership approached 65,000 (40%) in 1996 (Arat 1999: 378). Beyond forming women's commissions, the WP introduced crash courses on public speaking and interpersonal skills, equipping them for neighborhood recruitment. The Women's Commission in Istanbul drew on 18,000 volunteers to turn out female voters for the 1994 elections, securing mayoral posts in Istanbul and Ankara. Survey data indicate that female candidates, with and without headscarves, have become acceptable to a majority of voters; party affiliation is a much more compelling variable in determining electoral preferences (KONDA Research and Consultancy 2011; Matland and Tezcür 2011).

---

11 Included among the participants were the IHD, the Human Rights Foundation of Turkey (TIHV), and *Mazlum Der*, as well as smaller associations such as the Helsinki Citizens' Assembly, the Turkish branch of Amnesty International, think tanks, and professional and bar associations. See Negron-Gonzales 2012.

The period after 2000 saw a shift from informal to institutionalized cooperation, rooted in the positive collaborative experiences of the 1990s. Feride Acar and her colleagues counted 300+ Islamist women's associations focusing not only on headscarf bans and "inaccurate" readings of religious texts but also on changes in national legislation that work against women. The Rainbow Women's Platform encompasses forty-six working groups; others included the Plane Tree Women's Platform, the Capital City Women's Platform, and the Women's Rights Organization against Discrimination. In 2008, the AKP-dominated Grand Assembly changed the Constitution for the first time to permit religious attire at universities; rule changes for parliament and government offices followed in 2010.[12] Consequently, "when Islamist women in Turkey voice their 'equality' claims, they demand from the state the recognition of their difference as 'Muslim women' who might not be in an equal relationship (in the sense of sameness) with men" (Acar, Altunok, and Gözdasoglu-Kücükalioglu 2008: 15).

Developing equality claims of their own has occasionally exposed "feminists with a veil" to admonition and alienation within their own faith communities. They are also disparaged by secularist women who label them "fundamentalist feminists." Orthodox, non-feminist activists often oppose the externally funded "project culture" that has emerged in conjunction with EU pre-accession programs. Hidayet Tuksal, for example, sees these activities as propagating Western cultural outlooks and lifestyles rather than "genuine and sincere (*samimi*)" projects arising out of voluntary religious service commitment (Kuzmanovic 2010: 440–41).

---

12 The AKP circumvented an earlier Constitutional Court rejection of any change altering the secularist nature of the Turkish state, by revising Article 10 to include women's equality "in the procurement of public services" and amending Article 42 to read "no one would be deprived of the right to education unless openly articulated by law." See Arat (2010: 11).

7. Kurdish and Alevi women as ethnic minorities

Despite AKP insistence on the national order, Erdoğan's stress on "multi-culturalizing" Islam (to improve relations with neighboring states), coupled with his defense of individual religious freedom for veiled women, has engendered a new *democratic paradox*. As Yesim Arat observes, the exercise of religious freedoms, encouraged by a democratically elected AKP government, has been accompanied by real threats to gender equality. At the same time it has provided significant impetus to political cooperation among religious and ethnic women's rights advocates. Shortly after the ban on headscarves was lifted, devout Islamic women created a blog and circulated a petition, calling for equivalent Kurdish and Alevi human rights (Arat 2010: 869). Both groups have experienced more than their share of state oppression.

Not recognized as real Muslims by orthodox Sunni and Shia factions, Alevis have experienced "multiple discriminations" since the 1920s as non-recognized ethnic minorities (Kurds, Karamchis, Zazas, and others), then as leftist activists through the 1980s. Religious-cultural memory is rooted in massacres inflicted by the Turkish majority: e.g., the Dersim uprising of 1937; the Sivas slaughter of thirty-seven intellectuals and artists in 1993; and retaliatory police killings of twenty Alevi protestors in Istanbul's Gazi neighborhood in 1995 (Ulusoy 2013: 300). Once in power, the AKP sought to remedy the "Kurdish" problem by way of religious recognition and poverty alleviation without recognizing the specificity of ethnic persecution. Erdoğan permitted the reestablishment of the (banned) Union of Alevis in 2003 and creation of the first Alevi Institute in 2008. He has supported Alevi houses of worship (applying mosque exemptions to their water bills) and even attended ceremonies commemorating Alevi holy days. Ayse Dursan notes that Alevi houses of worship are still denied state funding commensurate with official status. AKP reforms have been limited to symbolic recognition, such as naming a public university after the Alevi mystic Haci Bektas-I Veli. Erdoğan nonetheless named his contested Bosporus bridge after Yavuz Sultan Selim "the Grim," who was responsible for the massacre of tens of thousands of Alevis in the early 1500s.

The violent suppression of Kurdish demands for independence took place largely at the hands of Turkish nationalist and military forces (including those under Çiller). According to state estimates, over 380,000 Kurdish residents were driven out of 905 villages and 2,523 hamlets by Turkish security forces and/or PKK combatants during the early 1990s; human rights activists report up to three million internally displaced persons (Ayata and Yükseker 2005). These persons included not only Kurds but also Assyrian Christians and Yezidi sect members. EU conditionality (i.e., minority protection mandated by the Maastricht and Amsterdam Treaties) finally moved the government to adopt a Return and Village Rehabilitation project in 2002. By 2009, a mere 151,469 had returned; out of 2,234 applications for property restitution, only 287 had been approved by then under the 2004 Law on Compensation of Losses resulting from Terrorist Acts (Yilmaz 2001; further, Ayata and Yükseker 2005).

Kurdish expulsions from the rural southeast played a key role in the mushrooming of illegal (*gecekondu*) "slum cities" outside major metropolitan areas, responsible for deep poverty among the displaced. The AKP initially sought to depoliticize the conflict by introducing policies to meliorate poverty and unemployment not by way of minority or human rights but rather as "development policy" (Yörük 2012: 523). Erdoğan's efforts to include Kurds in a new "Turkish Islam synthesis" (no longer pitting Islam against communism) has secured the AKP a growing segment of the East/Southeastern Anatolian vote. Cultural liberalization has permitted the founding of Kurdish language schools, expanded TV and radio broadcasting, and collaboration with the Kurdish Peace and Democracy Party (BDP). These efforts came to a halt after the 2015 elections. Now President, Erdoğan has renewed attacks against Kurds, even as the PKK battles against an even more radical "ISIS."

The European Parliament has taken a strong stand on human rights and against domestic violence, both very sensitive issues in the Anatolian and Kurdish regions. Candidacy brought 3.9 million Euros in subsidies for programs "Combating Violence against Women" and the "Promotion and Protection of Women's Rights." It committed another 5 million Euros in 2007 for capacity-building and technological assistance to foster the "Empowerment of Women and Women's NGOs in the Least Developed Regions of Turkey."

While domestic violence and sexual assault are prevalent throughout the country, both the state and international organs tend to

> externalize the problem, attributing it to tradition and/or ethnicity—a product of Kurdish and/or "feudal culture" in South-eastern Turkey—rather than attempting to understand its relationship to modern Turkey, its structures and its institutions. As the problems of "the other Turkey" and "other women" are externalized, gender issues or problems that "white Turk" women face in gender relations are often invisible or at best depoliticized in the way they are analyzed. (Arat-Koç 2007, cited in Acar, Altunok, and Gözdasoglu-Kücükalioglu 2008: 42)

This renders women's successful mobilization within the Peace and Democracy party all the more surprising. A self-proclaimed leftist party, the BDP dramatically increased its share of women officeholders over the last decade. Half of the female mayors elected since 2009 are DTP/BDP members (although women's share of all mayoral posts is only 6–7%). It makes use of the "zipper principle" for listing candidates, and applies a voluntary quota, which rose from 25% in 1999 to 40% in 2005. Women who have engaged in active struggle or who have lost relatives enjoy preferential status. While no women secured seats in 2002, eleven (34%) won parliamentary seats in 2011, despite the 10% threshold for entering the Grand Assembly. Their growing presence impelled the AKP and the opposition CHP to raise the number of female candidates they include in electoral lists, accounting for 13.5% and 14% of their respective mandates since 2011 (14.4% of all parliamentary seats). This is a dramatic improvement over the 4% figure for women's representation seen from 1935 to 2002.[13]

8. Radical/Autonomous feminists and single-issue activists

A multitude of women's studies centers and local initiatives against domestic violence and sexual assault also grew out of prohibitions on political activity

---

13   Interparliamentary Union figures

after the 1980 coup. Among the better-known groups are Purple Roof, Flying Broom, and Women for Women's Human Rights/New Ways. All have been active in raising public consciousness, to take advantage of the "pincer effect" described by Anna von der Vleuten: that is, increasing "top-down" (EU, UN, NGO) and "bottom-up" (local/provincial) pressures on lawmakers to induce policy change (van der Vleuten, 2012).

Founded in 1990, the Purple Roof Shelter Foundation faces special challenges, given the archconservative judicial responses to abuse cases. In one instance, a judge dismissed charges after asserting that a man should "never leave a woman's back without a stick and her belly without a baby." This triggered a 1987 Mother's Day protest in Ankara with banners reading "Do you love your mother and beat your wife?" (Marshall 2013: 67). Radical feminists engage in direct actions, one of the more (in)famous being the distribution of seven-centimeter "Purple Needles" for use against sexual harassers. In 2009, a Parliamentary Commission on Equal Opportunity for Women recognized sex crimes against *individuals*, rather than stressing *family honor* – regardless of one's "virgin" status. The Ministry of Justice recorded 61,469 rapes between 2002–2008, and another 29,980 from 2009–2011. The state no longer grants impunity to rapists who marry their victims, but the AKP has yet to end "virginity testing" for civil servants, or to try so-called honor killings as aggravated homicide (Acar and Uluğ 2014).

The Association to Support and Educate Women Candidates (known as KADER, meaning "destiny") supports only women who accept its norms, i.e., gender sensitivity and the commitment to ending discrimination and secularism. It relies on a decentralized, democratic structure based on committees, loosely bound to the center. Another example of autonomous mobilization, Young Civilians, appeals to a new generation committed to pluralism and multiculturalism. It uses Facebook to link an estimated 10,000 Turks, Kurds, Armenians, Jews, Muslims, Christians, gays, and other "civilian-democrats." An earlier survey indicated that 8% deemed communication among civil society actors "insignificant," 73% as limited; women's organizations constituted the exception to the rule (Kuzmanovic 2010: 434). Over the last five years, women's groups have generally credited new communication technologies and the Internet with helping them to mobilize issue-groups faster than was possible during the 1980s and 1990s (Marshall 2013: 67).

Any project or issue that fosters dialogue, informational exchanges, and the sharing of resources with groups formerly construed as "the other" generates internal change in otherwise bounded communities, proving that such boundaries are permeable (Arat 2010). Even "puritanical fundamentalists" have been transformed by the experience, gradually shifting from an exclusive concentration on their "difference" to realizing that they share certain forms of oppression and inequality. The AKP's neo-liberal, privatization push has destroyed many historical sites and neighborhoods. Istanbul's iconic Blue Mosque is now surrounded by skyscrapers. In Tarlabasi, Istanbul ("little Kurdistan"), the state tore down 278 buildings, 210 of which were under "monument protection" regulations, before turning the land over to a company owned by the Prime Minister's son-in-law (Yücel 2014: 57). Erdoğan's mega construction plans are clearly at odds with his insistence on the superiority of Turkish "cultural traditions"; the latter only seems to apply to woman's subordination to husband, household, and nation.

Women's groups have expanded the arena for civil rights mobilization by challenging the authority of a patriarchal state that justifies real-existing inequality by way of a mythical "unity" of national interests (Arat 2010: 879). Earlier versions of the identity claims raised by diverse groups were detrimental to their cause: female citizens were viewed as political subjects only to the extent that they accepted the dominant discourse without questioning pre-assigned gender roles. "Bottom-up" experiences have led them to develop a consciousness distinct from male leaders of all sorts who have instrumentalized them for their own political purposes.

The state's overwhelmingly economic interest in EU membership has been subverted over time by other normative demands for pluralist democracy, minority rights, equal treatment, non-violence, social inclusion, environmental sustainability, etc. Although some women's organizations enjoy more financial and institutional support than others, all activists increasingly realize that "the reforms we demand should take place not because of Turkey's candidacy to the EU, but because WE, AS WOMEN LIVING IN TURKEY WANT THEM and because we have a full right to gender equality as equal citizens"

(Marshall 2013: 114). The paradigm shift in women's consciousness was clearly manifested in the protests exacerbated by Erdoğan's response to the occupation of Gezi Park.

9. The *Spirit of Gezi*: young, political, and female

My emphasis on domestic political dynamics notwithstanding, the summer 2013 protests triggered by Gezi Park mirrored social movement trends witnessed on other continents, largely in the spirit of an "anti-globalization" movement. What began as a pattern of "patchwork politics," that is, as "the pursuit of policies ... disintegrating the political space into disconnected spheres ... and disregarding the axes of junction among these spheres," eventually turned into a blanket of protest, covering the nation (Coşar and Yeğenoğlu 2011: 556).

According to Amnesty International, efforts to save the Gezi Park/Taksim Square area in 2013 unleashed protests across 79 of 81 provinces, attracting an estimated 3.5 million participants. The period May to September produced 7,832 recorded injuries and nine deaths.[14] Police fired over 150,000 tear gas canisters and arrested 3,773 participants. Nearly 50,000 (but only five police) were indicted across 17 provinces for violating the Law on Meetings and Demonstrations, evincing ties to Taksim Solidarity (a legal coalition of 100+ NGOS), organized crime, or "terrorist organizations." The Interior Ministry registered the destruction of 14 party and 58 state buildings, 68 surveillance cameras, 337 shops, 90 public buses, 214 private autos, 240 police cars, and 45 ambulances, amounting to 140 million Lira (63 Million USD) in damages (Guttstadt 2014: 14). These sobering figures aside, many cities saw the subsequent rise of *citizen fora*, promoting public dialogue on social issues. Noteworthy is the extent to which participants are including previously shunned groups:

---

14 Amnesty International Report, p. 15. On June 16, a fourteen-year-old boy from an Istanbul working class district, Berkin Elvan Okmeydanı, fell into a coma after being allegedly hit in the head by a gas canister fired at close range by a police officer. The day after he died, March 12, 2014, an estimated one million people took to the streets to attend his funeral.

Gendering of Civil Society in Turkey 207

roughly 50,000 attended the parade in Istanbul marking LGBT Pride Week (June) after the Gezi crackdown, for example (Yücel 2014: 48).

While concentrated populations and better organizational resources make it easier to promote civic activism in urban areas, the "Kodak moment" afforded by Gezi suggests that citizen engagement has increased significantly over the last decade. In a 1999 survey, only 7.8% claimed membership in a civil society organization (CSO), despite a deeply rooted tradition of religious voluntarism: 80% contributed to charitable causes but only 18% directly supported CSOs. Membership data reveal a clear gender gap: 80% viewed women as significantly underrepresented, 73% found upper class elites overrepresented. The Department of Associations pegged the number of female members at 770,671 in 2005, compared to 3,555,577 males. Generational change and new communication technologies are narrowing the gap, at least in urban areas. Expanding educational opportunity is also a contributing factor.

The sea change in women's willingness to engage directly with or against the state is best illustrated by the findings of an on-site survey conducted during the Gezi protests, prior to the brutal evacuation of June 13–15. On June 6–7, the independent polling institute KONDA Research and Consultancy interviewed 400 participants at two-hour intervals across thirty hours, accruing 4,411 responses. Questions of "statistical representativeness" aside, the survey attests to a great deal of diversity among the participants.

The so-called *Spirit of Gezi* is, first and foremost, young and techno-savvy. Authoritarian regimes become particularly fragile at twenty-year intervals in countries where women produce children at earlier ages. While 43% of Turkey's citizens are under 25, 60% are under 35, all too young to recall the 1980 coup; 17% were not old enough to vote in 2011. The average age among Istanbul demonstrators was 28. Among the 69% who first heard about the protests via social media, the average age was 26, but 40 (7%) among those who relied on television. Instead of covering protest developments, state controlled TV aired a BBC documentary film on "Penguins: Spy in the Huddle"; outfitted with a gas mask, the bird immediately became an anti-censorship symbol. Erdoğan's disparaging label "marauders" (*çapulcu*) was also seized as a badge of distinction by activists. An estimated 1.6 million "tweets" were sent under #DirenGeziParki between May 29 and June 3, 400,000 of which included photos or videos, another 1.6 mil via #Occupygezi and 1 million by way of #Diren Ankara (Yücel 2014: 152). AKP officials failed in their efforts to "tweet" rumors regarding pizza and alcohol consumption in mosques.

One could argue, secondly, that the *Spirit of Gezi* is "the child of the prime minister" himself. Nearly half (47%) first came to the Park or Square after witnessing police violence against demonstrators; 53% had no previous direct action experience. A clear majority (58%) cited violations of political freedom as their core concern, 37% opposed AKP policies, and 30% Erdoğan's anti-protest stance. Only 20% stressed the original grounds for the site occupation, protecting the Park's existence. Police brutality brought people into the streets, but their diversity added ever more democratic demands to the agenda. When police threw gas grenades, people lobbed them back, chanting "Olley!" a common soccer stadium refrain. As journalist Tayfun Guttstadt noted, it was "a big mistake" for security forces to take on a group that had grown up shooting police and/or other bad guys on video games (Guttstadt 2014: 7).

Third, the *Spirit of Gezi* is intent on redefining politics, policies, and the nature of political participation. Among those eligible to vote in 2011, 13% had not cast ballots, 10% chose "independent" candidates, and 7% submitted blank ballots. While 15.8% had supported the AKP in 2009, one-third identified with no political party; 58% of those who lack such ties identified with a group experiencing human rights violations. In urban crowds in which everyone was an "other" of some kind, individual rights took precedence over national, ethnic, or religious grievances: "We don't need the AKP for religion, no CHP for the republic, no BPD for the Kurds and no MHP to preserve the nation. We are the people." However, "a generation that questions everything cannot be [construed as] apolitical" (Yücel 2014: 37). While they do take cues from other protest movements (Occupy, Arab Spring), even starkly religious groups have no interest in allowing a Muslim Brotherhood to dominate their movement. Indeed, Erdoğan's attempt to play the religious card backfired.

Just as importantly, in a political culture scarred by repeated military coups, corruption, and distrust, the *Spirit of Gezi* proved to be friendly, humorous, respectful, and even romantic. Journalist Deniz Yücel observed that there was so much smoke caused by people grilling meat to share with protestors that many joked Erdoğan had sent the former instead of tear gas refills for the police. Marking the month of Ramadan, neighborhoods like Fatih organized fast-breaking meals after sunset, joined by secularists abiding by a self-imposed alcohol ban. Anticipating protest graffiti, police attacked one man who was innocently painting his steps in Cihangir, leading prominent writers, actors, and artists who lived there to start coloring all steps; some now face blacklisting. Owned by one of Turkey's wealthiest families, the luxury-class Divan Hotel opened its lobby and restrooms, provided tea, and then a space for medical treatment when protestors sought refuge: police teargassed the lobby in return. The owners were later hit with a €175 million fine for "false financial reporting" (Yücel 2014: 94). After "morality-defenders" at Ankara's Kurtulus subway station used a loud-speaker to admonish a kissing couple in mid-May, 200 young people showed up to stage a *Kiss-In* (Yücel 2014: 35).

Last but not least, the *Spirit of Gezi* revealed itself as female. Women comprised 50.8%, men 49.2% of those surveyed. Hailing from 30 districts, 52% labeled themselves "workers" and 37% students; 6% were unemployed and 2% were "housewives." Among those active across Istanbul, 41% were workers, 14% were retired, and 33% identified themselves as housewives. Some 43% had graduated from high school, compared to 13% who held university degrees at Gezi (27% and 11%, respectively, across Turkey). Erdoğan's exhortation to women to produce more offspring resulted in posters and tweets with the slogan, *Do you really wants us to have three children like us?* Less amusing is the fact that many female activists received anonymous rape threats.

Although the women came to Gezi Park and other sites across Turkey as "protestors, not pin-up girls," the media quickly adopted "the woman in red" as its favorite icon. A doctoral student in urban planning, Ceyda Sungur was photographed while being sprayed point-blank with a police tear gas gun. She had no intent on becoming the poster girl of the resistance, but her image was quickly reproduced on websites, buttons, and posters, "prompting a whole heap of marriage proposals from rebellious romantics" (Fitch Little 2013). Other photos depicted women suggesting a variety of lifestyles, including a headscarf wearer with a sign declaring "We're here too, Girlfriend."

Rather than heed the Prime Minister's calls for parents to "bring their children home," a group of mothers formed a "human chain" between protestors and the police on June 13; their YouTube images went viral. The maternal emphasis generated ambivalence among some feminists; as one declared, "I came here as an individual, not as a role." It nevertheless denied the state a chance to attribute the protests to "extremists." Turkish women are unlikely to experience the fundamentalist backlash and dramatic upsurge in sexual assault witnessed in conjunction with Arab Spring protests in Egypt and elsewhere (Manea 2014). As Harriet Fitch Little reported:

> When women raised concerns early on about possible harassment in the occupation, they organised a march and flyering campaign to make it clear that it wouldn't be tolerated, and it worked; in a camp crammed with over 1,000 adrenaline pumped rebels there was ... an atmosphere of complete security and respect. When protest chants labelled Erdogan the son of a whore, women held seminars to explain issues the insult prompted. And when similarly unimaginative graffiti surfaced, they methodically painted over it. It didn't come back. (Fitch Little 2013)

10. Conclusion: occupying "a room of one's own"

Patriarchal leaders and entrenched bureaucratic elites thought that they could pour Turkey's new wine of globalization into the old bottles of Kemalist or neo-religious nationalism, but the combined effects of demographic change, expanding educational opportunity, and EU conditionality have rendered their traditional gender role mandates obsolete. In 2013, a new formula, "add women, technology and stir," helped to rally demonstrators faster than authorities could respond. Gender-sensitive political change, however, not only depends on the number of citizens who mobilize but also on the quality of their participation. The discovery of shared grievances, along with technological access to like-minded groups via the Internet and social media has expanded average citizens' understanding of democracy.

Nearly 60% of Turkey's citizens are under 35; younger cohorts who have come of political age since the 1980 coup have succeeded in "shedding 'the unbearable lightness of authoritarianism'."[15] EU monetary infusions dating back to the 1990s helped to promote women's rights, adult literacy, and grassroots organizational skills, but their domestic mobilization has taken on a life of its own. At the same time, the state's efforts to uphold a paternalistic, monocultural identity is out of sync with diversity among Turkey's own citizens. The establishment of activist networks has solidified the position of new stakeholders willing to build bridges among groups who used to target each other as much as they did the state. Minorities realize that their own appeals for human rights will be better served if reform demands encompass all persecuted groups.

Although the EU has contributed significantly to Turkish democratic pursuits, the community is a long way from practicing the gender equality it preaches to all member-states. EU-28 leaders have yet to recognize that the rise of an indigenous civil society, the professionalization of stake-holder groups, and youth's identification with "think globally, act locally" campaigns since the 1990s will make it difficult for Turkey to reverse its course. As Mehmet Ogutcu describes it, EU politicians "are still on 'rewind' instead of 'play'" (Ogutcu 2005: 3). External factors alone rarely precipitate the political-cultural changes needed to consolidate democratic pluralism and civil society. That requires "the interplay of internal contradictions and the decision of in-group actors to opt for a new identity synthesis that eventually brings about the actual change" (Johansson-Nogués and Jonasson 2011: 115).

Surveys show that most Turkish citizens are tired of being put on hold by EU politicians, although an overwhelming majority welcome the reforms brought about by the processes of Europeanization. Neo-liberal austerity programs imposed in the wake of the 2008–2009 financial crisis have shown "western" women that their own equality paradigms are vulnerable to attack. Although the strategies of younger Turkish women are grounded in very different nationalist, ethnic, and religious prerequisites, indigenous gender advocates "have a great deal to lose, and they know it" (Kandiyoti 2010: 175). As

---

15 Authoritarian regimes are often more fragile than they appear, following decades of coercion, corruption, and co-optation. The problem is that neither analysts, rulers, or protestors anticipate a full-scale collapse "because ferocity and strength [are] so easily conflated." See Teti and Gervasio (2011).

one woman wearing a tear gas canister necklace told a reporter for the *New Statesman* (savor the irony of that magazine title), "[H]ere women fought with men, resisted with them, and changed their opinions ... I hope that is the lesson that people remember" (Fitch Little 2013: 3).

Postscript

When I began this project in 2013, I had no way of anticipating that an alleged coup attempt in 2016 would undercut much of the democratic progress documented in this chapter. The growing confidence that many women's organizations had developed in their own ability to foster greater gender equality has been seriously undermined by over 79,000 arrests and the mass firing of 110,000 journalists, academics and other civil servants. Newly created private universities have been shut down or taken over by the state, given their affiliation with Gülen supporters, whom Erdoğan has charged with masterminding the coup. Over 4,330 Turks applied for asylum in Germany during the first half of 2018, added to 5,742 in 2016 and 3,200 during the first six months of 2017.

Given his belief that women, by nature, should be largely confined to traditional roles, it is harder for Erdoğan to accuse women of "terrorist" activities, with noteworthy exceptions like journalists Zehra Doğan, Ayşenur Panldak and Meşale Tolu. Having changed the constitution to grant himself major decree powers, the president has packed the courts, the police and the military with personally loyal supporters, after completely reneging on earlier promises to tackle corruption, i.e., by placing key state functions in the hands of family members. He has even accused 680 German companies (including Daimler and BASF) of "supporting terrorists," likely to chip away at foreign direct investment.

Given the fact that 43% of the population were under 25 in 2013, I am still optimistic that younger cohorts will tire of authoritarian rule, especially as economic conditions deteriorate further. The good news is that they are a lot more tech-savvy and will develop alternative communication channels. Those who do not "vote with their feet" by way of migration will eventually move to fill the associational vacuum, although that could take up to ten years. These developments testify to the fragility of the "rule of law," making it all the more important for the EU to continue investing in civil society groups outside its own borders, while insisting on "conditionality" mechanisms.

References

Abels, Gabriele/Mushaben, Joyce Marie (2012): Gendering the European Union: New Approaches to Old Democratic Deficits. Basingstoke UK: Palgrave Macmillan.

Acar, Feride/Altunok, Gülbanu, and Gözdaşoğlu-Küçükalioğlu, Elif (2008): Report Analysing Intersectionality in Gender Equality Policies for Turkey and the EU – European Commission Sixth Framework Programme, QUING Project, Vienna: Institute for Human Sciences.

Acar, Yasemin/Uluğ, Melis (2014): The Body Politicized: The Visibility of Women at Gezi. In: ROAR Collective.

Amnesty International (2014): Adding injustice to injury: One year on from the Gezi Park protests in Turkey. http://www.amnesty.org/en/library/info/EUR44/010/2014/en. (20.02.2018)

Arat, Yeşim (1998): A Woman Prime Minister in Turkey: Did It Matter? In: Women & Politics 19, 4, pp. 1-22.

Arat, Yeşim (1999): Democracy and Women in Turkey: In Defense of Liberalism. In: Social Politics 6, 3, pp. 370-387.

Arat, Yeşim (2010): Religion, Politics and Gender Equality in Turkey: Implications of a Democratic Paradox? In: Third World Quarterly 31, 6, pp. 869-884.

Arat-Koç, Sedef (2007): (Some) Turkish Transnationalism(s) in an Age of Capitalist Globalization and Empire: "White Turk" Discourse, the New Geopolitics and the Implications for Feminist Transnationalism. In: Journal of Middle East Women's Studies 3, 1, pp. 35-57.

Avci, Gamze/Çarkoğlu, Ali (2011): Taking Stock of the Dynamics that Shape EU Reforms in Turkey. In: South European Society and Politics 16, 2, pp. 209-219.

Ayata, Bilgin/Yükseker, Deniz (2005): A belated awakening: National and international responses to the internal displacement of Kurds in Turkey. In: New Perspectives on Turkey 32, pp. 5-42.

Blaser, Noah (2013): Amid alcohol row, treatment options for alcohol abuse remain 'almost non-existent'. In: Today's Zaman.

Canan-Sokullu, Ebru Ş. (2011): Turcoscepticism and Threat Perception: European Public and Elite Opinion on Turkey's Protracted EU Membership. In: South European Society and Politics 16, 3, pp. 483-497.

Coşar, Simten/Yeğenoğlu, Metin (2011): New Grounds for Patriarchy in Turkey? Gender Policy in the Age of AKP. In: South European Society and Politics 16, 4, pp. 555-573.

Dedeoglu, Saniye (2012): Equality, Protection or Discrimination: Gender Equality Policies in Turkey. In: Social Politics 19, 2, pp. 269-290.
Fitch Little, Harriet (2013): The women of Gezi Park are protestors, not pin-up girls. In: New Statesman.
Göçek, Fatma Müge (1999): To Veil or not to Veil: The Contested Location of Gender in Contemporary Turkey. In: Interventions 1, 4, pp. 521-535.
Guttstadt, Tayfun (2014): çapulcu: Die Gezi Park Bewegung und die neuen Proteste in der Türkei. Münster: Unrast.
Hancock, Claire (2008): Spatialities of the Secular. Geographies of the Veil in France and Turkey. In: European Journal of Women's Studies 15, 3, pp. 165-179.
Hassan, Mona (2011): Women Preaching for the Secular State: Official Female Preachers (Bayan Vaizler) in Contemporary Turkey. In: International Journal of Middle East Studies 43, pp. 451-473.
Hürriyet Daily News (2013): Joblessness among young Turks surges. http://www.hurriyetdailynews.com/joblessness-among-young-turks-surges-46944 (30.06.2013)
Ilkkaracan, Pinar (2004): How Adultery Almost Derailed Turkey's Aspiration to Join the European Union. In: Sex politics: Reports from the Front Lines, pp. 247-275.
Kandiyoti, Deniz (1987): Emancipated but Unliberated? Reflections on the Turkish Case. In: Feminist Studies 13, 2, pp. 317-338.
Kandiyoti, Deniz (2010): Gender and Women's Studies in Turkey: A moment for reflection? In: New Perspectives on Turkey, 43, pp. 165-176.
Kiliç, Azer (2008): The Gender Dimension of Social Policy Reform in Turkey: Towards Equal Citizenship? In: Social Policy & Administration 42, 5, pp. 487–503.
Knapp, Gundrun Axeli (2005): Race, Class, Gender – Reclaiming Baggage in Fast Traveling Theories. In: European Journal of Women's Studies 12, 3, pp. 249-265.
KONDA Research and Consultancy (2011): Representation of Women in Politics. http://konda.com.tr/wp content/uploads/2017/03/2011_04_KONDA_Representation_of_Women_in_Politics.pdf (20.02.2018)
Kuzmanovic, Daniella (2010): Project Culture and Turkish Civil Society. In: Turkish Studies 11, 3, pp. 429-444.
Manea, Elham (2014): The Arab Popular Uprisings from a Gender Perspective. In: Zeitschrift für Politik, 61, 1, pp. 81-100.
Manning, Nick (2007): Turkey, the EU and Social Policy. In: Social Policy & Society 6, 4, pp. 491-501.
Matland, Richard E./ Tezcür, Güneş Murat (2011): Women as Candidates: An Experimental Study in Turkey. In: Politics & Gender 7, pp. 365-390.
Marshall, Gül Aldikaçti (2013): Shaping Gender Policy in Turkey: Grassroots Women Activists, the European Union and the Turkish State. Albany: SUNY Press.
Müftüler-Baç, Meltem (2005): Turkey's Political Reforms and the Impact of the European Union. In: South European Society and Politics 10, 1, pp. 16-30.

Mushaben, Joyce Marie (2014): The Summer of Our Discontent": Demography, Democracy and the Gezi Park/Taksim Square Protests, paper presented at the ISA-Midwest, St. Louis.

Negron-Gonzales, Melinda (2012): Cooperation Between Secular and Religious Rights Organizations in Turkey. In: Turkish Studies 13, 3, pp. 415-430.

Munin, Nellie (2011): Female Employment and Turkey's EU Accession Process. In: Mediterranean Politics 16, pp. 449-457.

Özal, Mehmet (2012): Entpolitisierung in Raten? Die neue Rolle des türkischen Militärs nach dem Machtkampf mit Ministerpräsident Erdoğan. In: Zeitschrift für Außen- und Sicherheitspolititk 5, pp. 379-390.

Ogutcu, Mehmet (2005): Turkey and the European Union: How to Achieve a Forward-looking and 'win-win' Accession by 2015. In: Civitas International.

Ozcurumez, Saime/ Sayan-Cengiz, Feyda (2011): On resilience and response beyond value change: Transformation of women's movement (sic) in post-1980 Turkey. In: Women's Studies International Forum 34, pp. 20-30.

Elisabeth Johansson-Nogués and Ann-Kristin Jonasson (2011): Turkey, Its Changing National Identity and EU Accession: Explaining the Ups and Downs in the Turkish Democratization Reforms. In: Journal of Contemporary European Studies 19, 1, pp. 113-132.

Ruthenberg, Ina-Marline et al. (2012): Towards Gender Equality in Turkey: A Summary Assessment. Washington DC: World Bank. http://documents.worldbank.org/curated/en/377191468120289049/pdf/NonAsciiFileName0.pdf (20.02.2018)

Steinvort, Daniel (2013): A Zone of Freedom: Youth Insurgency Challenges Erdoğan. In: Der Spiegel. http://www.spiegel.de/international/world/turkish-youth-insurgency-poses-challenge-to-erdogan-a-904984.html. (20.02.2018)

Teti, Andrea/ Gervasio, Gennaro (2011): The Unbearable Lightness of Authoritarianism: Lessons from the Arab Uprisings. In: Mediterranean Politics 16, 2, pp. 321-327.

Ulusoy, Kivanc (2013): The 'Europeanization' of the Religious Cleavage in Turkey: The Case of the Alevis. In: Mediterranean Politics 18, 2, pp. 294-310.

Valance, Elizabeth/Davies, Elizabeth (1986): Women of Europe: Women Members of the European Parliament and Equality Policy. Cambridge: Cambridge University Press.

van der Vleuten, Anna (2012): Gendering the Institutions and Actors of the EU. In: Abels, Gabriele/Mushaben, Joyce Marie (Eds.): Gendering the European Union: New Approaches to Old Democratic Deficits. Basingstoke UK: Palgrave Macmillan, pp. 41-62.

Yavuz, M. Hakan/Özcan, Nihat Ali (2006): The Kurdish Question and Turkey's Justice and Development Party. In: Middle East Policy 13, 1, pp. 102-119.

Yilmaz, Gözde (2011): Is there a Puzzle? Compliance with Minority Rights in Turkey (1999-2010). KFG Working Paper, 23, The Transformative Power of Europe.

Yöruk, Erdem (2012): Welfare Provision as Political Containment: The Politics of Social Assistance and the Kurdish Conflict in Turkey. In: Politics & Society 40, 4, pp. 517-547.

Yücel, Deniz (2014): Taksim ist überall. Die Gezi-Bewegung und die Zukunft der Türkei. Hamburg: Nautilus Flugschrift.

Between Provocation and Incorporation – Social Gender Activism in the Hybrid Regime of the PRC

Stephanie Bräuer

1. Introduction

The People's Republic of China (PRC) is a hybrid regime in two ways: it maintains authoritarian and patriarchal legacies while promising democracy and gender equality. This particular institutional context puts a double burden on gender activists, who have to meet the demands of *social* and *gender* activism simultaneously. Not only is their burden doubled but their risks are heightened as well. This article investigates exactly this tension and questions how social gender activism can evolve under such adverse conditions.

The first part of the chapter analyzes the specific institutional configurations: in a first step, the political system and its authoritarian legacy are scrutinized. In a second step, the ambivalent gender regime of the PRC is examined, which cultivates features of the traditional gender order, on the on hand, and imposes gender equality on the other. The investigation of the institutional context is based predominately on an analysis of secondary data. The second part of this chapter is a case study of anti-domestic violence (ADV) activism in Beijing. After a brief discussion of the general development of domestic violence (DV) in the PRC, it turns to the composition and tactical alignment of the initial strand of Beijing ADV activism. The second part considers a more recent strand in the ADV movement, which is characterized as more provocative and confrontational than its predecessor.

This chapter will show that both tactical approaches are interlinked and that the latter form of activism would not have been possible without the former. Moreover, it will demonstrate that a nonconfrontational, less provocative tactical approach is better suited to influence policy decision-making. The hybrid regime places by the same token a double burden on gender activists, who are not only confronted and limited by the repressing state measures of policy elites with regard to their *social* activism but are also refused by society and policy elites due to the *gender*-related nature of their activity. The chapter will show that, as a consequence of the double burden, gender activists are especially vulnerable to harsh state repression.

2. The case of the PRC

2.1 The PRC as hybrid regime[1]

The PRC was founded in 1949 by the Chinese Communist Party (CCP) under the leadership of Mao Zedong,[2] thereby ending the Chinese civil war.[3] The new state was associated with the hope for a modern and democratic future. Despite these high expectations and the institutionalization of formal democratic elements, such as the National People's Congress (NPC), authoritarian traits have prevailed. Studies of the PRC's political system find that it still shows clear authoritarian traits (Teets 2013; Ho and Edmonds 2008a; He and Warren 2011). It has been depicted as a semi-authoritarian regime (Ho and Edmonds 2008), a deliberative authoritarian regime (He and Warren 2011), and a consultative authoritarian regime (Teets 2013, 2014). The authoritarian

---

1   This article reflects the author's thinking in 2015.
2   It stretches over a territory of 9.6 million square kilometers. Traditional and agricultural communities of more than 1.3 billion people (United Nations Economic and Social Commission for Asia and the Pacific [ESCAP] 2014) are pushing more and more into the urban centers; the urban population increased from 26.4% in 1990 to 54.4% in 2014 (United Nations Economic and Social Commission for Asia and the Pacific [ESCAP] 2014).
3   The Chinese civil war started in 1927 when the First United Front between the Nationalist Guomindang Party and the CCP was dissolved. The civil war continued formally until the foundation of the PRC in 1949 and was effectively ended in the 1950s (cf. Fairbank and Goldman 2006; Gernet 1988).

features are obvious: the party and government functions are synchronized and the power supremacy remains with the CCP (Heilmann 2004: 90; Heberer 2003: 70) and here in particular with the President, the Politburo, and the Politburo Standing Committee (Mercator Institute of China Studies [MERICS] 2014).

Although the situation of social actors has improved greatly since the late 1970s (Milwertz and Wei 2008: 121), they remain subjects of restrictive measures and curtailed freedom (Chin 2015; Chin and Chen 2015; Wong 2015; Ho 2007). Nonetheless, the PRC also exhibits more liberal or even *democratic* features, prompting some scholars to conclude that it is a hybrid regime bearing both authoritarian and democratic features simultaneously: democratic elections at the local level and residents' committees in urban areas became reestablished in the late 1990s (Heberer 2003: 97); the CCP increasingly relies on experts from social organizations to serve as advisors for, among other things, the design of new social directives and policies (Yang and Alpermann 2014); following the slogan "Small Government, Big Society" (Xiaozhengfu, da shehui, 小政府大社会) social organizations are urged to provide social services for the population (Schwartz, Shieh 2009)[4]; and technological empowerment, which led to a sharp increase in online activism, has enabled social actors to voice their political discontent and organize social activism (Yang 2009). However, this does not imply that China is democratizing in the Western sense. Rather, it makes the PRC a typical representative of a hybrid regime, in which political liberties, civic rights, and the rule of law bear authoritarian legacies while appearing under the guise of a democratic system (Croissant 2002: 32).

---

4   This became necessary after the socioeconomic reforms beginning in the late 1970s abolished the iron rice bowl and shifted social responsibilities in general from state to social actors. This is a development often described under the label of the privatization perspective (Hsu 2010).

2.2 Social activism in the authoritarian context of the PRC

Although the PRC has clear characteristics of an authoritarian regime, it is also conducive to collective social actors (Ho and Edmonds 2008b). Since the onset of the reform and open policies and hence the initiation of the post-socialist era, China has witnessed a sharp increase in (collective) social action. Before the reform, social activism was only permitted under the leadership of official party-state mass organizations (Ma 2009), such as the All-China Women's Federation (ACWF) or the All-China Federation of Trade Unions. In 2012 the number of officially registered civic groups amounted to 499,000, which consisted of 271,000 social organizations (Shehui tuanti, 社会团体), 255,000 non-profit organizations (Minban feiqiqiye danwei, 民办非企业单位), and 3209 foundations (Jijinhui, 基金会) (Yang and Alpermann 2014). Due to the rather difficult registration practices and the political control accompanying such registrations, approximately 80% of China's social actors remain unregistered and in legal limbo (Yang and Alpermann 2014). The registration practices are especially demanding because the CCP aims to incorporate social organizations in the official polity and thereby to mitigate confrontational acts. Despite these attempts, there are still social organizations with anti-state rhetoric such as Greenpeace surviving in China (Teets 2014: 1).

Social actors and an autonomous civil society simultaneously assist and threaten non-democratic regimes (Teets 2014: 2). The Chinese government seems to be aware of this, and has therefore attempted to incorporate pluralistic aspects of democratic governance into authoritarian state control mechanisms (Teets 2014: 2). The CCP encourages the development and formation of social action while it creates new, more indirect methods of state control (Teets 2014: 2). These new measures supplement established mechanisms. For example, nongovernmental organizations are obligated to register with a mother organization (Lingdao Danwei, 领导单位) in order to obtain an official status (Ma 2009), and they experience difficulties meeting registration requirements to become a nongovernmental organization, which would grant them possible tax benefits and/or the possibility of obtaining funding from foreign organizations (Ma 2009).

In this context the situation of social actors remains ambiguous and uncertain. On a positive note, social actors today not only operate under much better conditions than like-minded actors pre-1980, but are also engaged in a broad range of areas, such as social service provision (Fulda et al. 2012), advocacy (Guo et al. 2013), or in policy formulation processes (Yang and Alpermann 2014).

Although they are enjoying more freedom and rights than pre-1980, Damocles' sword is still hanging over them. For instance, 2015 marked a distressing climax of the Xi Jinping era. Legal activism – in particular human rights lawyers and legal advocates – experienced intense pressure in 2015 when more than a hundred human rights lawyers were targeted in a nationwide crackdown and wave of arrests (Amnesty International 7/13/2015).

2.3 The current gender regime in the PRC

Not only was the political system of China reset in 1949, but the established gender regime also underwent fundamental changes. These changes were implemented in a top-down manner through the establishment of a communist and hence surpassingly gender egalitarian political system. The establishment of the new gender regime was predominately carried out by communist policy elites and officially sanctioned organizations, such as the ACWF. And especially the ACWF played a decisive role. Due to its heterogeneous organization with branches on all administrative levels, it functioned as a good disseminator and propagator of Maoist gender politics (Kaufman 2012; Hershatter 2004; Chen 2011). As such the ACWF held a central role in the production of the gender regime, because it initially had the power to dominate all inscriptions of womanhood in the official discourse (Barlow 2004).

2.3.1 Historic legacies: the Confucian gender regime

China was a patrilineal society until the twentieth century. Confucian notions persisted: girls must obey fathers before marriage, their husbands thereafter, and sons in old age (Kaufman 2012: 588; Tang et al. 2002: 976). Until colonialism, gender and gender roles were largely defined by Confucian notions (Barlow 1994, 2004, 1993; Ko et al. 2003b; Ko 1994; Mann 1997).[5] Within Confucian ethics, the family was the basic unit of society and the five cardinal relations within a family, i.e., father and son, husband and wife, man and woman, older brother and younger brother, and patriarch and clan member (Li 1991: 53), were fundamental to all other relationships in a society (Moritz and Lee 1998).[6] Confucianism as a family philosophy was a specialized style of theoretical writing about being a person in the patriline,[7] and it was exactly this patriline of all Confucian thoughts that was held to be the literal foundation of the central government (Barlow 2004: 37).

---

5   This is a simplification since even in China the Confucian discourse had to compete with other philosophical and ethical systems with equally universalistic claims, often subsumed under the rubrics *Buddhism* and *Daoism* (Ko et al. 2003a: 3). Nonetheless, Confucian ethics had tremendous impact on social and state structures in China (Moritz et al. 1998; Ko et al. 2003a; Ko 1994; Croll 1995; Li 2000). Confucianism in itself consists of many variations. To account for the internal variety and changes over time scholars tend to talk about *Confucian discourses* rather than Confucianism and thereby acknowledge that there is not one but many forms of Confucianism (Ko et al. 2003a: 3; Li 2000: 2). Moreover, there is no exact Chinese counterpart to the English term *Confucianism*. The Chinese term often used in similar contexts is *Rujia* (儒家, the school of the literati). The term *Rujia* has also been used to include later developments of Confucian thought. In this analysis I understand Confucianism as institutional structures that directly impinge on people's lives (Li 2000: 5). For the sake of readability, when I refer to Confucianism, I am in fact speaking about the discourses of Confucianism. Confucianism is an ethics of the family or the clan. It encourages the socialization of practices that stabilize the clan and family (Moritz and Lee 1998: 15). It is also an ethics of the state, since it regulates the state structures and the relation between power and morality (Moritz and Lee 1998: 15; Ko et al. 2003a: 8).

6   With regard to Chinese women, the relationship between man and woman and husband and wife are of particular importance.

7   The patrilineal family structure is often combined with patrilocal or virilocal post-marriage residence patterns. Patrilocal residence patterns refer to arrangements in which the newlywed couple lives close to or with the husband's family. In that sense it differs from the uxorilocal marriage pattern in which a husband moves in with his wife's family (Zhang 2008). To increase gender equality the CCP, as early as 1950, started to encourage uxorilocal residence patterns (Zhang 2008), as I will discuss in more detail below.

A truly educated woman (*Funü*, 妇女)[8] devoted herself to the service of her husband and his family (Barlow 1994: 256). She could only gain social rank through marriage and, hence, the only available roles for women in Confucian China were as wives and mothers (Croll 1995: 37).[9] Woman's role and appropriate behavior were prescribed by the five cardinal relations outlined above (Barlow 1994: 260) and the *Three Obediences and Four Womanly Virtues* (*Sancong, Side,* 三从四德) (Croll 1995: 13). In the Confucian discourse the husband is responsible to secure the (material) survival of the family, while the wife is in charge of all decisions within the family, similar to a managing director of the private sphere (Li op. 1991: 55). This division of rights and duties became the cornerstone of the so-called *nei-wai* binary (*Nan zhuwai, Nü zhunei,* 男主外, 女主内), one of the fundamental principles of the Confucian gender regime and the moral justification for the exclusion of women from the public and particularly the political sphere (Li 2000: 3; Croll 1995: 13).[10]

The "three obediences" prescribe women's subordination to the father and elder brother when young (*Weijia congfu,* 未嫁从父), to the husband when married (*Jijia congfu,* 既嫁从父), and to the husband and son in old age (*Fusi*

---

8   The discursive sign *Funü* slowly emerged at the end of the twentieth century and indicates women's role outside of the family and hence the beginning of the decoupling of family and women from women's identity (Barlow 2004: 40ff.). Moreover, woman is not a stable category but is divided by social class, age, geography, and time. Confucian discourses envisioned a universal and undifferentiated womanhood, defined as the mutually constitutive other of manhood (Ko et al. 2003a: 2).

9   This is a generalization and simplification, since there are records of elite women in late imperial China who were artists and participated in the public sphere (Ko et al. 2003b; Ko 1994).

10 We have to treat these guidelines for an adequate code of conduct carefully, since they aimed to establish an *ideal type* and are not necessarily found as such in the reality of Chinese history. Ko et al., for instance, reject the image of Confucian women as cloistered beings who had no access to the public sphere, regardless of authoritative texts prescribing such isolation (Ko et al. 2003a: 7). Rather, they list examples of women who, despite this dictate, participated in public life. However, we have to treat this finding with equal caution. Chinese women in the late imperial era by and large were likely to act according to these widely accepted norms of adequate behavior.

congzi, 夫死从子).[11] Since a wife was not only a wife but also a daughter-in-law, she was expected to be filial and hence obedient to her in-laws (Li 2000: 55ff.). The "four womanly virtues" refer to the morality of women (*Fude*, 妇德) and advise them to know their place in the universe (their *li*) and to behave in total compliance with the time-honored ethical code (Croll 1995: 13). Secondly, women were supposed to be reticent and to take care not to chatter too much or bore others, in short, there was a proper womanly speech (*Fuyan*, 妇言). Thirdly, women had to be clean of person and habits and adorn themselves with a view pleasant for the opposite sex, i.e., they had to have a modest appearance that was appealing to the opposite sex (*Furong*, 妇容). Finally, Chinese women were supposed to be diligent in their household duties (*Fugong*, 妇功) (Croll 1995: 13).

The Confucian gender regime, although abolished in 1949, had long-lasting effects. Remnants of this regime are still evident today. For instance, the *nei-wai* binary still guides the everyday behavior of the Chinese. One reason for this can be traced back to its origin. Early Confucian scholars adapted and condensed established sociopolitical practices in their ethical systems (Woo 1999: 110ff.). Because Confucian notions reflected existing practices, they were readily adopted by Chinese people. Moreover, Confucian precepts were frequently reduced to one-line quotations, proverbs, and folk sayings for oral repetition among the literate and illiterate, such as, "To be a woman means to submit" (Lee Swann 1999; Croll 1995: 14). This mineralization of foundational gendered norms guiding everyday practices supported a strong anchoring of such codes of conduct in the sociopolitical sediment of every Chinese.

2.3.2   The Communist gender regime

The founding of the PRC drastically changed the existing gender regime. Mao propagated that women should be equal to men and "hold up half the sky" (*Chengqi ban bian tian*, 撑起半边天) (Chen 2011: 42). Thus the equality of

---

11   These are not literal translations. Literally translated, the three obediences state, "unmarried, obey the father" (*Weijia congfu*), "already married, obey the husband" (*Jijia congfu*), and "after the husband's death, obey the son" (*Fusi congzi*).

men and women (*Nannü pingdeng*, 男女平等) was included in the Constitution of the PRC in 1950 (Chen 1999). The Communist gender regime can be divided into two major phases: before and after the reform and open policies at the end of the 1970s (Spakowski 2014; Hershatter 2004).[12]

2.3.3. Maoist gender egalitarianism

Before the reform and open policies, Mao's gender politics can best be described as *Maoist egalitarianism*. The equality of men and women (*Nannü pingdeng*) was symbolized as the core of the Constitution, and women were supposed to assimilate to male-oriented norms (Spakowski 2014: 23). Women were encouraged to fully participate in the socialist construction (Hershatter 2004: 1036). The resulting "iron girl" was able to do the work of men and could simultaneously carry (alone) the burden of housework, while encouraging her family to give their all for the greater social good (Honig 2000). The Maoist gender politics degenderized society and aimed at the establishment of non-difference of the two main sexes (Chen 2011: 42), which led to the emergence of the socialist androgyne (Hershatter 2004; Spakowski 2014; Chen 2011). The rationale underlying Mao's egalitarianism was the subordination of gender issues to class questions. Gender issues were ruled obsolete, and women's liberation was perceived as an integral part of the communist revolution (Chen 2011; Spakowski 2014; Xu 2009). The main advocate of this gender politics was the ACWF, an institutional vehicle for Mao's gender politics, directed by the CCP (Chen 2011: 42; Howell 1997). The ACWF was set up to organize women from the central government down to the local level, execute all the communist political decisions related to women, and rally support for the incorporated policies (Chen 2011: 42; Kaufman 2012: 589; Hershatter 2004: 1035). Due to these features, the ACWF is often described as a typical transmission-belt organization.

---

12 Other classifications are possible. For our purpose, the distinction between two major developmental phases seems practicable. However, the time before and after the reform and open polices, as well as the post-socialist era in itself, could be divided into several development phases.

2.3.4. Gender politics after the reform and open policies

The reform and open policies of the late 1970s had a profound impact on the existing gender order and led to the reemergence of women's issues in public and policy debates (Spakowski 2014: 229). Concerning gender politics, core elements of the socialist order remained while the party-state withdrew the provision of gender-related services (Milwertz and Bu 2009: 228; Chen 1999; Evans and Strauss 2010). Gender equality (*Nannü pingdeng*) remained the core element, and the ACWF was reestablished after its disbandment in the Cultural Revolution as the institutional vehicle of CCP's gender politics (Spakowski 2014: 230; Chen 1999).[13]

On the one hand, in the reform era women's rights were formally backed by several laws that aimed to improve women's situation by rectifying specific problems, e.g., the Law for the Protection of Women's Rights and Interests (*Zhonghua renmin gongheguo funü quanyi baozhangfa*, 中华共和国妇女权益保障法) was implemented in 1992 and the Marriage Law was amended in 1980. Despite the new opportunities, increased social space, improved economic conditions, and enhanced legislation, women were negatively impacted by the socioeconomic transformation. The downsizing and economic restructuring of state-owned industries pushed women *en masse* out of the labor market (Spakowski 2014; Liu 2007; Kaufman 2012; Wesoky 2002). Women were, and still are, discriminated in higher education (Spakowski 2014), restricted by the well-known one-child policy (Hong 1987), and excluded from high leadership roles within the party and enterprises (Chen 2011; Croll 1995).

Moreover, women's situation is also influenced by informal gender institutions. Gendered expectations and arrangements of family life and marriage persist (Evans and Strauss 2010). And the socially institutionalized discourse of the *nei-wai* binary continues to function as a cognitive framework molding many aspects of gendered behavior and practices (Evans and Strauss 2010; Evans 2010), often discouraging women from participating fully and equally in socioeconomic life (Hong Fincher 2013). A regular survey by the National

---

13 For a more detailed inquiry into the Cultural Revolution, cf. Fairbank and Goldman (2006) and Gernet (1988); for a more in-depth discussion of women's situation during the Cultural Revolution, cf. Croll (1978).

Bureau of Statistics even warns that the social support for the *nei-wai* binary might be on the rise again (Department of Social, Science and Technology, and Cultural Statistics, National Bureau of Statistics 2012). In 2000 44.4% of the surveyed respondents approved the notion, "A good marriage is better than a good job for women" (Department of Social, Science and Technology, and Cultural Statistics, National Bureau of Statistics 2012: 126). In 2004 53.9% of the male respondents and 50.4% of the female respondents supported the notion, "Men should mainly work outside, women should mainly do housework" (Department of Population, Social Science, and Technology, National Bureau of Statistics 2004: 107), and in 2012 61.6% of the male respondents and 54.8% of the female respondents approved the same notion (Department of Social, Science and Technology, and Cultural Statistics, National Bureau of Statistics 2012: 126), which indicates a slow but steady increase in the approval rates for the *nei-wai* binary, the cornerstone of the traditional Confucian gender regime. These statistics parallel the decline in women's political participation in recent years. The proportion of women in the Party's Central Committee (CCP), after increasing from 5–13% between the 1960s–70s, declined to 7.69% in 2002 (Guo and Zheng 2008) and dropped to a devastating low of 4.9% in the recent party congress (Zheng 2014). Moreover, in the eighteenth Politburo Standing Committee only two out of twenty-five members, Liu Yandong and Sun Chunlan, were women (Yuen 2013). Furthermore, traditional Confucian gender institutions were reemphasized in public debates to address the pending problems related to socioeconomic hardship. For instance, when women were pushed *en masse* out of the labor market in the 1980s, the public discourse "women should return home" (*Funü huijia*, 妇女回家) became dominant (Zhang 2005: 377).

Against this background, the ambivalence of the current Chinese gender regime is striking. It follows the legacy of the traditional Confucian patriarchal gender regime, which is predominately manifested today in the form of informal gender institutions (established cognitive frameworks, Chinese proverbs, stories). Simultaneously, it is formally manifested as a gender egalitarian regime with formal institutions that secure and prescribe gender equality. Gender activism in the Chinese hybrid regime is therefore challenged on two fronts: The authoritarian legacy limits civil rights, including, among others, freedom of press, the right to free assembly, and the right of free speech; in addition, the traditional informal gender institutions of the patriarchal legacy have created a hostile atmosphere for gender activists, who are rejected by society and/or policy elites.

3. Beijing anti-domestic violence activism: a form of Chinese gender activism

The relationship between gender equality and DV is complex. Evidence suggests that gender inequalities increase the risk of violence by men against women and inhibit the ability of victims to seek protection (World Health Organization 2009). When gender inequalities prevail, women are often subordinated to men, which results in a lower social status of women and allows men control over them and a greater decision-making power (World Health Organization 2009; Hanser 2007: 208; Berkel and LaVerne 2007: 13; Walker 1999: 22; Hester 2004: 1433; Tang et al. 2002: 975). Such situations make women more vulnerable to physical, psychological, and sexual violence by men and hinder victims from getting help. As such, how a state deals with DV is a good indicator in understanding how well gender equality is supported and implemented by that state.

Gender relations are power relations.[14] Unequal gender relations can be manifested in the form of laws and regulations and gender politics and policies, such as the one-child policy, or in informal institutions, such as the aforementioned *nei-wai* binary. As a result, gender-specific formal and informal institutions can express and consolidate unequal gender relations. In this way, the prevalence of DV is largely influenced by the existing gender politics and the resulting gender relations, making Beijing ADV activism a good case to exemplify how Chinese gender activism is wedged between the patriarchal and authoritarian legacy.

---

14 Power can be understood as a relationship between actors. This relationship is defined through actions that relate to the actions of another actor (cf. Foucault et al. 2005, 252).

3.1 From superficial public displays of goodwill to improved legal protection against DV

DV remains a severe problem in the PRC.[15] Depending on the study, between 24.7% and 54.6% females are victims of DV (All-China Women's Federation, Oct. 21, 2011: 4). It is not a new political issue, but resurfaced as a central topic in the mid-1990s. Until then most state measures were superficial public displays of goodwill (Milwertz 2003: 630). The reform and open policies marked a turning point for ADV activism. The reforms led not only to a boom of social organizations but also to an increase in women's organizations (Milwertz 2003; Zhang 2009; Kaufman 2009). This enhanced interest in women's issues was due to the aforementioned emerging negative outcomes of the reforms for women (Spakowski 2014; Xu 2009; Chen and Cheung 2011). Moreover, a growing number of women's organizations began engaging with the DV issue. DV reemerged as an important issue for several reasons. Besides a greater general awareness of women's issues, the PRC signed and ratified the Convention on the Elimination of All Forms of Discrimination Against Women (Human Rights in China [HRIC] 2006). By doing so, they committed themselves internationally to combatting DV and hence increased national support for ADV. Furthermore, Beijing hosted the "Fourth World Conference of Women" in 1995, which was organized and directed by the United Nations. DV was one of the four core issues broadly discussed by international scholars and – for the first time – Chinese practitioners and scholars (interview #2 with a founder and legal expert of a professional organization). In the following years, DV became more and more public. Especially since the beginning of the twenty-first century, much has been improved in the legal sphere with regard to DV, for instance, the Marriage Law was revised in 2001 to include DV as an acceptable reason for divorce (Lü 2011), and local rules or policies dealing with DV in 28 out of 34 provinces or equivalent administrative regions were created (Creasey et al. December 2013). Nonetheless, DV remains a severe issue, and the

---

15 *Domestic violence* refers in the context of the PRC mostly to three sets of actions: physical violence (*Shenti baoli*, 身体暴力), psychic violence (*Jingshen baoli*, 精神暴力), and/or sexual violence (*Xingbali*, 性暴力). For an in-depth discussion, cf. Zhang and Liu Meng (2004).

official Anti-Domestic Violence Law of the PRC was only introduced in the spring of 2016 (Li Jianhua 2016; Gao 2016; Gao et al. 2016).[16]

3.2 Main actors of Beijing ADV social and gender activism

Beijing ADV activism is mostly comprised of expert organizations, which are driven by charismatic leaders rather than individual activists (interview #3 with the administrative director of a professional organization). The founders, employees, and volunteers of such organizations are mostly experts in their particular fields; for instance, there are legal scholars in legal aid organizations and social workers in organizations providing educational seminars for cadres. Most experts have been committed to tackling DV for a long time (interviews with a co-founder and legal expert, with a founder and legal expert, with a social work expert, and a managing director and media expert of professional organizations) and have well-established links to the political system, either through their networks or as a result of being embedded in established political and academic institutions (interviews with a cofounder and legal expert and a managing director and media expert of professional organizations). In Beijing, four organizations are crucially important to the ADV professional movement, all of which hold official registrations. To obtain an official registration status, organizations must be associated with state entities (Ma 2009); the state entities are responsible for their activities and thus function as a control mechanism. As a result of being highly networked and supervised, Beijing ADV organizations have a rather corporatist and nonconfrontational tactical orientation. Nonetheless, two of the four organizations lost their registration status in 2010 and had to reapply as independent nonprofit entities (interviews with a cofounder and legal expert and a managing director and media expert of professional organizations). This marks an important caesura in the Beijing ADV

---

16 For the entire law please check: http://news.xinhuanet.com/legal/2015-12/27/c_128571791. htm. An unofficial translation can be found here: https://www.chinalawtranslate.com/%E5% 8F%8D%E5%AE%B6%E5%BA%AD%E6%9A%B4%E5%8A%9B%E6%B3%95-2015/? lang=en.

activism. Since all of these social organizations depend on external funding, which for most of them consists of international giving,[17] Beijing ADV actors are especially vulnerable to changes in international funding trends.

The networks between all organizations were well institutionalized.[18] Employees of all organizations were members of the same formal women's rights networks, which disseminate national and international gender-specific information mostly through internet channels, such as mailing lists and webpages. Moreover they frequently worked together on diverse projects, ranging from gender discrimination lawsuits to conferences and workshops. The offices of two of the four organizations were located in the same building, providing an infrastructure for easy informal exchange. This combination of institutionalized communication and geographic proximity led to strong networks that could be easily maintained and actions that could be easily coordinated.

3.3 Strategic alignment of Beijing ADV actors

Prior to 1995, psychological and emotional support for DV victims were cornerstones of ADV organizations' efforts. After 1995, this tactical approach changed; they increasingly turned to the legal dimension of DV and to raising awareness about the issue (interview #8 with a managing director and media expert of a professional organization). However, the nonconfrontational tactical approach adopted by ADV actors toward the party-state remained the same pre- and post-1995: they adapted to the prevailing political environment in which the party-state officially remained the dominant policy decision-maker – one of the two Goliaths, the authoritarian legacy. As such, ADV

---

17 These organizations are reluctant to provide detailed listings of the funds they receive. They are afraid that public knowledge of their predominant dependence on foreign donors puts them at higher risk for backlashes by party-state actors.
18 The alliance changed profoundly in 2014 with the dissolution of one of the organizations, an umbrella organization which held a central role in the mobilization process of Beijing ADV activism. The organization claimed on their now inactive webpage that the main reason for its dissolution was that the draft for an ADV law was accepted for discussion into the NPC in 2013 and hence their proclaimed superordinate goal was achieved.

organizations provided legal recommendations, seminars, and workshops for policy cadres and other multipliers and conducted pilot projects on DV prevention. Especially awareness raising campaigns were supported by the ACWF.

These mobilization efforts were framed as supportive to the CCP's efforts. As a result, the organizations were able to establish themselves as important advisors for policy cadres regarding legal protection against DV (interview #1 with a co-founder and legal expert of a professional organization). In this sense, professional ADV organizations functioned as service providers and professional advocates simultaneously. Their advocacy was directed to a wide range of recipients from policy elites (such as members of the ACWF and NPC) to lawyers and judges. All of them were key figures in implementing formal and informal institutional change top-down.

On the other hand, the tactical approach of Beijing ADV activism was limited by the second Goliath, the patriarchal legacy. The ADV activists adapted their tactical approach to the narrow space open to gender activities. DV has long been a taboo topic, traditionally confined to the private sphere. This confinement to the private sphere is deeply rooted in the traditional Confucian gender regime in which female obedience to father, husband, son, and, as their representatives, the in-laws, is strongly anchored in considerable parts of society even today. Moreover, the *nei-wai* binary confines woman to the house and makes the family, where she has a subordinate role, her main frame of reference. Instead of disappearing, the *nei-wai* binary is, as discussed previously, advancing once again. Consequently female victims of DV face rather unsurmountable difficulties to defend themselves. If they remain in the rather traditional gender regime, they are expected to be obedient to the male family members and their representatives (the in-laws) and are not supposed to discuss their family matters in public. In fact it is exactly this behavior that is prohibited in the traditional Chinese proverb "Don't wash your dirty linen in public" (*Jia chou bu ke waiyang*, 家丑不可外扬), which effectively contains family quarrels and is often used to circumscribe DV as well.

Beijing ADV activism, for instance, designed their tactical approach to address the increasing sensitivity of the issue, in order to avoid scaring off possible recipients by violating DV taboos during awareness raising campaigns (interview #6 with a founder and legal expert of a professional organization). Most of the Beijing ADV activists followed a scattergun approach directed at policy elites, as they intended to mobilize key figures and gatekeepers who are better able to implement useful measures to fight DV. Moreover, by focusing the activism on policy elites, the activists emphasized the supportive, nonconfrontational nature of their initiatives; they simply framed themselves as *providing expertise to policy elites* and as *raising their awareness of emerging and existing blind spots*. As such, they framed themselves as neither challenging the party-state (authoritarian legacy) nor traditionalists (patriarchal legacy).

And, finally, Beijing ADV activists navigated between formal gender equality institutions and lingering informal Confucian gender institutions condemning DV to the private sphere. They clearly aligned their claims with the established gender equality of the Constitution or the Women's Law, but they designed their activities in a manner that did not vehemently contradict the prevailing condemnation of DV to the private sphere. Their campaigns are predominately designed for policy elites and as such are not public disturbances. If public awareness raising campaigns are held, they are not designed as huge events. Rather, they are planned in collaboration with other social organizations and the local ACWF branch. Since the ACWF is aware of the *local culture,* they can adapt the events to the specific micro-institutional context.

The composition and tactical alignment of Beijing ADV activism only recently underwent fundamental changes. Since 2012, individual volunteers have begun associating themselves with established ADV organizations and they have increasingly made their concerns public through staged public disturbances, thus deviating from the highly sensitive, nonconfrontational approach. This tactical approach was first applied in Beijing ADV activism, but has spread like wildfire to other issues of gender activism.

3.4 Recent trends of Beijing ADV activism: We are here, we are visible, and we demand change!

ADV activism in Beijing has undergone drastic changes in terms of its personnel composition and tactical approaches since 2012. Although the changes were initiated by Beijing ADV activists, the new tactical approach has spread like wildfire, first in the nationwide ADV mobilization and then to other subjects of gender activism, such as the Occupy Men's Bathroom[19] and Equal University Access[20] campaigns.

This new tactical approach is often labeled "performance art public advocacy," which consists of live performances in public places for public audiences (Guo et al. 2013) and thus differs significantly from traditional advocacy tools such as lobbying (Wang Man 2012) or the compilation of (legal) recommendations for policy elites. It is an inclusive strategy and has the potential to receive broad media coverage due to its public event character; as such, it is an apt tool to raise public awareness and rally support for policy reforms. However, unlike ex-ante expectations, the actual media response is strikingly low, as I argue elsewhere.

> The young people have a different way than the old ... the previously existing approach based on experience and expert knowledge is completely different ... The old approach relied on articles, experts, or the ACWF. But this new approach is a very direct activity; it is the freedom of speech of the public ... These activities try to spur the public to discuss such hot topics. (Interview #4 with a resort manager of a professional organization, translation by author)

---

19   Occupy Men's Bathroom (*Zhanlin Nan Cesuo*, 占领男厕所) was initiated by feminist activists in Guandong in 2012 and was quickly taken up by feminist activists in many major cities in the PRC to tackle the problem of the limited number of public toilets for women. Women occupied men's public bathrooms to call for improved and increased facilities for women and the incorporation of women's needs in day-to-day activities.

20   Equal University Access activism refers to activities in 2012 in which young female activists used performance art public advocacy to demonstrate for the equal treatment of women in the university entry exams.

3.4.1 The Injured Brides as forerunner of a new tactical approach

In 2012 three women in Western wedding dresses adorned with red "blood" stains paraded down the *Qianmen* pedestrian street with signs drawing attention to the social problem of DV (Chen Di 2012). Their signs stated that love is no excuse for violence (*Ai bushi baoli de jiekou.* 爱不是暴力的借口), proclaimed a violence-free zone since equality is the precondition for harmony (*Baoli wutequ: pingdeng cahexie.* 暴力无特区: 平等才和谐), and questioned why the majority stayed silent despite DV occurring in close proximity to them (*Ni yiran chenmo? Baoli zai shenbian.* 你依然沉默？暴力在身本). *The Injured Brides* event is the first known occurrence of public performance art advocacy used in the Chinese women's movement (interviews with a social work expert and a managing director and media expert of professional organizations).

To stress the symbolism of the event, *The Injured Brides* took place on Valentine's Day 2012. The day is widely perceived as a special date (*Qingrenjie*, 情人节) symbolizing the celebration of harmonious intimate relationships. Within the women's movement, and particularly among ADV activists, Valentine's Day is also significant as the date of the international "V Day" campaign. V Day was initiated by Eve Ensler; inspired by reactions to her play *The Vagina Monologues*, the campaign calls for creative, simultaneous actions worldwide on Valentine's Day to raise awareness of and demand an end to violence against women. During *The Injured Brides* performance, DV was portrayed as symbolizing the dark side of intimate relationships, in sharp contrast to the romantic image of love that is commonly propagated on Valentine's Day. By using a topic relevant to every Chinese – love and marriage – and by contrasting the ideal of harmonious intimacy with DV, the activists hoped to draw attention to and rally support against DV (interview #4 with a resort manager of a professional organization).

The activists chose to parade down the famous *Qianmen* pedestrian street because it is known as one of the last remnants of the business center of old Beijing and is one of the top tourist locations. Given the high pedestrian traffic, the performance had the potential to reach a substantial audience: "Qianmen … is also Beijing's business district and there are quite a lot of people on the streets" (interview #5 with a public performance art activist; translation by author).

Moreover, *The Injured Brides* was repeatedly framed as the activism of independent volunteers, which emphasized the activists' separation from professional ADV organizations (Wang Man 2012; interview #4 with a resort manager of a professional organization). This framing stemmed from fear of reprisals against the ADV organizations involved (interview with a resort manager of a professional organization) if these collective social actors were perceived as initiators of public disturbances:

> We always say it is an activity organized by volunteers, because it can bring along threats for the organizations. ... The reporters are always very keen to know what organization we are representing, but if we would give them a name, the organization could experience diverse risks. ... In Beijing we can discuss, organize, and conduct almost any activity, but if the police find out about it, if too many people know that we work this way, they [the authorities] can easily find a reason to shut us [the organizations] down. (Interview #4 with a resort manager of a professional organization; translation by author)

3.4.2 Features of a new tactical turn

This new tactical approach is innovatively enacting performances in public settings. Such performances are not directed at the attention of policy elites but media representatives (and through the latter, the broader public), who are drawn to the scene by means of the element of public disturbance: "They [the authorities] simply don't want to have any kind of controversy or incident; they simply don't want any kind of controversy or activity out on the street" (interview #4 with a resort manager of a professional organization; translation by author).

Disturbing the social order is part of the Chinese penal code, but due to its broad scope it is hard to define exactly which actions may constitute such a disturbance. It is a widespread practice to round up undesirable social elements, such as dissidents, labor activists, or initiators of other forms of disruption of the social order (Johnson 2005: 294).

This new tactic is in sharp contrast to the tactics of professional ADV organizations in Beijing. Whereas the professional organizations are not interested in challenging the established regime – neither the CCP rule nor possible remnants of the Confucian gender regime – public performance art activism is meant to expose traditional taboos and disturb the social order. These activists therefore run the risk of violating the penal code and disturbing the deep-seated informal institutions. In doing so, they challenge both Goliaths, the authoritarian legacy and the patriarchal legacy. And the risks associated with such social and gender activism are doubled as well.

However, to ease this twofold confrontational tactical approach, the activists keep framing their activity as supportive of the CCP. "Harmonious society" (*Hexie shehui* 和谐社会) is one of the central *social and political leitmotifs* propagated by the CCP to encourage social and political stability. The CCP still spends considerable amounts of financial resources on the establishment of the harmonious society slogan as an important pillar of Chinese society (Holbig and Gilley 2010). Activists conducting performance art advocacy consciously used this leitmotif to legitimize their claims (interview #4 with a resort manager of a professional organization). The signs carried down the *Qianmen* during *The Injured Brides* stated "Violence Free Zone: Equality is the Precondition of Harmony." The message hence emphasized the ongoing gender inequality in the PRC and brought out how a harmonious society could only be achieved after gender equality was established. The activists thus framed their public disturbance activity as supportive of official party-state propaganda, thereby trying to ease the confrontational character of the event.

Nonetheless, because this new tactical approach challenges the authoritarian and patriarchal legacies, activists are put at increased risk. This became most evident in March 2015 when five gender activists, three of whom were directly and indirectly involved in the introduction of this new approach, were detained by the CCP. The Beijing police charged them with "gathering crowds to disturb public order," not only for their conduct at *The Injured Brides* performance but also for the Occupy Men's Bathrooms campaign (Zhao 2015). Even Chinese feminist experts were surprised by the unexpected harsh behavior toward the gender activists (Zhao 2015). Ai Xiaoming, a well-known Chinese feminist scholar, argues that the detained activists became influential advocates and that the Chinese policy elites are most afraid of the entry of citizen expression in the public sphere. Therefore, these activists constituted a sustainable threat to social stability and were seen as uncontrollable because they seemed to have the potential to mobilize huge parts of the Chinese society (Zhao 2015).

4. Conclusions: gender activism wedged between authoritarian and patriarchal legacies

If we reflect on the forms of Beijing ADV activism, we find two interlinked tactical approaches. In the first stage of activism, the field was dominated by professional expert organizations, which were tightly embedded into the established control system of (collective) social actors. Their well-established networks with policy elites enabled them to function as advisors and experts and, hence, to some degree, to influence policy decision-making. Moreover, these organizations conducted important groundwork to raise awareness for DV. In the second stage of Beijing ADV activism, provocative, progressive, and rather independent activists appeared whose aims contrasted sharply with those of the professional ADV organizations; they sought a huge media impact, they wanted to shake-up and wake-up society.

The potential impact of gender activism largely depends on the selected tactical approach. Professional gender organizations are able to support (legal) improvements in the gender realm and in state-society relations. However, these changes do not reflect the *huge expectations* of a Western democratic and gender equal society. Professional gender organizations are able to consult with policy elites and participate as experts in decision-making process if they stick to the CCP's rules to operate in a nonconfrontational and incorporated manner. In such cases, they actually become important experts in their field and have an impact on the official policy process. Moreover, they are able to influence CCP gender politics, most notably the enacted legal improvements in the realm of DV. However, gender activism such as FEMEN[21] is far-fetched

---

21 According to the FEMEN website, "FEMEN is an international women's movement of brave topless female activists painted with the slogans and crowned with flowers." For more information please check: https://femen.org/about-us/

because it violates both the established gender institutions and the guidelines of the political regime.

Furthermore, it is obvious that the later tactical approach is built on the earlier one; without the awareness raising campaigns of the professional ADV organizations it seems unlikely that the performance art advocacy activists would have had any positive impact. In that sense the activism of the professional organizations created greater leeway for the subsequent young and provocative activists.

Moreover, gender activism remains wedged between two Goliaths – the authoritarian and patriarchal legacies. While this article indicates that both kinds of activists are able to influence policy elites and impact policy decision-making, it seems activists are more likely to be successful if they incorporate themselves into the control system established by the CCP for social actors and do not confront gender inequalities too loudly or publicly. When using the latter tactics, the activists' risk seems to double, most notably in the current unexpected and hard crackdown on social and gender activists.

References

All-China Women's Federation (Quanguo Fulian) (2011): Report on Major Results of the Third Wave Survey on The Social Status of Women in China (Disanqi Zhongguo Funü Shehui Diwei Diaocha. Zhuyao Shuju Baogao). http://www.china.com.cn/zhibo/zhuanti/ch-xinwen/2011-10/21/content_23687810.htm. (20.02.2018)

Amnesty International (2015): China: Latest information on crackdown against lawyers and activists. http://www.amnestyusa.org/news/news-item/china-latest-information-on-crackdown-against-lawyers-and-activists. (20.02.2018)

Barlow, Tani E. (1993): Introduction. In: Barlow, Tani E. (Ed.): Gender politics in modern China. Writing and feminism. Durham: Duke University Press, pp. 1–13.

Barlow, Tani E. (1994): Theorizing Women: Funü, Guojia, Jiating. In: Zito, Angela/Barlow, Tani E. (Eds.): Body, subject & power in China. Chicago: University of Chicago Press, pp. 253–291.

Barlow, Tani E. (2004): The question of women in Chinese feminism. Durham: Duke University Press.

Berkel, LaVerne, A. (2007): Domestic Violence in African American Community. In: Ali Jackson, Nicky (Ed.): Encyclopedia of domestic violence. New York: Routledge, pp. 11–18.

Chen, Mingxia (1999): From Legal to Substantive Equality: Realizing Women's Rights by Action. In: Violence Against Women 5, 12, pp. 1394–1410. DOI: 10.1177/10778019922183444.

Chen, Xue Fei/Cheung, Fanny M. (2011): Feminist Psychology in China. In: Rutherford, Alexander (Ed.): Handbook of international feminisms. Perspectives on psychology, women, culture, and rights. New York, London: Springer (International and cultural psychology), pp. 268–293.

Chen, Ya-chen (2011): The many dimensions of Chinese feminism. New York: Palgrave Macmillan (Breaking feminist waves).

Chen Di (2012): Beijing Students initiate a performance art on Valentine's Day to oppose intimate partner violence (Beijing Nüren Xuesheng Qingrenjie Faqi Xingwei Yishu Fandui Banghuo Baoli). In: China Daily, 2/14/2012. http://www.chinadaily.com.cn/hqzx/2012-02/14/content_14607836.htm.

Chin, Josh (2015): China Frees Detained Women's-Rights Activists. In: The Wall Street Journal, 4/13/2015. http://www.wsj.com/articles/china-frees-three-womens-rights-activists-1428934300.

Chin, Josh; Chen, Te-Ping (2015): China Targets Human-Rights Lawyers in Crackdown. In: The Wall Street Journal, 7/12/2015. http://www.wsj.com/articles/china-targets-human-rights-lawyers-in-crackdown-1436715268.

Creasey, Daniel/Coventry/Miller, David (2013): A landscape analysis of domestic violence laws. Thomas Reuter Foundation, checked on 4/24/2014.

Croissant, Aurel (2002): Von der Transition zur defekten Demokratie. Demokratische Entwicklung in den Philippinen, Südkorea und Thailand. Wiesbaden: Westdt. Verl. (Politik in Afrika, Asien und Lateinamerika).

Croll, Elisabeth (1978): Feminism and socialism in China. London, Boston: Routledge & K. Paul.

Croll, Elisabeth J. (1995): Changing Identities of Chinese Women. Rhetoric, Experience and Self-Perception in Twentieth-Century China. London: Zed Books.

Department of Population, Social, Science and Technology, National Bureau of Statistics (2004): Women and Men in China: Facts and Figures. http://www.stats.gov.cn/english/Statisticaldata/OtherData/200509/U020150722579392934100.pdf. (20.02.2018)

Department of Social, Science and Technology, and Cultural Statistics, National Bureau of Statistics (2012): Men and Women in China. Facts and Figures 2012. Beijing, checked on 8/21/2015.

Evans, Harriet (2010): The Gender of Communication: Changing Expectations of Mothers and Daughters in Urban China. In: The China Quarterly 204, pp. 980–1000. DOI: 10.1017/S0305741010001050.

Evans, Harriet/Strauss, Julia C. (2010): Gender, Agency and Social Change. In: The China Quarterly 204, pp. 817–826. DOI: 10.1017/S0305741010000974.

Fairbank, John King/Goldman, Merle (2006): China. A new history. Cambridge, Mass.: Belknap Press of Harvard University Press.

Fulda, Andreas/Li, Yanyan/Song, Qinghua (2012): New Strategies of Civil Society in China: a case study of the network governanceFehler! Textmarke nicht definiert. approach. In: Journal of Contemporary China 21, 76, pp. 675–693. DOI: 10.1080/10670564.2012.666837.

Foucault, Michel (et al.) (2005): Analytik der Macht. Frankfurt a.M.:Suhrkamp.

Gao, Li/Zhou, Liting/Lin, Mu/Ru, Xijia (2016): National dissemination activities against domestic violence. Local women's federations organize activities to promote the anti-domestic violence law. (Fandui jiating baoli quanguo jiasu xingding. Gedi fulian zhuzhi kaizhan fanjiabaofa xuanchuan huodong.) In: Zhongguo fulian xinwen, 3/2/2016. http://acwf.people.com.cn/n1/2016/0302/c99057-28164801.html. (07.03.2016).

Gao, Shan (2016): Mainland China is currently enacting the first "Anti-Domestic Violence Law". (Zhongguo dalu zhengzai zhiding diyibu "fanduijiabaolifa".) In: Ziyou yazhou diantai putonghua, 3/4/2016. http://www.rfa.org/mandarin/yataibaodao/renquanfazhi/hc-03042015113916.html. (07.03.2016).

Gernet, Jacques (1988): Die chinesische Welt. Die Geschichte Chinas von den Anfängen bis zur Jetztzeit. Frankfurt am Main, Germany: Suhrkamp (Edition Suhrkamp, 1505).

Guo, Ting/Fu, Tao/Liu, Haiying (Eds.) (2013): The Diversification of Public Advocacy in China (Zhongguo Gongyi Changdao de Duoyuanhua Fazhan). A CDB Special Report. Beijing: The China Development Brief (Zhongguo Fazhan Jianbao).

Guo, Xiajuan/Zheng, Yongnian (2008): Women's political participation in China. In: Briefing Series (34), checked on 8/29/2014.

Hanser, Robert D. (2007): Cross-cultural examination of domestic violence in China and Pakistan. In: Ali Jackson, Nicky (Ed.): Encyclopedia of domestic violence. New York: Routledge, pp. 208–212.

He, Baogang/Warren, Mark E. (2011): Authoritarian Deliberation: The Deliberative Turn in Chinese Political Development. In: Persp on Pol 9, 2, pp. 269–289. DOI: 10.1017/S1537592711000892.

Heberer, Thomas (2003): Das politische System der VR China im Prozess des Wandels. In: Derichs, Claudia/Heberer, Thomas (Eds.): Einführung in die politischen Systeme Ostasiens. VR China, Hongkong, Japan, Nordkorea, Südkorea, Taiwan. Opladen: Leske + Budrich (UTB Politikwissenschaft, 8233), pp. 19–123.

Heilmann, Sebastian (2004): Das politische System der Volksrepublik China. Wiesbaden: VS Verl. für Sozialwiss.

Hershatter, Gail (2004): State of the Field: Women in China's Long Twentieth Century. In: Journal of Asian Studies 63, 4, pp. 991–1065. DOI: 10.1017/S0021911804002396.

Hester, M. (2004): Future Trends and Developments: Violence Against Women in Europe and East Asia. In: Violence Against Women 10, 12, pp. 1431–1448. DOI: 10.1177/1077801204270559.

Ho, Peter (2007): Embedded Activism and Political Change in a Semiauthoritarian Context. In: China Information 21, 2, pp. 187–209. DOI: 10.1177/0920203X07079643.

Ho, Peter/Edmonds, R. L. (Eds.) (2008a): Chinas embedded activism: Opportunities and constraints of social movement. London and New York: Routledge, Taylor & Francis Group.

Ho, Peter/Edmonds R. L. (2008b): Perspectives of time and change. Rethinking green environmental activism in China. In: Ho, Peter/Edmonds, R. L. (Eds.): Chinas embedded activism: Opportunities and constraints of social movement. London and New York: Routledge, Taylor & Francis Group, pp. 216–225.

Holbig, Heike/Gilley, Bruce (2010): Reclaiming Legitimacy in China. In: Politics & Policy, 28, 3, pp. 395–422, checked on 7/7/2014.

Hong, Lawrence K. (1987): Potential Effects of the One-Child Policy on Gender Equality in the People's Republic of China. In: Gender and Society 1, 3, pp. 124–141, checked on 11/10/2014.

Hong Fincher, Leta (2013): Leftover women. The resurgence of gender inequality in China (Asian arguments).

Honig, Emily (2000): Iron Girls Revisited: Gender and the Politics of Work in the Cultural Revolution. In: Entwisle, Barbara/Henderson,Gail (Eds.): Re-drawing boundaries. Work, households, and gender in China. Berkeley: University of California Press, pp. 97–110.

Howell, Jude (1997): Post-Beijing Reflections: Creating Ripples, But Not in Waves in China. In: Women's Studies International Forum 20, 2, pp. 235–252.

Hsu, Carolyn (2010): Beyond Civil Society: An Organizational Perspective on State–NGO Relations in the People's Republic of China. In: Journal of Civil Society 6, 3, pp. 259–277. DOI: 10.1080/17448689.2010.528949.

Human Rights in China (HRIC) (2006): Implementation of the Convention on the Elimination of All Forms of Discrimination against Women in the People's Republic of China. A Parallel NGO Report by Human Rights in China June 2006. http://www.hrichina.org/sites/default/files/PDFs/Submissions/HRIC_CEDAW-2006.pdf.

Johnson, Ian (2005, c2004): Wild grass. Three portraits of change in modern China. New York: Vintage Books.

Kaufman, Joan (2009): The role of NGOs in China's AIDS crisis: challenges and possibilities. In: Schwartz, Jonathan/Shieh, Shawn (Eds.): State and society responses to social welfare needs in China. Serving the people. New York: Routledge, pp. 156–175.

Kaufman, Joan (2012): The Global Women's Movement and Chinese Women's Rights. In: Journal of Contemporary China 21, 76, pp. 585–602. DOI: 10.1080/10670564.2012.666830.

Ko, Dorothy (1994): Teachers of the inner chambers. Women and culture in seventeenth-century China. Stanford, Calif.: Stanford University Press.

Ko, Dorothy/Haboush, JaHyun Kim/Piggott, Joan R. (2003a): Introduction. In: Ko, Dorothy / Kim Haboush, JaHyun/Piggott, Joan R. (Eds.): Women and Confucian cultures in premodern China, Korea, and Japan. Berkeley: University of California Press, pp. 1–24.

Ko, Dorothy/Haboush, JaHyun Kim/Piggott, Joan R. (Eds.) (2003b): Women and Confucian cultures in premodern China, Korea, and Japan. Berkeley: University of California Press.

Lee Swann, Nancy (1999): Ban Zhao: Admonitions for Women (Nüjie). In: De Bary, William Theodore/Bloom, Irene/ Chan, Wing-tsit/Adler, Joseph/Lufrano, Richard John (Eds.): Sources of Chinese tradition. 2nd ed. New York: Columbia University Press (Introduction to Asian civilization), pp. 821–824.

Li, Chenyang (2000): Can Confucianism Come to Terms with Feminism? In: Li, Chenyang (Ed.): The sage and the second sex. Confucianism, ethics, and gender. Chicago, Ill.: Open Court, pp. 1–23.

Li, Hanlin (op. 1991): Die Grundstruktur der chinesischen Gesellschaft. Vom traditionellen Klansystem zur modernen Danwei-Organisation. Opladen: Westdt. Verl.

Li, Jianhua (2016): China's First Anti-domestic Violence Law Takes Effect. In: CRI English, 3/1/2016. http://english.cri.cn/12394/2016/03/01/4204s918561.htm.

Liu, Jieyu (2007): Gender and Work in Urban China. Women workers of the unlucky generation. New York: Routledge, Taylor & Francis Group.

Lü, Pin (2011): Report on Anti-Domestic Violence Actions in China. (Zhongguo fan jiating baoli xingdong baogao.) Di 1 ban. Peking: Zhongguo she hui ke xue chu ban she (Fan dui jia ting bao li li lun yu shi jian cong shu).

Ma, Qiusha (2009): Non-governmental organizations in contemporary China. Paving the way to civil society? Digital print. London [u.a.]: Routledge.

Mann, Susan (1997): Precious records. Women in China's long eighteenth century. Stanford, Calif.: Stanford University Press.

Mercator Institute of China Studies (MERICS) (2014): Wer hat's geMACHT? Das Kräftefeld in der chinesischen Politik. http://www.merics.org/merics-analysen/china-mapping/wer-hats-gemacht-das-kraeftefeld-in-der-chinesischen-politik.html (09.01.2015).

Milwertz, Cecilia (2003): Activism Against Domestic Violence in the People's Republic of China. In: Violence Against Women 9, 6, pp. 630–654. DOI: 10.1177/1077801203009006002.

Milwertz, Cecilia/Bu, Wei (2009): Non-governmental Feminist Activism in The People's Republic of China: Communicating Oppositional Gender Equality Knowledge. In: Gilles Guiheux/Eng Kuah, Khun (Eds.): Social movements in China and Hong Kong. The expansion of protest space. Amsterdam: Amsterdam University Press.

Milwertz, Cecilia/Wei, Bu (2008): Consciousness-Raising among and beyond Women's Movement Activists in China. In: Burghoorn, Wil (Ed.): Gender politics in Asia. Women maneuvering within dominant gender orders. Copenhagen: NIAS, pp. 121–144.

Moritz, Ralf/Lee, Ming-huei (1998): Einführung. In: Moritz, Ralf /Li, Minghui/Goldfuss, Gabriele/Jansen, Thomas (Eds.): Der Konfuzianismus. Ursprünge, Entwicklungen, Perspektiven. Leipzig: Leipziger Universitätsverlag (Mitteldeutsche Studien zu Ostasien, 1), pp. 11–55.

Moritz, Ralf/Li, Minghui/Goldfuss, Gabriele/Jansen, Thomas (Eds.) (1998): Der Konfuzianismus. Ursprünge, Entwicklungen, Perspektiven. Leipzig: Leipziger Universitätsverlag (Mitteldeutsche Studien zu Ostasien, 1).

Schwartz, Jonathan/Shieh, Shawn (2009): Serving the people? The changing roles of the state and social organizations in social service provision. In: Schwartz, Jonathan /Shieh, Shawn (Eds.): State and society responses to social welfare needs in China. Serving the people. New York: Routledge, pp. 177–188.

Spakowski, Nicola (2014): Feminismus in China im Kontext von Postsozialismus und internationalem Feminismus. In: Mae, Michiko/Saal, Britta (Eds.): Transkulturelle Genderforschung. Ein Studienbuch zum Verhältnis von Kultur und Geschlecht. Wiesbaden: Imprint: Springer VS (Geschlecht und Gesellschaft, 41), pp. 229–249.

Tang, C. S.-K/Wong, D./Cheung, F. M.-C (2002): Social Construction of Women as Legitimate Victims of Violence in Chinese Societies. In: Violence Against Women 8, 8, pp. 968–996. DOI: 10.1177/107780102400447096.

Teets, Jessica C. (2013): Let Many Civil Societies Bloom: The Rise of Consultative Authoritarianism in China. In: The China Quarterly, pp. 1–20. DOI: 10.1017/S0305741012001269.

Teets, Jessica C. (2014): Civil society under authoritarianism. The China model. Cambridge: University Press.

United Nations Economic and Social Commission for Asia and the Pacific (ESCAP) (2014): Statistical Yearbook for Asia and the Pacific 2014. China - Country profiles, provides a brief overview of main development indicators for China. http://www.unescap.org/sites/default/files/China_Country-profiles_SYB2014.pdf. (20.08.2015).

Walker, Lenore E. (1999): Psychology and domestic violence around the world. In: American Psychologist 54, 1, pp. 21–29. DOI: 10.1037/0003-066X.54.1.21.

Wang Man (2012): Carrying Out Public Advocacy Through Performance Art. Edited by China Development Brief (China Development Brief, 53). http://www.chinadevelopmentbrief.cn/?p=2190.

Wesoky, Sharon (2002): Chinese feminism faces globalization. New York: Routledge (East Asia).

Wong, Edward (2015): China Releases 5 Women's Rights Activists Detained for Weeks. In: The New York Times, 4/13/2015. http://www.nytimes.com/2015/04/14/world/asia/china-releases-3-of-5-detained-womens-rights-activists.html?_r=0.

Woo, Terry (1999): Confucianism and Feminism. In: Sharma, Arvind/Young, Katherine K. (Eds.): Feminism and world religions. Albany, N.Y.: State University of New York Press (McGill studies in the history of religions), pp. 110–148.

World Health Organization (2009): Promoting gender equality to prevent violence against women, pp. 1–28, checked on 8/29/2014.

Xu, Feng (2009): Chinese Feminisms Encounter International Feminisms. In: International Feminist Journal of Politics 11, 2, pp. 196–215. DOI: 10.1080/14616740902789567.

Yang, Guobin (2009): The power of the Internet in China. Citizen activism online. New York: Columbia University Press (Contemporary Asia in the world).

Yang, K. M.; Alpermann, B. (2014): Children and youth NGOs in China: Social activism between embeddedness and marginalization. In: China Information 28, 3, pp. 311–337. DOI: 10.1177/0920203X14554350.

Yuen, Lotus (2013): China's Glass Ceiling: Women Still Excluded from High-Level Politics. In: The Atlantic, 2013.06. http://www.theatlantic.com/china/archive/2013/06/chinas-glass-ceiling-women-still-excluded-fromhigh-. (29.08.2014).

Zhang, Jian (2005): "Women Returning Home" - A Topic of Chinese Women's Liberation. In: Leutner, Mechthild/Spakowski, Nicola (Eds.): Women in China. The Republican period in historical perspective. Münster [Germany], New Brunswick, NJ: Lit; Distributed in North America by Transaction Publishers (Berliner China-Studien, 44), pp. 376–396.

Zhang, Lixi/Meng, Liu (2004): Zhongguo Jiatingbaoli Yanjiu (Research on Domestic Violence in China). 1st Edition. Beijing: Zhongguo she hui ke xue chu ban she (Fan dui jia ting bao li li lun yu shi jian cong shu).

Zhang, Lu (2009): Transnational feminisms in translation. The making of a women's anti-domestic violence movement in China. Saarbrücken: VDM Verlag Dr. Müller.

Zhang, Weiguo (2008): State Gender and Uxoriloal Marriage in Contemporary China. In The China Journal 60, pp. 111–132, checked on 3/11/2015.

Zhao, Sile (2015): The Inspirational Backstory of China's Feminist Five. In: Foreign Policy, 4/17/2015. http://foreignpolicy.com/2015/04/17/china-feminist-bail-interview-released-feminism-activist/.

Zheng, Benxiang (2014): Women's Political Participation in China: Improved or Not? In: Journal of International Women's Studies 15, 1, pp. 136–150. http://vc.bridgew.edu/jiws/vol15/iss1/9. (22.09.2014).

Appendix

Interviews

Interview # 1: Beijing, August 2012, co-founder and legal expert, professional organization
Interview # 2: Beijing, January 2012, founder and legal expert, professional organization
Interview # 3: Beijing, August 2012, administrative director, professional organization
Interview # 4: Beijing, August 2012, resort manager, professional organization
Interview # 5: Beijing, August 2012, public performance art activist
Interview # 6: Beijing, December 2011, founder and legal expert, professional organization
Interview # 7: Beijing, August 2012, social work expert, professional organization
Interview # 8: Beijing, August 2012, managing director and media expert, professional organization

In the Shadow of Autocracy. Gender Politics in Chile

Patricia Graf

1. Introduction

Women's movements have become an established area of research in the analysis of democratization processes. A wide range of studies show that women's movements have influenced democratization throughout the world by integrating women's rights into policy making processes (Boris 1998; Jaquette 1994). Women's movements thus play an important role not only in overcoming autocratic regimes but also in shaping democracy. Under this view, women's movements in democratic transitions are acclaimed for their emancipatory potential; however, the fact that authoritarian regimes in transition are also working to consolidate their authoritarian ideals of gender relations often fades into the background. For instance, the study of Woods and Frankenberger (2016) on family policy in authoritarian states showed that "electoral autocracies" – autocracies in which staged elections take place – are able to preserve their traditional gender policies. They allow the opening process while maintaining control over national identities and existing gender relations.

The mechanisms and discourses that might lead to such a consolidation are examined in this chapter in light of the role of women's movements in Chile's democratic transition. The case of Chile was selected, on the one hand, because it exhibits particularly resistant authoritarian institutional enclaves. On the other, Chilean women's movements are often cited as a paragon of women's movements in transitions. In public opinion and scientific literature (Valenzuela 1998; Jaquette 1994; Franceschet and Macdonald 2004), Chilean women's movements are regarded as playing a decisive role in resistance to the dictatorship. Despite the central role of Chilean women's movements as a strong civil society force, especially for gender politics, institutions and gender images inherited from the autocratic regime (e.g., conservative divorce and reproductive rights) have remained dominant. I argue that in the time of transition there was a "normalization of hegemonic discourses of the authoritarian" (Graf, Schneider, and Wilde 2017: 79) that stabilized conservative institutions and gender images. In this chapter, I examine the nature of these normalization processes, as well as the role played by civil society in this normalization. The theoretical basis of this chapter is the governmental perspective on gender relations, which assigns an important role to civil society in the stabilization of transitioning regimes; the focus of this chapter is on the predominant discourses in democratic opening and closing processes (Graf, Schneider, and Wilde 2017).

The study of Chilean women's movements is based on a literature review of the role of women's movements in transition politics and on a secondary analysis of speeches and interviews of movement members and members of the transition regime. In the first step, the case study focuses on a concrete legislative process, the Law on Domestic Violence. This policy was chosen because its analysis clearly demonstrates how the conservative family image from the dictatorship was normalized in a democratic context. In a second step, I examine the role of women's movements in democratic transitions. For this purpose, the initial situation of the women's movement at the end of the dictatorship is presented. On this basis, I analyze how the women's movement became more and more divided after the end of the dictatorship and how this was accompanied by a normalization of authoritarian discourse. It will be shown how this normalization has even influenced the gender policies of recent president in office Michelle Bachelet.

2. Theoretical background

Gender relations play an important role in securing the stability of authoritarian regimes and in de-democratization. Numerous cases, such as the military dictatorship in Spain or the Peruvian gender policy under Fujimori, highlight the influence of autocratic regimes on gender relations. There are, however, large gaps in research on gender relations in autocracies and transitional regimes. The gender images and roles often found in informal institutions and power relations are neglected due to the common focus on the "deficits" of formal institutions. Studies in comparative analysis have emerged that systematically explore the role of gender relations in autocracies. In recent times, this strand of research has focused on the legitimacy of autocratic regimes (cf. Gerschewski et al. 2013). This approach assumes that autocratic regimes not only accumulate output legitimacy, for example by means of political results and regime performance, but also generate input legitimacy.

Democratic regimes achieve input legitimacy through democratic consent. It has long been assumed that among autocratic regimes only the electoral autocracies could access this source of input legitimacy, because they connect the population by means of pseudo-elections (Buzogány, Frankenberger, and Graf 2016). As Hannah Arendt asserted, authoritarian regimes still have other sources of input legitimacy, with ideologies and identity policies playing central roles. Ideology "promises to explain all historical happenings, the total explanation of the past, the total knowledge of the present, and the reliable prediction of the future" (Arendt 1951/1966: 470). Recent reflections on the role of legitimacy in autocracies are taking up this perspective once again (for an overview, see Kailitz and Wurster 2017).

As Arendt pointed out in her remarks on totalitarian rule, totalitarian systems seek to destroy social pluralism: "Ideologies always assume that one idea is sufficient to explain everything in the development from the premise, and no experience can teach anything because everything is comprehended in this consistent process of logical deduction" (Arendt 1951/1966: 471). In terms of gender relations, this means that pluralist gender subject positions are replaced with uniform images. These images – embedded in ideologies and identity policies – are very influential (Wilde 2012). I argue that this holds true for autocracies, too. Authoritarian regimes can use their gender policies to transport their ideologies and express their visions of family, social security, education, and gender roles (cf. Woods and Frankenberger 2016).

What is the relationship between the gender policies of autocracies and transitional regimes? Gender research so far has mainly analyzed the effects of gender on formal and informal institutions (Waylen 2015). The research strand of historical institutionalism (Mahoney and Thelen 2010) assumes that both formal and informal institutions are not simply replaced but can be "deposited" in later regimes. During regime transitions, powerful actors negotiate which institutions of the authoritarian system will be "inherited" and the limits of civilian rule (Fuentes 2000: 112). Who are the actors of negotiation? Studies on women's movements in Latin America (Franceschet and Macdonald 2004; Valenzuela 1998), authoritarian Spain (Threlfall 2013), and Eastern Europe (Jaquette and Wolchik 1998) indicate that some of them exerted pressure on authoritarian regimes.

Literature on international norm creation and norm entrepreneurs suggests that organized civil society can contribute to political opening by pressuring the regime to implement international women's rights on a national level (Finnemore and Sikkink 1998; Rošul-Gajić 2014). These women's movements successfully linked national and international levels, which enabled them to influence and shape discourse about gender. Knowledge of how discourses are negotiated and shaped is helpful when considering gender in autocracy and transition scholarship for two reasons. On the one hand, it shows that discourse is also subject to powerful negotiations in autocracies. On the other, such an understanding offers another perspective in contrast to the monolithic field of populism, which emphasizes the discourse of charismatic leaders who seek to generate input legitimacy by exalting the people and who ascribe traits to the actors of civil society.

Literature on norm creation is helpful for investigating the breakdown of autocratic discourse, as it emphasizes the dynamics of change and the significance of networked actors in an organized civil society. However, literature on international norm entrepreneurs has a strong normative foundation. Organized civil society is automatically perceived as the antithesis to autocrats; it is a "school of democracy" (Graf, Schneider, and Wilde 2017: 73). This normative assumption is also expressed in the standard definitions of civil society: "Civil society is the realm of organized social life that is voluntary, self-generating, (largely) self-supporting, autonomous from the state, and bound by a legal order or set of shared rules" (Diamond 1999: 221). But such a normative assumption obscures the internal power relations of actors of movements or of state institutions.

On the one hand, the "voluntary" aspect of civil society automatically connects its actors to instruments of deliberation; actors are seen as persons who would not resort to coercion or oppression. Yet, there are examples of social movements that are not based on internal democratic processes, such as the Peruvian guerrilla movement Luminous Path. All in all, "social movements cannot simply be equated with democracy" (Roth 1999: 48). On the other hand, definitions of civil society like the one provided by Diamond position social movements outside of the power and hierarchy of the state. To understand the power of civil society in transitions, we must consider its connection to the government apparatus. As Wilde (2014) shows, in accordance with Gramsci, civil society has the function of supporting the transition regime's institutions. It can thus serve to stabilize conservative institutions and gender images. This stabilization is referred to by Graf et al. as a "normalization of antifeminist and conservative gender images" (2017: 82): there is the generation of norms on the one hand, and on the other gender images are being explained as "normal," everyday practices – despite their contestation by parts of civil society. This process of normalization, however, generates input legitimacy for the transition regime because it helps to form a "we-feeling," or a collective identity.

To refer to such conservative institutions and gender images, I use the term "authoritarian gender regime." According to Henninger and Ostendorf, gender regimes focus on "the core political question of politics and power" (2005: 20). The focus is thus not only on how formal and informal institutions shape gender relations, but also on the power and domination relations underlying discursive practices and gender norms (Bothfeld 2008).

How can we define authoritarian gender regimes? Friedrich und Brzezinski define authoritarianism as "any political system in which the rulers are insufficiently, or not at all, subject to antecedent and enforceable rules of law – enforceable, that is, by other authorities who share in the government and who have sufficient power to compel the lawbreaking rulers to submit to the law" (1965: 5). In the absence of pluralism and diversity, autocracies are based on ideologies and mentalities that support the regime and maintain a unified national identity (Buzogány, Frankenberger, and Graf 2016). Authoritarian gender regimes are thus characterized by the fact that political positions and resources influencing gender relations are beyond the scope of state institutions and practices. Second, the gender norms and discourses of authoritarian gender regimes are based on ideologies and mentalities that do not allow a variety of gender images. Gender norms that could become "dangerous" for the regime are thus precluded. In transitions, authoritarian gender regimes must compete with democratic gender regimes. The authoritarian gender regime can become normalized in this process.

The mechanisms and discourses contributing to this normalization are investigated in the following in the case of Chilean gender policy during the transitional government of Patricio Aylwin (1989–1994). Subsequently, I analyze the aftereffects of gender norms established during the transitional government and how they shaped the scope of reform of gender policy under Michelle Bachelet (2006–2010, 2014–2018).

3. Gender policies in Chile

Among Latin American countries, Chile is often presented as a model for the successful transition to democracy. Chile is seen as exemplary in terms of it rule of law and economic performance (Hillebrand 2004). It is categorized as a consolidated democracy and depicted as a successful system transformation (Merkel 2010). When Patricio Aylwin, the first democratically elected president, took over the political leadership in Chile after sixteen years of military rule, he removed the last military dictatorship in the southern part of Latin America. Nevertheless, authoritarian ideologies are still at work in the subjects, mentalities, and institutions and guide the thoughts and actions of the people. Authoritarian enclaves – authoritarian institutional "islands" within a democratic political system – contribute to this effect. These enclaves are still apparent in several policy areas, including the area of gender policy. In the following, I will examine which mechanisms and discourses led to the negotiation and stabilization of these enclaves.

4. The establishment of an authoritarian gender regime during military dictatorship

Chilean women's movements played an important part in the transition to democracy. They are considered as one of the few movements capable of acting during the military dictatorship, since civil society organizations operating within the parties and trade unions were violently oppressed (Boris 1998). The motives of the women who organized during the military dictatorship were highly varied. On the one hand, women of different backgrounds organized soup kitchens in poverty-stricken areas (Boris 1998). On the other, women increasingly took over the role of breadwinners due to the "disappearance" of many men during the military dictatorship. Also, the neo-liberal, export-oriented policy created new employment opportunities for women, especially in the agricultural sector. Toward the end of the military dictatorship, these women workers organized themselves in the fight for better labor rights (Tinsman 2000). They also organized to protest human rights violations and to search for those who disappeared.

The military regime was not blind to the formation of the women's movement. In an effort to suppress alternative visions of society, eliminate anti-regime tendencies, and control gender relations, Augusto Pinochet created the National Women's Office (SERNAM). His wife, Lucia Hiriart, served as director and was joined by several officers' wives and upper-class women in the administration (Chuchryk 1994, 2016). SERNAM was intended to generate legitimacy for the military regime and to propagate Pinochet's vision of the "patriarchal family" as the ideal order. In Pinochet's vision, women were to concentrate on family affairs, patriotic childhood upbringing, welfare, and the fight against poverty (Thomas 2016). This traditional division (vision) of gender roles was not unique to Pinochet, as it had already been promoted under the rule of Salvador Allende: the slogan of the leading parties under Allende was "Give land to the man who works it," which institutionalized gender-specific land rights (Tinsman 2000: 158). Fischer describes the Chilean agrarian reform under Allende as representing a "monstrous" masculine, heteronormative ideal (2016: 41). To sum up, during the final period of the military dictatorship there was a broad women's movement which made demands on the military regime. The military regime responded by founding SERNAM as the first Chilean institution for gender policy.

5. Normalization of authoritarian gender images during the transition

In 1988 Pinochet lost his own referendum, which would have secured him a "second term." This opened the way for Chile's transition to democracy. However, the conservative gender and family images of the dictatorship survived this referendum and were normalized during the first years of the transition.

The focus of the first democratically elected transitional government under Patricio Aylwin was how to cope with past human rights abuses. Here, too, conservative gender images were passed down. Since Aylwin was severely restricted and under pressure by numerous prerogatives still possessed by the military, he chose the discourse of the *Reconciliación* in order to enforce a human rights policy oriented toward reconciliation and forgiveness. Aylwin applied the strategy of non-cooperation with the military and tried to limit the constitutional power of the military, i.e., the authoritarian enclaves within the democratic constitution. Aylwin's establishing of the Rettig Commission to investigate human rights violations led to the *Día de Enlace*: In response to the commission's institutionalization, Pinochet ordered unannounced military exercises throughout the country (Fuentes 2000). In terms of human rights policy, Aylwin made concessions.

This influenced Aylwin's understanding of the transition, which he claimed was completed with the first democratic election, as well as his assertion that the view should now be directed toward the future (Forstenzer 2017). Human rights violations should only be pursued "as far as possible" (Hiner and Azocar 2015). Above all, the Catholic Church was able to make use of its proximity to the Christian Democratic Party in order to implement its vision of reconstruction. Actors of the Church and of the conservative parties were key to shaping the discourse of the *Renacimiento*, the rebirth of Chile. For this rebirth, a consensus was necessary. Victims of political or sexualized violence as well as of ill treatment and other criminal acts that did not end with death were excluded from the first report on the crimes of the dictatorship, the so-called Rettig report. Correspondingly, the report produced a picture of a dictatorship that had mainly been violent to men (Hiner and Azócar 2015). The fact that women during the military dictatorship engaged in acts of political resistance and suffered massive human rights violations is usually excluded from the debates accompanying this development (Hiner and Azócar 2015). At the presentation of the report, Aylwin reiterated the formula of reconciliation: "For the good of Chile we must look to the future that unites us more than the past that separates us ... Forgiveness requires regret by one party and generosity by the other" (cited in Hiner and Azócar 2015: 57).

The discourse of reconciliation and consensus meant the continuation of the dictatorship's gender policies, namely, they were left untouched or even linked to liberal norms. This is reflected in domestic violence legislation. It was a major concern of feminist organizations in the first years of transition to pass legislation in this arena (Haas 2010). In 1994 the Chilean Government signed the Inter-American Convention on the Prevention, Punishment, and Elimination of Violence against Women. This increased the pressure of feminist activists on the Chilean Government to become active in this area, which Aylwin seemed open to, as he had already put stopping violence against women on the reform agenda. However, when the Socialist Party introduced a corresponding bill, the Senate called for cooperation with SERNAM (Haas 2010). SERNAM converted the draft into a bill for the prevention and punishment of "family violence" to protect the family (and the woman in it with her "natural" role) (Ríos Tobar and Marcela 2007). Right-wing parties were bothered by the term "family violence," since it questioned the natural order of the institution of marriage (Hiner and Azócar 2015). Aylwin solved the dilemma once again by founding a National Family Commission. As in the case of the Rettig Commission, the aim was to establish a consensus and an expert committee. Aylwin stated that he wanted to avoid "to go to the press, get involved in controversies or produce spectacular effects." He continued, "[I]t is a commission like the Rettig Commission, which accomplished its mission well, that aims to work in silence and with due gravitas" (speech by Patricio Aylwin cited in Hiner and Azócar 2015: 62).

When the bill finally entered the conservative Senate in 1993, the debate on family violence was framed in antifeminist terms: "[T]here is no worse family violence than abortion and divorce," noted Senator Eugenio Cantuarias, member of the right-wing party *Unión Demócrata Independiente*. Senator of the ruling Christian Democratic Party Nicolas Díaz expressed his opinion, which still influences the discussion on women's and reproductive rights: "[T]he most brutal violence is that used to assassinate a child in the uterus" (cited in Hiner and Azócar 2015: 62–63). From an initially feminist reform proposal emerged a discussion that granted antifeminist discourse a prominent place.

SERNAM assumed a moderate position in this dispute to avoid damaging its own institution. Controversial issues such as domestic violence and reproductive rights were downplayed and less controversial issues of gender equality were taken up. Differences – deviant gender images or identities (e.g., indigenous groups such as the Mapuche) – had no room in this conception of gender policy; the intersectionality of discrimination on the basis of race and sex was therefore neglected by SERNAM (Richards 2005). An activist who identifies as Mapuche describes her interaction with SERNAM concerning the acceptance of intersectionality in politics in the following passage:

> "It hasn't been talked about [intersectionality], this is only starting recently. But generally before, they talked about the issue of gender, and that doesn't fit, because the relations between men and women in Western culture is one, and within Mapuche culture, it's another. Our way of relating with men is different. So long as they don't recognize us as a people, they are always going to try to assimilate us, so that we will be the same as the Chileans". (Richards 2005: 212)

Considering the broad landscape of feminist organizations and women's movements that contributed decisively to ending the Pinochet dictatorship, how was such a normalization of antifeminist and conservative gender models possible at all? First, it must be noted that social movements generally lost their influence in the transition to democracy, as political participation – similar to the time before the dictatorship – was concentrated strongly on the political parties. If the "public invisibility" (Chuchryk 1994) of women had opened a window of opportunity for political organization during the dictatorship, it now limited their engagement: the candidates of the first elections were mostly male. This is also the fault of the binominal electoral system, which is advantageous for well-known politicians from established families and disadvantageous for less-familiar female candidates.

For this reason, a group of women belonging to the parties of the center-left coalition came together with independent feminists in the *Concertación de Mujeres por la Democracia* (Coalition of Women for Democracy). They formulated a program to be included in the election program *Concertación* (Chuchryk 1994). However, this led to further divisions between the women's movements: The presence of a common enemy, Pinochet, had bonded the extremely heterogeneous women's movements. Many leftist activists had already established close ties with the Left and Center parties during the dictatorship. This close connection to the state provoked protest among many smaller radical organizations and led to the division of the movements. This division was encouraged by the institutionalization of women's policy in expert committees and institutions, such as SERNAM, and the establishment of a state feminism in which, most importantly, the "institutionalists" (Forstenzer 2017: 171) among the activists were included. Their strategy was to adapt feminist demands to the dominant power relations and social narratives. In addition to the institutionalists and radical activists, there was another group of young women who, after the end of the dictatorship, focused their efforts on organizations that reflected traditional gender roles, e.g., parent organizations and religious associations (Marques-Pereira 2005). In general women only rarely became political party members or worked actively in political parties. And Marques-Pereira noted the political disinterest of young Chileans during the transition period, which was evident in their low rates of electoral registration, i.e., a large portion of young Chileans passed up their chance to vote.

To sum up, during the transition to democracy, Chilean gender policies, as well as the treatment of dictatorship violence, focused on generating a politics of consensus in expert committees. As a result, everyday violence and oppression in Chilean society remained in the dark: "After so many years of violent dictatorship, we as a society were inclined to blame the military and thus were unable to recognize the daily violence in our families" (Bacigalupe 2000: 438).

A hegemonic discourse became in due time the norm. This discourse determined societal relations and the way to deal with the authoritarian past: through the narrative of reconstruction, Chilean society was depicted as a whole. Key to this discourse was the hegemonic unity of the Chilean people, which excluded deviant gender images or identities. This normalization was made possible by a division of civil society in view of its relation to the transition state. The price paid for the institutionalization of gender policies and for allowing female activists to hold political positions was an extreme narrowing of women's and gender policies to the dominant narrative. Thus, parts of the gender regime were democratized, the parts that had access to political power and resources. But in concrete policies – in the underlying mentalities and attitudes of those who took part in shaping these policies – there was also a normalization of aspects of the authoritarian gender regime. How do these gender policies of the transition affect Chile today? In the following, I consider Chilean gender policy under the two presidencies of Michelle Bachelet and show how the narrow discursive window of gender policy has influenced reform efforts.

6. Chile under Bachelet

President Michelle Bachelet has faced high expectations regarding reforms in the field of gender policy. Because she represents the Socialist Party, there was great hope that she would tackle social inequality. And because Bachelet herself is a victim of the dictatorship, many expected her to bring new momentum to the debate on the accountability of past crimes. She also represented feminist positions and advocated gender justice (Stevenson 2012).

Nevertheless, Bachelet's own resume is ambivalent. On the one hand, she pushed forward several important changes: SERNAM has been reformed several times and has gained importance. In her first term (2006–2010), Bachelet succeeded in strengthening SERNAM institutionally, and in her second term (2014–2018) SERNAM was institutionalized as a full-fledged ministry. Furthermore, more and more female politicians connected to feminist groups and

NGOs and with political experience in the field of women's policy have taken up SERNAM leadership positions (Thomas 2016).

Another milestone is Bachelet's important reforms, such as the introduction of legislation to decriminalize therapeutic abortion, which was adopted in September 2016 by the Senate. That women have been waiting for this law since the beginning of the transition – twenty-seven years – shows how powerful discourses about the "holy family" and the role of woman still are, even today. According to Stevenson (2012), Bachelet had to bring in all her presidential power to get this law passed. The fact that such a bill could pass the Senate in conservative Chile, in the end, testifies to the power and patience of women's movements and feminist activists.

Bachelet also succeeded in increasing women's descriptive representation. Chile has historically been a country with low female representation both in politics and in the economy. In 2014, only 15.8% of all senators were female (Gender Inequality Index). And access to executive positions in the economy has grown only slightly since the transition (UNDP 2010).

As discussed above, low female representation is mainly due to the binominal electoral system. Bachelet took this as her starting point and in her second term finally pushed through a reform of the electoral system that she had been preparing for many years. With the election of the Chamber of Deputies in November 2017, the reformed electoral system enters into force, which includes the introduction of gender quotas: On the party lists, the number of female and male candidates must not exceed 60% of the total candidates. For every female candidate, the party will be "rewarded" by the state. Parties receive $20,000 (Gamboa and Morales 2016) for each elected female representative or senator. Even more important is Bachelet's reform of the executive branch to include more women's appointments, as the executive has greater power than congress in the centralized political system of Chile (Stevenson 2012). Bachelet pursued this practice at least at the beginning of the first term; after several political crises, two female ministers were replaced by male colleagues.

Despite these milestones, Bachelet faces strong criticism and seems to disappoint many. For example, leading women's and indigenous organizations complain that SERNAM still pursues family rights at the expense of women's rights. And the intersectionality of discrimination due to race and gender is completely dismissed in official policies (CEDEM 2012). The criticism of women's organizations is directed at all areas: sexualized violence by policemen; weak legislation on sexual harassment; inadequate protection of gays and lesbians; inadequate protection and social security of indigenous peoples, especially the Mapuche; and the existing gender wage gap, to name only a few.

Another point of criticism is the insufficient reform of the pension system. This has been a problem since Pinochet's pension privatization. To receive the guaranteed minimal pension, a minimal number of monthly payments has to be paid. However, given the little competition among private providers, three large financial groups are able to hold a quasi-monopoly position. A great deal of criticism arose because a large proportion of Chileans could not reach the minimum pension from the second pillar, since at least 240 regular monthly pensions had to be paid. In the year 2000, 56.7% of all Chileans failed to reach this number. Informal workers in the low-wage sector with frequent work interruptions were particularly disadvantaged (Staab 2016).

With the reforms, the third pillar of voluntary amounts was strengthened, and these were now tax deductible. But this only created incentives for those who earned more. In 2008 Bachelet tried to reform the pension system once again. The reform was explicitly connoted as a "gender reform," and Bachelet pointed to gender injustices in the pension system as the main motivation. The most important element of this reform was the consideration of unpaid care work (regardless of the gender of the care worker). However, the pension reform had to pass Congress and Senate, where an alliance of economic interests and right-wing parties was opposed to a gender-independent payment of care work. The compromise was a maternalist policy exclusively for women: women received child "bonuses," or supplements, for their unpaid care work (Staab 2016). Bachelet wanted to involve the interests of many women's organizations. But because the importance of gender equality in care work was not heeded, the traditional image of the caring mother was strengthened (Staab 2017). A former minister commented on the persistence of these gender images in social policy: "I would say that [the social security system] is like a building with a strong conceptual foundation" (cited in Staab 2016: 125). And this building could not be completely remodeled.

7. Conclusion

In the transition to democracy, conservative gender images and roles that emerged during the military dictatorship or even earlier were perpetuated. This was possible due to the establishment of a discourse of reconciliation, which conceived of Chileans as a unified whole in an effort to prioritize (economic) progress. Divergent roles, gender images, and conflictive topics had no place in this discourse. Attempts to implement international standards on the national level were unsuccessful, because they were reinterpreted and integrated into conservative notions of gender relations. The politics of reconciliation led to a division of organized civil society, as only parts of society found a place in the "rebirth" of Chile.

The establishment of a hegemonic discourse was possible by establishing a state feminism and integrating the "institutionalists" among the women's movements into SERNAM. This integration divided radical women's movements and institutionalists; it also weakened feminist demands, because in the desire to extend the influence of the SERNAM the institutionalists adapted feminist demands to the dominant power relations and societal narratives. Thus, the authoritarian gender regime was only partially reformed: access to positions of power and resources were changed, but the conservative discourses and gender images of the old military dictatorship were carried over to the new democratic regime. Young Chileans, who could have potentially brought about change, were rather apathetic and stayed away from the ballots and from political organizations.

More than two decades after the end of the dictatorship, these conservative discourses still limit the political frame and possibilities of Bachelet, who explicitly sought gender and social policy reform. In the area of care and pension policy, traditional gender roles are extremely persistent. This is also due to socially divided attitudes toward gender equality and the gendered division of labor. A survey by the United Nations Development Programme (UNDP) shows that while 62% of the population strongly support or at least accept the traditional role distribution (UNDP 2010, 5), 38% of the population, especially young adults and women, at least support the equal distribution of roles or believe that the state should be more committed to gender equality and diversity. The reform of the electoral system will hopefully lead not only to an increase in descriptive representation but also substantial representation. It might also lead to the integration of feminist demands and issues of gender justice and intersectionality on a broader basis into the political system. It can be stated that the previous electoral system brought about a narrowing of political content, since candidates representing critical issues did not receive a place on the party lists. As Waylen (2006) shows in the example of the constitutionalization process in Iraq, the guarantee of descriptive representation is not enough if in the transition process there are already elements of an authoritarian gender regime in the constitution.

References

Arendt, Hannah (1951/1966): The Origins of Totalitarianism. New York: Schocken Verlag.
Bacigalupe, Gonzalo (2000): Family Violence in Chile. In: Violence Against Women 6, 4, pp. 427-228.
Boris, Dieter (1998): Soziale Bewegungen in Lateinamerika. Hamburg: VSA-Verlag.
Bothfeld, Silke (2008): Under (Re-) Construction – Die Fragmentierung des deutschen Geschlechterregimes durch die neue Familienpolitik. In: ZeS-Arbeitspapier (1).
Buzogány, Aron/Frankenberger, Rolf/Graf, Patricia (2016): Policy-Making und Legitimation in Autokratien. Das Beispiel der Innovaionspolitik. In: Totalitarismus und Demokratie 13, pp. 257–279.
CEDEM/Corporaciones Homanas/Domos/OBSERVATORIO CIUDADANO/RED CHILENA CONTRA LA VIOLENCIA DOMÉSTICA Y SEXUAL/OBSERVATORIO DE GÉNERO Y EQUIDAD/CENTRO DE ESTUDIOS DE LA MUJER (2012): Joint submission: Comments and Contributions from Civil Society related to the Fifth and Sixth Periodic Report of the State of Chile, for the 53rd Session of the CEDAW Committee.
Chuchryk, Patricia M. (1994): From Dictatorship to Democracy: the Womens Movement in Chile. In: Jaquette, Jane S. (Ed.): The women's movement in Latin America. Participation and democracy. Boulder: Westview-Press, pp. 65–108.
Diamond, Larry Jay (1999): Developing Democracy. Toward Consolidation. Baltimore: Johns Hopkins Univ. Press.

Finnemore, Martha/Sikkink, Kathryn (1998): International Norm Dynamics and Political Change. In: International Organization 52, 4, pp. 887–917.

Fischer, Carl (2016): Queering the Chilean Way. Cultures of Exceptionalism and Sexual Dissidence 1965-2015. London: Palgrave Macmillan.

Forstenzer, Nicole (2017): Feminism and Gender Policies in Post-Dictatorship Chile (1990–2010). In: Donoso, Sofia/Bülow, Marisa von (Eds.): Social Movements in Chile. New York, pp. 161–189.

Franceschet, S./Macdonald, L. (2004): Hard times for citizenship. Womens movements in Chile and Mexico. In: Citizenship Studies 8, 3–23.

Friedrich, Carl Joachim/Brzezinski, Zbigniew K. (1965): Totalitarian Dictatorship and Autocracy. Cambridge Mass: Harvard Univ. Press.

Fuentes, Claudio (2000): After Pinochet. Civilian Policies Toward the Military in the 1990s Chilean Democracy. In: Journal of Interamerican Studies and World Affairs 42, 3, pp. 111–142.

Gamboa, Ricardo/Morales, Mauricio (2016): Chile's 2015 Electoral Reform. Changing the Rules of the Game. In: Latin American Politics and Society 58, 4, pp. 126–144.

Gerschewski, Johannes/Merkel, Wolfgang/Schmotz, Alexander/Stefes, Christoph H./Tanneberg, Dag (2013): Warum überleben Diktaturen? In: Kailitz, Steffen/Köllner, Patrick (Eds.): Autokratien im Vergleich. Baden-Baden, pp. 111–136.

Graf, Patricia/Schneider, Silke/Wilde, Gabriele (2017): Geschlechterverhältnisse und die Macht des Autoritären. In: Femina Politica. 26, 1, pp. 68–85.

Haas, Liesl (2010): Feminist policymaking in Chile. University Park, Pa: Pennsylvania State University Press.

Henninger, Annette/Ostendorf, Helga (2005): Einleitung: Erträge feministischer Institutionenanalyse. In: Ostendorf, Helga/Henninger, Annette (Eds.): Die politische Steuerung des Geschlechterregimes. Beiträge zur Theorie politischer Institutionen. Dordrecht, pp. 9–36.

Hillebrand, Ernst (2004): Chile - Auf der Suche nach einem neuen Wirtschafts- und Gesellschaftsmodell. In: FES-Analyse. Januar 2004.

Hiner, H./Azocar, M. J. (2015): Irreconcilable Differences. Political Culture and Gender Violence during the Chilean Transition to Democracy. In: Latin American Perspectives 42, 3, pp. 52–72.

Jaquette, Jane S. (Ed.) (1994): The women's movement in Latin America. Participation and democracy. Boulder: Westview Press.

Jaquette, Jane S./Wolchik, Sharon L. (Eds.) (1998): Women and democracy. Latin America and Central and Eastern Europe. Baltimore, Md: Johns Hopkins University Press.

Kailitz, Steffen/Wurster, Stefan (2017): Legitimationsstrategien von Autokratien. In: Zeitschrift für Vergleichende Politikwissenschaft 11, 2, pp. 141–151.

Mahoney, James/Thelen, Kathleen Ann (2010): A Theory of Gradual Institutional Change. In: Mahoney, James/Thelen, Kathleen Ann (Eds.): Explaining institutional change. Ambiguity, agency, and power. Cambridge, New York: Cambridge Univ. Press, pp. 1–37.

Marques-Pereira, Bérengère (2005): Le Chili. Une démocratie de qualité pour les femmes? In: Politique et Sociétés 24, 2-3, S. 147.
Merkel, Wolfgang (1999): Systemtransformation. Tübingen: Leske+Budrich.
Merkel, Wolfgang (2010): Systemtransformation. Eine Einführung in die Theorie und Empirie der Transformationsforschung. Wiesbaden: VS-Verlag.
Richards, Patricia (2005): The Politics of Gender, Human Rights, and Being Indigenous in Chile. In: Gender and Society 19, 2, pp. 199-220.
Ríos Tobar/Marcela (2007): How Pink is the Pink Tide. Chilean Feminism and Social Democracy From the Democratic Transition to Bachelet. In: Nacla Report on the Americas (March/April), pp. 25–29.
Rošul-Gajić, Jagoda (2014): Rošul-Gajić, Jagoda: Gleichstellungspolitischer Wandel durch Engagement und Handeln der Frauenorganisationen. Kroatien auf dem Weg zur Gleichstellung. In: Femina Politica 23, 1, pp. 62–76.
Roth, Roland (1999): Neue soziale Bewegungen und liberale Demokratie. Herausforderungen, Innovationen und paradoxe Konsequenzen. In: Klein, Ansgar/Legrand, Hans-Josef/Leif, Thomas (Eds.): Neue soziale Bewegungen. Impulse, Bilanzen und Perspektiven. Wiesbaden: Springer VS, pp. 47–63.
Staab, Silke (2016): Opportunities and Constraints on Gender-Egalitarian Policy Change: Michelle Bachelet's Social Protection Agenda. In: Waylen, Georgina (Ed.): Gender, institutions, and change in Bachelet's Chile. Houndmills, Basingstoke, Hampshire, New York: Palgrave Macmillan, pp. 121–146.
Staab, Silke (2017): Gender and the politics of gradual institutional change. Social policy reform and innovation in Chile/Silke Staab. Cham, Switzerland : Springer International Publishing.
Stevenson, Linda S. (2012): The Bachelet Effect on Gender-Equity Policies. In: Latin American Perspectives 39, 4, pp. 129–144.
Thomas, Gwynn (2016): Promoting Gender Equality: Michelle Bachelet and Formal and Informal Institutional Change within the Chilean Presidency. In: Waylen, Georgina (Ed.): Gender, institutions, and change in Bachelet's Chile. Houndmills, Basingstoke, Hampshire, New York: Palgrave Macmillan, pp. 95–120.
Threlfall, Monica (2013): Women's Movement in Spain. In: Snow, David A./Della Porta, Donatella/Klandermans, Bert/McAdam, Doug (Eds.): The Wiley-Blackwell Encyclopedia of Social and Political Movements. Chichester, UK Wiley-Blackwell.
Tinsman, Heidi (2000): Reviving Feminist Materialism. Gender and Neoliberalism in Pinochet's Chile. In: Signs - Journal of Women in Culture and Society 26, 1, pp. 145-188.
UNDP (2010): Human Development in Chile 2010. Gender: the challenges of equality.
Valenzuela, Maria Elena (1998): Women and the Democratization Process in Chile. In: Jaquette, Jane S./Wolchik, Sharon L. (Eds.): Women and democracy. Latin America and Central and Eastern Europe. Baltimore, Md: Johns Hopkins University Press, pp. 47–74.
Waylen, Georgina (2006): Constitutional engineering. What opportunities for the enhancement of gender rights? In: Third World Quarterly 27, 7, pp. 1209–1221.

Waylen, Georgina (Ed.) (2016): Gender, institutions, and change in Bachelet's Chile. Houndmills, Basingstoke, Hampshire, New York: Palgrave Macmillan.

Wilde, Gabriele (2012): Totale Grenzen des Politischen: Die Zerstörung der Öffentlichkeit bei Hannah Arendt. In: Femina Politica 21, 1, pp. 17-28.

Wilde, Gabriele (2014): Zivilgesellschaftsforschung aus Geschlechterperspektive. Zur Ambivalenz von Begrenzung und Erweiterung eines politischen Handlungsraumes. In: Zimmer, Annette/Simsa, Ruth (Eds.): Forschung zu Zivilgesellschaft, NPOs und Engagement. Quo vadis? Wiesbaden: Springer VS, pp. 209–227.

Woods, Dorian/Frankenberger, Rolf (2016): Examining the Autocracy-Gender-Family Nexus. In: Femina Politica 25, 1, pp. 112-121.

Authors

Bräuer, Stephanie, M.A., Political Scientist at WWU Münster.
E-Mail: braeuer@uni-muenster.de

Graf, Patricia, Prof. Dr., Political Scientist at BSP Business School Berlin.
E-Mail: patricia.graf@businessschool-berlin.de

Hinterhuber, Eva Maria, Prof. Dr., Sociologist at Rhine-Waal University of Applied Sciences.
E-Mail: eva-maria.hinterhuber@hochschule-rhein-waal.de

Mushaben, Joyce, Prof. Dr., Political Scientist at University of Missouri, St. Louis.
E-Mail: mushaben@umsl.edu

Obuch, Katharina, Dr., Political Scientist at WWU Münster.
E-Mail: k.obuch@uni-muenster.de

Panreck, Isabelle-Christine, Dr., Political Scientist at WWU Münster.
E-Mail: isabelle.panreck@uni-muenster.de

Sandhaus, Jasmin, M.A., Project Manager at Academy for Research and Teaching of Practical Politics Bonn.
E-Mail: jasmin.sandhaus@uni-bonn.de

Schneider, Silke, Dr., Political Scientist at University of Hagen.
E-Mail: silke.schneider-ksw@fernuni-hagen.de

Wilde, Gabriele, Prof. Dr., Political Scientist at WWU Münster.
E-Mail: gabriele.wilde@uni-muenster.de

Zimmer, Annette, Prof. Dr., Political Scientist at WWU Münster.
E-Mail: zimmean@uni-muenster.de

Index

antagonism 87, 90, 109
citizenship 27, 32, 34, 41, 47, 109f., 113f., 167
discrimination 14, 16, 37, 40, 55, 112f., 119, 177-180, 190, 192, 204, 231, 256, 260
dispositive 104, 110, 114
emancipation 13, 36, 75, 84, 91, 95, 156
equal opportunities 36, 76, 169, 176f., 181
equality 12, 14, 18ff., 31f., 37, 39, 42-46, 51f., 54f., 75f., 79, 84, 88, 90, 95, 99, 102, 108, 113, 119, 142, 149, 159, 166ff., 173, 176ff., 180f., 185, 187f., 190, 192-197, 200f., 205, 211f., 217, 222, 224-228, 233, 235, 237, 256, 260f.
exclusion 14, 16, 19, 31, 102, 113, 178, 223
gender gap 207
gender identification 14
gender identity 14ff., 114
gender inequality 28, 45, 79, 156, 189, 237

gender justice 12, 14, 55f., 258, 262
gender order 14f., 46, 53, 99, 114, 138, 142, 154f., 158ff., 217, 226
gender roles 15, 19, 21, 35, 48, 53, 122, 126, 129, 137ff., 142, 144, 178, 205, 222, 249, 253, 257, 261
governance 9, 10, 42, 48, 80, 83, 142, 167, 189, 220
governmentality 102
modernization 13, 41, 78f., 84, 88, 92ff., 137f., 155, 158ff., 196
populism 14f., 119, 121, 250
power structures 14, 17, 105, 121f., 146
re-traditionalization 16, 126, 139
sexual contract 29, 108
strategic framing 124, 127
traditional family images 16, 43ff., 53, 179
visibility 124, 128, 132, 179

Political Science

 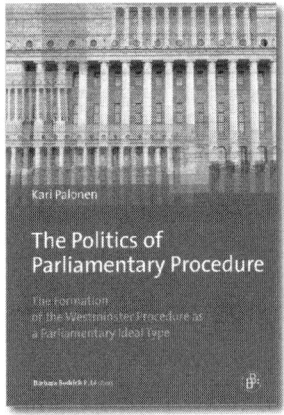

Kia Lindroos
Frank Möller (eds.)
Art as a Political Witness

2017. 239 pp. Pb. 48,00 € (D),
GBP 43.95, US$63.00
ISBN 978-3-8474-0580-1

The book explores the concept of artistic witnessing as political activity. In which ways may art and artists bear witness to political events? The Contributors engage with dance, film, photography, performance, poetry and theatre and explore artistic witnessing as political activity in a wide variety of case studies.

Kari Palonen
The Politics of Parliamentary Procedure
The Formation of the Westminster Procedure as a Parliamentary Ideal Type

2016. 274 pp. Pb. 34,90 € (D),
GBP 31.95, US$49.95
ISBN 978-3-8474-0787-4

Currently, parliament as a political institution does not enjoy the best reputation. This book aims to recover less known political resources of the parliamentary mode of proceeding. The parliamentary procedure relies on regulating debates in a fair way and on constructing opposed perspectives on the agenda items.

 www.shop.budrich-academic.de

The ANTICORRP Project:
The Anticorruption Report

 vol. 1

 vol. 2

2013. 128 pp.
Pb. 19,90 € (D),
US$26.00,
GBP 17.95

2013. 128 pp.
Pb. 19,90 € (D),
US$26.00,
GBP 17.95

Alina Mungiu-Pippidi (ed.)
Controlling Corruption in Europe
ISBN 978-3-8474-0125-4
eISBN 978-3-8474-0381-4

Alina Mungiu-Pippidi (ed.)
The Anticorruption Frontline
ISBN 978-3-8474-0144-5
eISBN 978-3-8474-0276-3

 vol. 3

 vol. 4

2015. 128 pp.
Pb. 19,90 € (D),
US$26.00,
GBP 17.95

2017. 128 pp.
Pb. 19,90 € (D),
US$26.00,
GBP 17.95

Alina Mungiu-Pippidi (ed.)
Government Favouritism in Europe

ISBN 978-3-8474-0795-9
eISBN 978-3-8474-0921-2

Alina Mungiu-Pippidi
Jana Warkotsch (eds.)
Beyond the Panama Papers. The Performance of EU Good Governance Promotion
ISBN 978-3-8474-0582-5
eISBN 978-3-8474-0405-7

 www.shop.budrich-academic.de

Pamela M. Barnes | Ian G. Barnes

The Politics of Nucelar Energy in the European Union

Framing the Discourse: Actors, Positions and Dynamics

For the foreseeable future the overall use of nuclear electricity in the European Union is unlikely to change significantly despite the controversies surrounding its use amongst the EU's nation states. The author questions the role that nuclear electricity plays in meeting the challenges of providing secure, competitive and sustainable energy to support the development of the low carbon economy in the EU.

2018 • 292 pp. • Pb.
58,00 € (D) • 59,70 € (A)
ISBN 978-3-8474-0687-7
eISBN 978-3-8474-0831-4

Maria Marczewska-Rytko (Ed.)

Handbook of Direct Democracy in Central and Eastern Europe after 1989

Since the collapse of the Soviet Union the political history of Central and Eastern Europe has been mainly the story of arise, consolidation, transformation and struggles of new democratic regimes and societies. This handbook offers an instructive approach to that history focusing on the relevance of practices and institutions of direct democracy.

2018 • 351 pp. • Pb.
64,90 € (D) • 66,80 € (A)
ISBN 978-3-8474-2122-1
eISBN 978-3-8474-1110-9

www.barbara-budrich.net

Erratum

Due to a technical failure there are some misprints to be found that we would like to correct as follows:

p. 60, references

- Barnovský, Michal/Cambel, Samuel/Čierny, J./Kamenec, Ivan/Šťastný, Jiri/Vrablic, Emil (1988): *Dejiny Slovenska VI*. Bratislava: Veda.
- Bašovský, Oliver/Divinský, Boris, (1991): The development of modern urbanisation in Slovakia and its present problems. In: *Revue Belge de Géographie*, 115, #1-2-3, pp. 265-277.
- Čulík, Jan (2008): Den, kdy tanky zlikvidovaly české sny Pražského jara. *Britské Listy*. http://www.britskelisty.cz/9808/19980821h.html (2008-23-01)

p. 83, 3rd paragraph

- The other two coalition parties, mainly ĽS-HZDS, had long had difficulty affiliating with some of the European political parties.

p. 83, 6th paragraph

- Although ĽS-HZDS had had three MEPs since the 2004 elections, it had not managed to join any European political party. ... ĽS-HZDS had a detailed electoral program, in which it vowed to balance continuation of the integration processes and reform the Lisbon treaty, while advocating the preservation of tax sovereignty and the suitable regulation of financial capital.

p. 185, references

- Učeň, Peter (2009): Approaching National Populism, in: Petőcz, Kálmán (ed.) National Populism and Slovak-Hungarian Relations in Slovakia 2006-2009. Šamorín: Forum Minority Research Institute, pp. 13-38.

p. 189, 4th paragraph

- The Christian Democratic Movement (KDH) was founded by leading Catholic dissidents in February 1990 (Kostelecký 2002: 47), and is the only party that has been represented in all parliaments since 1990.

p. 205, references

- Kostelecký, Tomáš (2002): Political Parties after Communism. Developments in East-Central Europe. Washington D.C.: Woodrow Wilson Center Press.

Baldersheim, Harald/Bátora, Jozef (eds.): The Governance of Small States in Turbulent Times. The Exemplary Cases of Norway and Slovakia. Barbara Budrich Publishers, Opladen, Berlin, Toronto 2012. ISBN: 978-3-86649-430-5